Microsoft RPC Programming Guide

Microsoft RPC Programming Guide

John Shirley and Ward Rosenberry
Digital Equipment Corporation

O'Reilly & Associates, Inc.
103 Morris Street, Suite A
Sebastopol, CA 95472

Microsoft RPC Programming Guide

by John Shirley and Ward Rosenberry

Editor: Andy Oram

Production Editor: Clairemarie Fisher O'Leary

Printing History:

> March 1995:   First Edition.

ISBN: 1-56592-070-8

Table of Contents

List of Figures

List of Tables

Preface

Remote Procedure Call (RPC) is a unique facility in the Microsoft environment. It is a glue that binds together MS-DOS, Windows, and Windows NT—and connects them to the world of the Distributed Computing Environment (DCE). One RPC protocol works across all of these systems. Thus, you can use a single Application Programming Interface (API) to create distributed programs across DOS, Windows, and Windows NT. While the API is somewhat different from that used by DCE, the presence of an identical protocol allows you to reach DCE systems as well. In this book we describe how to develop application programs that use Microsoft RPC to run applications across multiple systems.

To successfully use this book you need to know the C programming language, be experienced with common programming techniques, and understand some basic networking concepts. We designed this book for two levels of application developers:

- The developer of a client for an application that has an existing interface and server

- The developer of an interface and server

Microsoft RPC was based on the RPC protocols of DCE. This book, too, is the result of a DCE project. It is based on a book written at Digital Equipment Corporation for O'Reilly & Associates, called *Guide to Writing DCE Applications*. The current book has the same conceptual background material as that book, but entirely new examples and a lot of Microsoft-specific material.

If you are interested in making Microsoft systems communicate with DCE systems, you should also read O'Reilly & Associates' book *Distributing Applications Across DCE and Windows NT*.

Conventions

Throughout the book we use the following typographic conventions:

`Constant width`
>   indicates a language construct such as a MIDL keyword, a code example, system output, or user input. Words in constant width also represent application-specific variables and procedures.

`Constant Bold`
>   is used in examples to indicate text that is literally typed by the user.

Bold   introduces new terms or concepts.

Italic   in command syntax or examples indicates variables for which the user supplies a value. Italicized words in the text also represent system elements such as filenames and directory names, and user functions or RPC-specific routines.

[]
>   enclose attributes in interface definitions and Attribute Configuration Files (ACFs) and are part of the syntax. Note that this is different from the common convention in which brackets enclose optional items in format and syntax descriptions.

`C:\>`   represents system prompts.

`C:\SERVER>`
>   represents a server system prompt to distinguish it from a client system prompt.

`C:\CLIENT>`
>   represents a client system prompt to distinguish it from a server system prompt.

Book Organization

This book is divided into the following seven chapters and six appendices:

Chapter 1, *Overview of an RPC Application*, shows a complete, simple RPC application.

Chapter 2, *Using a Microsoft RPC Interface*, shows how to read an RPC interface definition (a file ending in *.idl*), which is a file that declares the remote procedures of an interface.

Chapter 3, *How to Write Clients*, discusses how to develop client programs for RPC interfaces. Topics include binding methods, finding servers, customizing binding handles, handling errors or exceptions, and compiling clients.

Chapter 4, *Pointers, Arrays, and Memory Usage*, shows how pointers and arrays are defined in an interface and how to develop applications to use them.

Chapter 5, *How to Write a Server*, discusses how to develop a server program for an RPC interface. Topics include initializing a server, writing remote procedures, and compiling servers.

Chapter 6, *Using a Name Service*, describes a name service database and how to use it with distributed applications.

Chapter 7, *Context Handles*, shows how to maintain a state (such as a file handle) on a specific server between remote procedure calls from a specific client.

Appendix A, *MIDL and ACF Attributes Quick Reference*, shows all the attributes in the Microsoft Interface Definition Language (MIDL) and Attribute Configuration File (ACF).

Appendix B, *RPC Runtime Routines Quick Reference*, shows all the RPC runtime routines organized into convenient categories.

Appendix C, *The Arithmetic Application*, is a small application that shows the basics of remote procedure calls.

Appendix D, *The Inventory Application*, is a somewhat richer application than that in Appendix C, showing different MIDL data types, how to use ACFs, and how to find servers by importing information from a name service database.

Appendix E, *The Rfile Application*, shows how to use context handles and how to find servers using strings of network location information.

Appendix F, *The Windows Phonebook Application*, offers a simple Windows-based client that uses RPC to get phone numbers from a database on the server.

How to Use This Book

If you are developing just a client for an existing RPC interface and server, read the following chapters first:

- Chapter 1, *Overview of an RPC Application*

- Chapter 2, *Using a Microsoft RPC Interface*

- Chapter 3, *How to Write Clients*

Read other chapters as needed to learn how to develop applications that use more features of interface definitions.

If you are developing a network interface with accompanying server, read the following:

- Chapter 1, *Overview of an RPC Application*

- Chapter 2, *Using a Microsoft RPC Interface*

- Chapter 3, *How to Write Clients*

- Chapter 4, *Pointers, Arrays, and Memory Usage*

- Chapter 5, *How to Write a Server*

Obtaining the Example Programs

The example programs in this book are available electronically in a number of ways: by CompuServe, FTP, FTPMAIL, and BITFTP. The fastest and easiest ways are listed first. If you read from the top down, the first one that works for you is probably the best.

Use CompuServe if you are accustomed to getting Microsoft-related software that way. Use FTP if you are directly on the Internet. Use FTPMAIL if you are not on the Internet, but can send and receive electronic mail to Internet sites (this includes CompuServe users). Use BITFTP if you send electronic mail via BITNET.

CompuServe

Sample programs from this book are available in the same CompuServe forum as other documents and code related to Microsoft RPC. Go to *mswin32*, ask for the Libraries Menu, and choose the API-WinNet/RPC item from the menu.

The sample code consists of four files in zip format:

- *arith.zip*, the basic arithmetic example from Appendix C.

- *inv.zip*, the inventory example from Appendix D.

- *rfile.zip*, the remote file example from Appendix E.

- *phnrpc.zip*, the Windows-based phonebook example from Appendix F.

The four examples are also available together in *orarpc.zip*.

Here is a captured CompuServe session showing how to obtain one of the files, with your input marked in bold:

```
Enter choice or <CR> for more !go mswin32

   You have left basic services

Personal Computing     MSWIN32


One moment please...

Welcome to Microsoft Win32 SDK Forum+, V. 3B(77)

Hello,
Last visit:  06-Jan-95 06:40:11

Forum messages:  85795 to  86881
Last message you've read:  85794

Section(s) Selected: All
```

Number of Members in Conference: None

Press <CR> !**lib**

Microsoft Win32 SDK Forum Libraries Menu

 1 MS Info and Index
 3 Far East Win32-beta
 4 API-User/GUI
 5 API-Graphics/GDI
 6 API-Base/Console
 7 API-Security
 8 Tools-Win32 SDK
 9 Tools-SCT
10 Tools-MS Test/Setup
11 Porting-OS/2 & UNIX
12 API-WinNet/RPC
13 Windows NT DDK
14 API-Win32s
15 API-Unicode/NLS
16 Tools-Third Party
17 FAQ Library

Enter choice !**12**

Microsoft Win32 SDK Forum+   Library 12

API-WinNet/RPC

 1 BROWSE Files
 2 DIRECTORY of Files

 3 UPLOAD a File (FREE)
 4 DOWNLOAD a file to your Computer

 5 LIBRARIES

Enter choice !**4**

File name: **orarpc.zip**

File ORARPC.ZIP, 41384 Bytes, Lib 12

File name for your computer: **orarpc.zip**

Press <CR> !dow orarpc.zip orarpc.zip

Microsoft Win32 SDK Forum+   Library 12

API-WinNet/RPC

 1 BROWSE Files
 2 DIRECTORY of Files

 3 UPLOAD a File (FREE)
 4 DOWNLOAD a file to your Computer

 5 LIBRARIES

Enter choice !**off**

Thank you for using CompuServe!

Off at 06:59 EST 11-Jan-95
Connect time = 0:06

FTP

To use FTP, you need a machine with direct access to the Internet. A sample session is shown, with what you should type in boldface.

```
% ftp ftp.uu.net
Connected to ftp.uu.net.
220 ftp.UU.NET FTP server (Version 6.34 Thu Oct 22 14:32:01 EDT 1992) ready.
Name (ftp.uu.net:andyo): anonymous
331 Guest login ok, send e-mail address as password.
Password: janetv@xyz.com (use your user name and host here)
230 Guest login ok, access restrictions apply.
ftp> cd /published/oreilly/nutshell/ms_rpc
250 CWD command successful.
ftp> binary (Very important! You must specify binary transfer for compressed files.)
200 Type set to I.
ftp> prompt (Convenient, so you are not queried for every file transferred)
Interactive mode off.
ftp> mget *
200 PORT command successful.
           .
           .
           .
ftp> quit
221 Goodbye.
%
```

Each *.Z* archive contains all source code and configuration information required for building one example. Extract each example through a command like:

```
% zcat arith.dec94.tar.Z | tar xf -
```

System V systems require the following *tar* command instead:

```
% zcat arith.dec94.tar.Z | tar xof -
```

If *zcat* is not available on your system, use separate *uncompress* and *tar* commands.

The *tar* command creates a subdirectory that holds all the files from its archive. The *README.dec94* file in this subdirectory describes the goals of the example and how to build and run it; the text is an ASCII version of the introductory material from the corresponding appendix in this book.

FTPMAIL

FTPMAIL is a mail server available to anyone who can send electronic mail to and receive it from Internet sites. This includes any company or service provider that allows email connections to the Internet. Here's how you do it.

You send mail to *ftpmail@online.ora.com*. In the message body, give the FTP commands you want to run. The server will run anonymous FTP for you and mail the files back to you. To get a complete help file, send a message with no subject and the single word "help" in the body. The following is an example mail session that should get you the examples. This command sends you a listing of the files in the selected directory, and the requested example files. The listing is useful if there's a later version of the examples you're interested in.

```
% mail ftpmail@online.ora.com
Subject:
reply-to janetv@xyz.com              Where you want files mailed
open
cd /published/oreilly/nutshell/ms_rpc
dir
get README.dec94
mode binary
uuencode                             (or btoa if you have it)
get arith.dec94.tar.Z
get inv.dec94.tar.Z
get rfile.dec94.tar.Z
get phnbk.dec94.tar.Z
quit
.
```

A signature at the end of the message is acceptable as long as it appears after "quit."

All retrieved files will be split into 60KB chunks and mailed to you. You then remove the mail headers and concatenate them into one file, and then *uudecode* or *atob* it. Once you've got the desired *.Z* files, follow the directions under FTP to extract the files from the archive.

BITFTP

BITFTP is a mail server for BITNET users. You send it electronic mail messages requesting files, and it sends the files back to you by electronic mail. BITFTP currently serves only users who send it mail from nodes that are directly on BITNET, EARN, or NetNorth. BITFTP is a public service of Princeton University. Here's how it works:

To use BITFTP, send mail containing your *ftp* commands to *BITFTP@PUCC*. For a complete help file, send HELP as the message body.

The following is the message body you should send to BITFTP:

```
FTP   ftp.uu.net   NETDATA
USER  anonymous
PASS  your Internet email address (not your bitnet address)
CD   /published/oreilly/nutshell/ms_rpc
DIR
GET README
BINARY
GET arith.dec94.tar.Z
GET inv.dec94.tar.Z
GET rfile.dec94.tar.Z
GET phnbk.dec94.tar.Z
QUIT
```

Once you've got the desired *.Z* files, follow the directions under FTP to extract the files from the archive. Since you are probably not on a UNIX system, you may need to get versions of *uudecode, uncompress, atob,* and *tar* for your system.

Questions about BITFTP can be directed to Melinda Varian, *MAINT@PUCC* on BIT-NET.

Acknowledgments

This book can be traced back to the DCE documentation set put out by Digital Equipment Corporation. John Shirley, working with Steve Talbott and Andy Oram from O'Reilly & Associates, wrote a DCE version of this book called *Guide to Writing DCE Applications.* Ward Rosenberry then took it over and thoroughly revised it to cover Microsoft RPC. While at first glance, it might seem that relatively little effort was required to write this new version, the work put into it was nevertheless considerable and required the cooperation and support of many individuals.

First off, I want to thank my editor at O'Reilly & Associates, Andy Oram, for his excellent advice and his persistence on this lengthy project.

For supporting this project I want to thank folks at Digital Equipment Corporation, in particular Jeff Shrieshiem, Frank Willison, and Michelle Chambers for funding various portions of the project. Also at Digital Equipment corporation, other major contributors to this book include Neil Miranda, who converted several DCE applications to Microsoft RPC Version 1.0 for use in this book. Riaz Zolfonoon later modified these applications for use with Microsoft RPC Version 2.0. Riaz also provided helpful advice on numerous aspects of Microsoft RPC.

Others at Digital who played central roles in developing the book include Jerry Harrow and Will Lees, who provided painstaking reviews of various drafts of sections of the book. Jim Teague provided a Microsoft RPC version of the phonebook application which was originally written for another O'Reilly book titled *Distributing Applications Across DCE and Windows NT.* Jim is a co-author of that book. Larry Friedman, Dick Annicchiarico, Michael Blackstock, Rob Philpott, and Andy Ferris provided bits and pieces of technical advice along the way. I also want to thank Ladan Pooroshani, Beth Benoit, and Brian Shimpf for their cooperation and support.

Credit for logistical support goes to several folks at Digital including Gerry Fisher, Evelyn McKay, Lisa Cozins, and Madeline Cormier, all of whom made sure I had what I needed to get things done.

Several people at Microsoft Corporation also deserve thanks for providing various inputs to the book. These people include Debbie Black, Dave Tanaguchi, and Craig Link (from Microsoft's Win32 SDK forum on CompuServe).

Additional help and support for the DCE version of the book came from Tony Hinxman, Al Simons, David Magid, Margie Showman, Ken Ouellette, Mary Orcutt, Marll McDonald, Mark Heroux, Clem Cole, Marty Port, Ram Sudama, Diane Sherman, Susan Scott, David Strohmeyer, Karol McIntyre, Wei Hu, Susan Hunziker, Vicki Janicki, Beth Martin, Dan Cobb, Lois Frampton, Steve Miller, Eric Jendrock, Gary Schmitt, Ellen Vliet, Judy Davies, Judy Egan, Collis Jackson, David Kenney, Suzanne Lipsky, Darrell Icenogle, Terry Tvrdik, Howard Mayberry, and John Shirley's wife, Linda McClary.

Joe Scandora was very helpful on the Microsoft version of the book.

Book design and production credits go to lots of the folks at O'Reilly & Associates who artfully turned many pieces of a stark manuscript into a real book. Edie Freedman designed the cover. Jeff Robbins and Chris Reilley created the figures. Kismet McDonough, Eileen Kramer, and Clairemarie Fisher O'Leary did the copy-editing and production management. Kiersten Nauman assisted with the production work. Seth Maislin refined the index.

Finally, I want to thank Frank Willison for giving me the opportunity to work on this book.

Joint Venture

This book was produced as a cooperative effort between Digital Equipment Corporation and O'Reilly & Associates. While we at O'Reilly & Associates frequently work closely with vendors of hardware and software, this book gave us an opportunity for much more extensive cooperation and mutual support than is customary. It is a model we like, and we believe the end result testifies to the value of sharing one's resources in this way.

1

Overview of an RPC Application

A traditional application is a single program running on a single computer system, where a procedure and its caller execute in the same address space. In contrast, the **client-server model** for distributed applications embodies a client program and a server program, usually running on different systems of a network. The client makes a request to the server, which is usually a continuously running daemon process, and the server sends a response back to the client (see Figure 1-1).

The **remote procedure call** (RPC) mechanism is the simplest way to implement client-server applications, because it keeps the details of network communications out of your application code. The idea is that each side behaves, as much as possible, the way it would within a traditional application: the programmer on the client side issues a call, and the programmer on the server side writes a procedure to carry out the desired function. To convey the illusion that you are working in a single address space, some hidden code has to handle all the networking. Many related issues are also involved, such as converting data between formats for different systems, and detecting communication errors.

Figure 1-2 shows the relationship between your application code and the RPC mechanism during a remote procedure call. In client application code, a remote procedure call looks like a local procedure call, because it is actually a call to a client stub. (A **stub** is surrogate code that supports remote procedure calls. Later in this chapter we'll discuss how stubs are created and what they do.) The **client stub** communicates with the **server stub** using the **RPC runtime library**, which is a set of standard runtime routines that supports all Microsoft RPC applications.

The server's RPC runtime library receives the remote procedure call and hands the client information to the server stub. The server stub invokes the remote procedure in the server application.

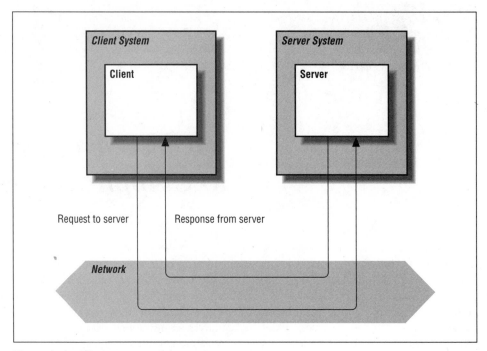

Figure 1-1. Client-server model

When the server finishes executing the remote procedure, its stub communicates output to the client stub, again by using the RPC runtime library. Finally, the client stub returns to the client application code.

Figure 1-3 shows the three phases required to develop a distributed application. An essential part of the RPC mechanism is an **interface**, which is a set of remote procedure declarations. Given the same interface, client and server development of an application can occur in parallel and on separate systems of the network.

In this chapter we will create an entire RPC application from scratch. Naturally, we'll use every shortcut and simplification the system offers to accomplish this feat. When you are done with the chapter, you will know the place of all the major RPC features, and how an application is developed.

You may not need to develop an entire application as shown in this chapter. If the interface and server already exist, your development may require only the client.

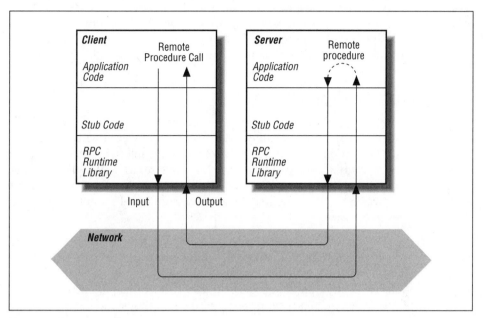

Figure 1–2. RPC mechanism

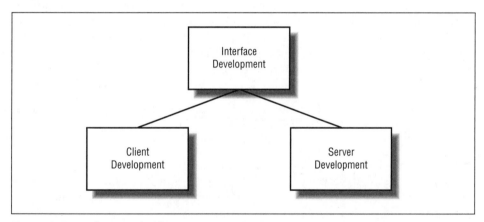

Figure 1–3. Application development

The arithmetic example in this chapter demonstrates a very simple one-client/one-server RPC application. Suppose a remote server system uses special hardware, such as an array processor. In our example, the client performs an arithmetic operation on arrays by calling a remote procedure that uses the array processor. The remote procedure executes on the server system, taking two arrays as arguments and adding together the elements of the arrays. The remote procedure returns the results to the client in a third array argument. Finally, the results of the remote procedure are displayed on the client system.

The arithmetic example is deliberately limited to demonstrate the basics of a distributed application implemented with RPC. We describe each portion of the application in this chapter, and Appendix C shows the complete code. The Preface tells you how to obtain source code online for this and other examples in the book.

A Simple Interface

When writing a local application, should you start by deciding exactly what functions you'll call and what arguments they take? Well, if you were dividing the work among multiple programmers and needed to clarify the interfaces between their work, you probably would proceed that way. The same reasoning applies to a distributed program: the client and server are being developed separately. Since the boundary or interface between them is the procedure call itself, you have to specify its attributes at the start.

So an interface consists of what the client and the server have to agree on; it contains some identifying information and a few facts about the remote procedures. Each **procedure declaration** includes the name of the procedure, the data type of the value it returns (if any), and the order and data types of its parameters (if any). An **interface definition** contains a set of procedure declarations and data types.

Just as programmers select functions from libraries, client application writers use interface definitions to determine how to call remote procedures. Server application writers use interface definitions to determine the data type of the remote procedure's return value, and the number, order, and data types of the arguments. The interface definition is like a design document that ties the client and server application code together. It is a formal definition describing the set of procedures offered by the interface.

You write the interface definition in **Microsoft Interface Definition Language** (MIDL). The MIDL closely resembles the declaration syntax and semantics of C, with the addition of attributes that allow information to be sent over a network.

You may think that we have introduced an unnecessary level of complexity here, but you will see that keeping the salient features of a distributed application in one file—the interface definition—makes it easier to scale up development to multiple servers and many clients for those servers.

Figure 1-4 shows the utilities used and the files produced when developing the arithmetic interface. The *uuidgen* utility generates a **universal unique identifier** (UUID) used in the interface definition to distinguish this interface from any other interface on the network. You use a text editor to write the rest of the interface definition, *arith.idl*. When the interface definition is complete, compile it with the MIDL compiler (*midl*) to generate stubs and a C header file that you use to develop the client and server programs.

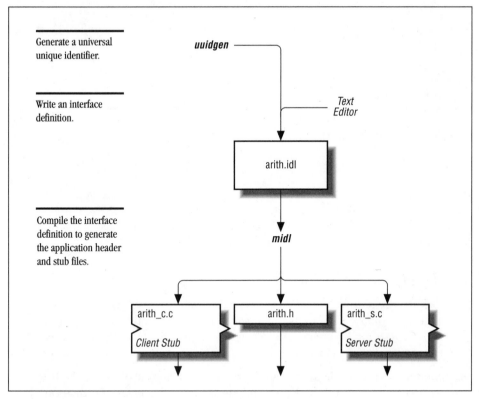

Figure 1–4. Arithmetic application: interface development

Universal Unique Identifiers

When you write a new interface, you must first generate a UUID with *uuidgen*. A UUID is simply a number that the *uuidgen* utility generates using time and network address information so that no matter when or where it is generated, it is guaranteed to be unique. A UUID is like a fingerprint that uniquely identifies something—such as an interface—across all network configurations.

An interface UUID is an excellent example of how you tie a client and server together through the MIDL file. When a client makes a remote procedure call, its UUID has to match that of the server. The RPC runtime library performs this check; this way you don't get unexpected results.

Generating a UUID in an interface definition template

To generate and display a UUID in a template for an interface definition, type the following command:

```
C:\> uuidgen -i
[
uuid(6AF85260-A3A4-101A-B1AE-08002B2E5B76),
version(1.0)
]
interface INTERFACENAME
{

}
```

In this example, the output appears at the terminal, but generally you save it in a file with the extension *.idl*. Replace the template name INTERFACENAME with a name you choose for the new interface. In the next section, we use a template like this to develop the arithmetic interface definition.

The Interface Definition

Now we are ready to write an interface definition. Here we put data type definitions and procedure declarations that need to be shared between server and client. Later, the MIDL compiler creates the header file and stubs from the interface definition, for use in your application.

The interface definition includes syntax elements called **attributes**, which specify features needed for distributed applications. Attributes convey information about the whole interface or items in the interface, including data types, arrays, pointers, structure members, union cases, procedures, and procedure parameters. For example, the in attribute specifies an input parameter for a remote procedure. You can pick out attributes in the file because they're enclosed in square brackets.

Example 1-1 shows a simple interface definition. The text consists of a **header** and **body**. The header contains a uuid attribute and the name assigned to the interface. The body specifies all procedures for the interface; it contains the procedure declarations with their data types and constants. There is only one procedure declared in our example. It adds two input arrays and returns the results in a third array.

Example 1–1: A Simple Interface Definition

```
/* FILE NAME: arith.idl */
/* This Interface Definition Language file represents a basic arithmetic */
/* procedure that a remote procedure call application can use.           */
[
uuid(6AF85260-A3A4-101A-B1AE-08002B2E5B76),     /* Universal Unique ID ❶ */
pointer_default(ref)              /* default pointer type is reference ❷ */
]
interface arith                         /* interface name is arith    ❸ */
{
    const unsigned short ARRAY_SIZE = 10; /* unsigned integer constant  ❹ */
```

Example 1–1: A Simple Interface Definition (continued)

```
    typedef long long_array[ARRAY_SIZE];   /* array type of long integers ❺ */

    void sum_arrays (    /* sum_arrays procedure does not return a value  ❻ */
        [in] long_array a,                  /* 1st parameter is passed in  */
        [in] long_array b,                  /* 2nd parameter is passed in  */
        [out] long_array c                  /* 3rd parameter is passed out */
    );
}
```

❶ The uuid attribute specifies the interface UUID. The interface definition header for any distributed application requires a uuid attribute.

❷ RPC provides three types of pointer, offering varying levels of complexity and overhead. Here, the pointer_default attribute specifies reference pointers as the default, because they offer the lowest overhead and are sufficient for our purposes.

❸ The last part of the interface definition header contains the keyword interface followed by the name chosen for the interface (arith).

❹ You can define constants for type definitions and application code. In this example, we define ARRAY_SIZE to set the bounds of arrays.

❺ You can define data types for use in other type definitions and procedure declarations. In this example, we define a data type that is an array of ten long integers. The indexes of arrays begin at zero, so the index values for this array range from zero to nine.

❻ The remainder of this interface definition is a procedure declaration. A procedure of type void does not return a value. The in and out parameter attributes are necessary so the MIDL compiler knows in which direction the data need to be sent over the network.

   [in]: A value is passed in to the remote procedure when it is called from the client.

   [out]: A value is passed back from the server to the calling procedure on the client when the procedure returns. A parameter with the out directional attribute must be a pointer or array so that the parameter can be passed to the client stub by reference. Note that the MIDL compiler requires more complex pointer types to have [in, out] attributes.

Stub and Header Generation Using the MIDL Compiler

When the interface definition is complete, you compile it with the MIDL compiler, which creates the following:

- A C language header file that contains definitions needed by the stubs and your application code. You can now include the header file in client and server application code.

- A client stub file, which you will link with the client portion of the application. During a remote procedure call, the client stub code is intermediate between your client application code and the RPC runtime library.

- A server stub file, which you will link with the server portion of the application. During a remote procedure call, the server stub code is intermediate between your server application code and the RPC runtime library.

- Client and server auxiliary stub files linked with the client and server portions of the application. The auxiliary stub files convert complex data structures like pointers to and from a data stream suitable for transmission over the network.

When you invoke the MIDL compiler, it generates the header file and intermediate C language stub files. Although we show a *midl* command by itself here, we recommend that you use a tool like *nmake* and a makefile to automate your entire build procedure. Such tools can hide differences between different hardware platforms making your code more portable. They can also relieve you from the drudgery of typing in long command strings over and over. Later, we'll show a makefile for use in building client and server applications.

To invoke the MIDL compiler and create the header and stub files for the arithmetic interface, type the following:

```
C:\> midl arith.idl
```

In this example, we generate the header file and the C language stub files of the client and server in one operation. The MIDL compiler produces auxiliary stub files by default, but you may suppress their generation by using appropriate MIDL compiler options.

If you develop the client and server on different systems, copies of the interface definition and the MIDL compiler must reside on both the client and server systems. To generate code correctly for different kinds of systems, compile the interface definition for the client stub on the client system, and for the server stub on the server system.

A Simple Client

We'll start our coding with the client, because it's so simple. In fact, you will not be able to detect any difference between our client and a traditional, single-system program! That's one of the beauties about Microsoft RPC—it hides most of the networking complexity from the client developer.

To develop a client, you must be able to read and interpret the interface definition. To use all the capabilities of RPC, you must also know the RPC runtime routines. The client in our simple example, however, requires no RPC runtime routines.

Figure 1-5 shows the files and utilities needed to produce a client. You write the client application code (*client.c*) in C. Currently, Microsoft RPC provides libraries only for C. Remote procedure calls in a client look like local procedure calls. (The server portion of the application implements the remote procedures themselves.) You must include the header file (*arith.h*) produced by the MIDL compiler, so that its type and constant definitions are available.

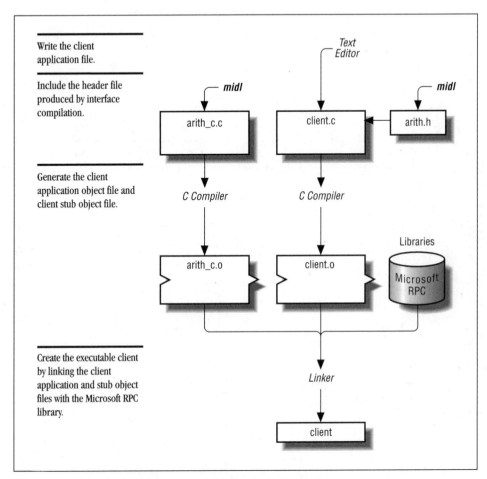

Figure 1–5. Arithmetic application: client development

After compiling *client.c* and *arith_c.c* with the C compiler, you can create the executable client by linking the client stub (*arith_c.o*) with the client object file and the Microsoft RPC library. Example 1-2 shows a simple client.

Example 1–2: A Simple Client

```
/* FILE NAME: client.c */
/* This is the client module of the arithmetic example. */
#include <stdio.h>
#include <stdlib.h>
#include "arith.h"        /* header file created by MIDL compiler ❶ */
```

Example 1–2: A Simple Client (continued)

```
long_array a ={100,200,345,23,67,65,0,0,0,0};
long_array b ={4,0,2,3,1,7,5,9,6,8};

main ()
{
   long_array    result;
   int i;

   sum_arrays(a, b, result);            /* A Remote Procedure Call ❷ */
   puts("sums:");
   for(i = 0; i < ARRAY_SIZE; i++)
      printf("%ld\n", result[i]);
}

/**********************************************************************/
/***              midl_user_allocate / midl_user_free           ***/
/**********************************************************************/

void * __RPC_API
midl_user_allocate               /* Procedures called by the stubs ❸ */
         (
          size
         )
size_t size;
{

    unsigned char * ptr;
    ptr = malloc( size );
    return ( (void *)ptr );

}

void __RPC_API
midl_user_free
         (
          object
         )
void * object;
{
    free (object);
}
```

❶   The client code includes the header file produced by the MIDL compiler.

❷   The client calls the remote procedure *sum_arrays* using the two initialized
    arrays as input. It then displays the elements of the resulting array.

❸   Two programmer-supplied procedures—*midl_user_allocate* and *midl_user_
    free*—may be called by client and server stubs for certain memory manage-
    ment functions. Although this simple application does not require these rou-
    tines, they are essential parts of many Microsoft RPC applications. Usually
    these are just wrapper routines for *malloc* and *free*. Chapter 4, *Pointers,
    Arrays, and Memory Usage*, contains more information about these proce-
    dures.

The following section shows how to write the server for the arithmetic application.

A Minimal Server

Developing a server requires you to know the interface definition and some RPC runtime routines. You write two distinct portions of code:

- The actual remote procedures—this portion is sometimes called the **manager**

- Code to initialize the server

You make calls to the RPC runtime routines mainly in the server initialization, which prepares the server to listen for remote procedure calls. For our arithmetic application, server initialization is the only code that requires the use of runtime routines.

Figure 1-6 shows the files and utilities needed to produce a server. You must write the remote procedures (*manager.c*) and server initialization code (*server.c*) in C. You need the header file (*arith.h*) produced by the MIDL compiler because it contains definitions required by the remote procedures and runtime calls.

After compiling the server application with the C compiler, you create the executable server by linking the server stub (*arith_s.o*) with the server application object files and the Microsoft RPC library.

Remote Procedure Implementation

The programmer who writes a server must develop all procedures that are declared in the interface definition. Refer to the interface definition (*arith.idl*) and the header file generated by the MIDL compilation (*arith.h*) for the procedure's parameters and data types. Example 1-3 shows the code for the remote procedure of the arithmetic application.

Example 1–3: A Remote Procedure Implementation

```
/* FILE NAME: procedure.c */
/* Implementation of procedure defined in the arithmetic interface. */
#include <stdio.h>
#include "arith.h"              /* header file produced by MIDL compiler ❶ */

void sum_arrays(a, b, c)        /* implementation of sum_arrays procedure ❷ */
    long_array a;
    long_array b;
    long_array c;
    {
    int i;

    for(i = 0; i < ARRAY_SIZE; i++)
        c[i] = a[i] + b[i];     /* array elements are each added together ❸ */
    }
```

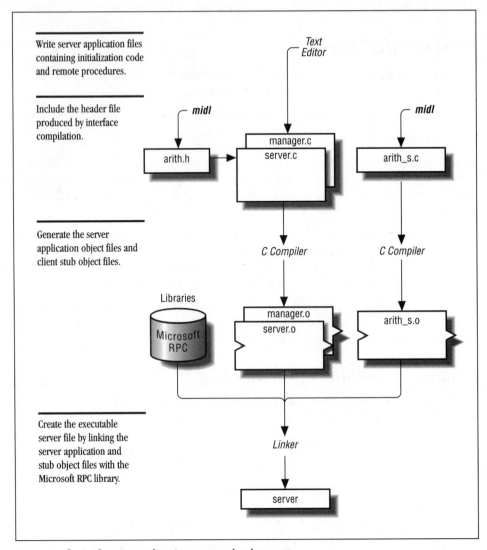

Figure 1-6. Arithmetic application: server development

❶   The server code includes the header file produced by the MIDL compiler.

❷   The procedure definition matches its corresponding declaration in the interface definition.

❸   The procedure implementation is completed.

So far, the client and server application code has been much like any other application. In fact, you can compile and link the client and remote procedures, and run the resulting program as a local test.

Before going on to write the server initialization code, we found it useful to discuss how the arithmetic application works in a distributed environment. This is the subject of the next section.

A Distributed Application Environment

When a client makes a remote procedure call, a binding relationship is established with a server (see Figure 1-7). **Binding information** is network communication and location information for a particular server. Conveniently, in the arithmetic application, the client stub and the RPC runtime library automatically find the server for you during the remote procedure call. Figure 1-8 illustrates how binding information acts like a set of keys to a series of gates in the path a remote procedure call takes toward execution.

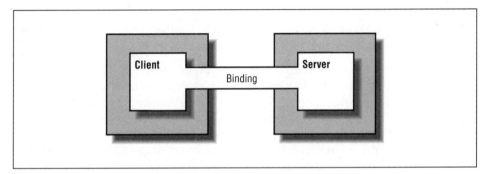

Figure 1-7. Binding

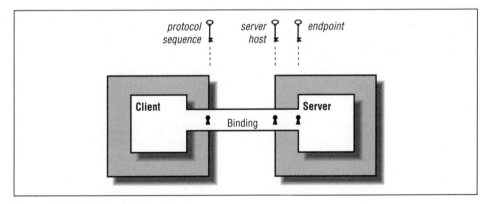

Figure 1-8. Binding information

Binding information includes the following:

1. **Protocol Sequence**

   A protocol sequence is an RPC-specific name containing a combination of communication protocols that describe the network communication used between a client and server. For example, ncacn_ip_tcp represents the protocol sequence for a Network Computing Architecture connection-oriented protocol, over a network with the Internet Protocol and the Transmission Control Protocol for transport.

2. **Server Host**

   The client needs to identify the server system. The server host is the name or network address of the host on which the server resides.

3. **Endpoint**

   The client needs to identify a server process on the server host. An endpoint is a number representing a specific server process running on a system.

To help clients find servers in a flexible and portable manner, Microsoft RPC provides a name service to store binding information. **Name service** is a general term for a database service that stores information for distributed applications—that is, a service that offers the same information to applications running on different systems. Using the name service, a server can store binding information that a client on another system can retrieve later. The particular name service offered with Microsoft RPC is called the Locator.

The RPC runtime library contains a general set of functions called **name service independent** (NSI) routines. Thus, to store binding information, your server calls an NSI routine. This routine internally communicates with the Locator to put information into the database. NSI routines are a level of abstraction above the particular name service on a system, and thus can be used to access whatever name service your system uses. For instance, if you shared a network with DCE systems, you could configure your Microsoft RPC system to use the DCE Cell Directory Service (CDS).

Distributed applications do not require the name service database, but we recommend that you use it. Alternatives to using the name service are to manage binding information directly in client and server code, or to create your own application-specific method of advertising and searching for servers. These alternatives present more maintenance problems than if you use the name service routines.

Figures 1-9, 1-10, and 1-11 show how the arithmetic application uses binding information, and how the remote procedure call completes.

A server must make certain information available to clients. Figure 1-9 shows the typical steps needed each time a server starts executing. A server first registers the interface with the RPC runtime library, so that clients later know whether they are

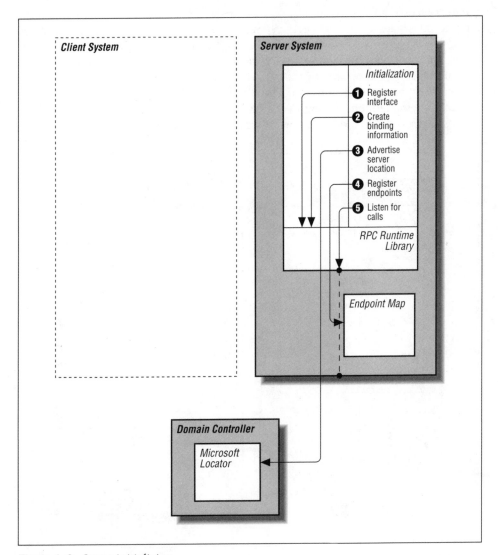

Figure 1–9. Server initializing

compatible with the server. The runtime library creates binding information to identify this server process. The server places the binding information in appropriate databases so that clients can find it. The server places communication and host information in the name service database. The server also places process information (endpoints) in a special database on the server system called the **local endpoint map**, which is a database used to store endpoints for servers running on a given system. In the final initialization step, a server waits while listening for remote procedure calls from clients.

When the server has completed initialization, a client can find it by obtaining its binding information, as illustrated in Figure 1-10. A remote procedure call in the client application code transfers execution to the client stub. The client stub looks up the information in the name service database to find the server system. The RPC runtime library finds the server process endpoint by looking up the information in the server system's endpoint map. The RPC runtime library uses the binding information to complete the binding of the client to the server. Chapter 3, *How to Write Clients*, discusses variations on how to obtain server binding information.

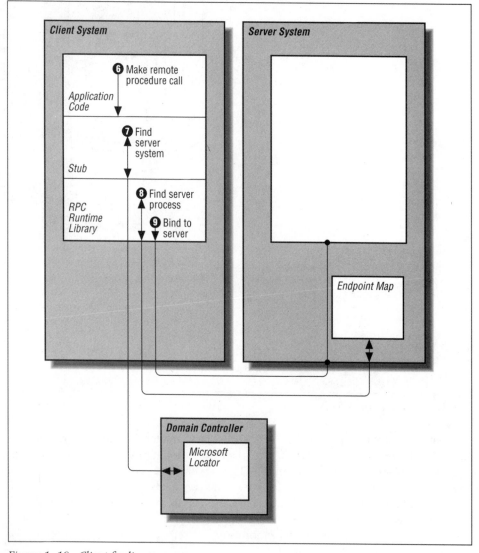

Figure 1–10. Client finding a server

As shown in Figure 1-11, the remote procedure executes after the client finds the server. The client stub puts arguments and other calling information into an internal RPC format that the runtime library transmits over the network. The server runtime library receives the data and transfers it to the stub, which converts it back to a format the application can use. When the remote procedure completes, the conversion process is reversed. The server stub puts the return arguments into the internal RPC format, and the server runtime library transmits the data back to the client over the network. The client runtime library receives the data and gives it to the client stub, which converts the data back for use by the application.

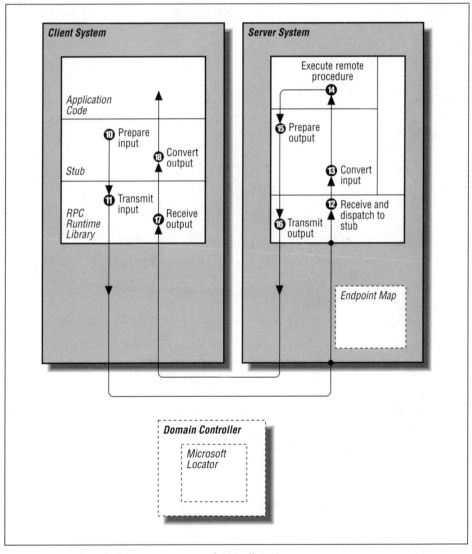

Figure 1-11. Completing a remote procedure call

Server Initialization

As illustrated in Figure 1-9, a server must make certain information available to the RPC runtime library and clients before it can accept remote procedure calls. Example 1-4 contains the server initialization code for the arithmetic application, illustrating the sequence of steps to initialize a typical RPC server.

Example 1-4: A Minimal Server Initialization

```
/* FILE NAME: server.c */
#include <stdio.h>
#include "arith.h"                   /* header created by the MIDL compiler */
#include "status.h"                  /* header with the CHECK_STATUS macro */

main ()
{
   unsigned long     status;                      /* error status */
   rpc_binding_vector_t *binding_vector;          /*set of binding handles */
   unsigned char     *entry_name;         /*entry name for name service */

   status =                                        /* error status */
   RpcServerRegisterIf(         /* register interface with the RPC runtime ❶ */
      arith_v1_0_s_ifspec,             /* interface specification (arith.h) */
      NULL,
      NULL
   );
   CHECK_STATUS(status, "Can't register interface", ABORT);

   status =
   RpcServerUseAllProtseqs(                 /* create binding information ❷ */
      RPC_C_PROTSEQ_MAX_REQS_DEFAULT,            /* queue size for calls */
      NULL                          /* no security descriptor is used */
   );
   CHECK_STATUS(status, "Can't create binding information", ABORT);

   status =
   RpcServerInqBindings(     /* obtain this server's binding information ❸ */
      &binding_vector
   );
   CHECK_STATUS(status, "Can't get binding information", ABORT);

   entry_name = (unsigned char *)getenv("ARITHMETIC_SERVER_ENTRY");
   status =
   RpcNsBindingExport(        /* export entry to name service database ❹ */
      RPC_C_NS_SYNTAX_DEFAULT,       /* syntax of the entry name        */
      entry_name,                    /* entry name for name service     */
      arith_v1_0_s_ifspec,         /* interface specification (arith.h)  */
      binding_vector,                /* the set of server binding handles */
      NULL
   );
   CHECK_STATUS(status, "Can't export to name service database", ABORT);

   status =
   RpcEpRegister(             /* register endpoints in local endpoint map ❺ */
      arith_v1_0_s_ifspec,         /* interface specification (arith.h)   */
```

Example 1–4: A Minimal Server Initialization (continued)

```
        binding_vector,              /* the set of server binding handles    */
        NULL,
        NULL
                    Can't add address to the endpoint map", ABORT);

                              /* free set of server binding handles ❻ */

                    "Can't free binding handles and vector", ABORT);
                    remote procedure calls...");

                                      /* listen for remote calls   ❼ */
                                      /* minimum number of threads  */
                    _CALLS_DEFAULT,        /* concurrent calls to server */
                        /* continue listening until explicitly stopped */

                , "rpc listen failed", ABORT);

          /*****************************************************/
          midl_user_allocate / midl_user_free          ***/
          /*****************************************************/

                    /* Procedures called by the stubs       ❽ */



          * ptr;
          size );
          i *)ptr );




          ct



          t);
```

❶ **Register the interface**. Register the interface with the RPC runtime library using
the *RpcServerRegisterIf* routine. The `arith_v1_0_s_ifspec` variable is called
an **interface handle**. It is produced by the MIDL compiler and refers to information that applications need, such as the UUID. We describe the NULL arguments in Chapter 5, *How to Write a Server*.

The CHECK_STATUS macro is defined in the *status.h* header file for the applications in this book. It is used to interpret status codes from runtime calls. (See Example 3-12 in Chapter 3.) Figure 1-9, step 1 is now complete.

❷ **Create binding information.** To create binding information, you must choose one or more network protocol sequences. This application, like most, calls *RpcServerUseAllProtseqs* so that clients can use all available protocols. During this call, the RPC runtime library gathers together information about available protocols, your host, and endpoints to create binding information. The system allocates a buffer for each endpoint, to hold incoming call information. Microsoft RPC sets the buffer size when you use the *RPC_C_PROTSEQ_MAX_CALLS_DEFAULT* argument.

❸ **Obtain the binding information.** When creating binding information, the RPC runtime library stores binding information for each protocol sequence. A **binding handle** is a reference in application code to the information for one possible binding. A set of server binding handles is called a **binding vector**. You must obtain this information through the *RpcServerInqBindings* routine in order to pass the information to other runtime routines. Figure 1-9, step 2 is now complete.

❹ **Advertise the server location in the name service database.** In this example, the server places (exports) all its binding information in the name service database using the *RpcNsBindingExport* runtime routine.

The *RPC_C_NS_SYNTAX_DEFAULT* argument tells the routine how to interpret an entry name. (The current version of Microsoft RPC has only one syntax.) The entry_name is a string obtained in this example from an environment variable set by the user specifically for this application, ARITHMETIC_SERVER_ENTRY (discussed at the end of this chapter when the application is run). The interface handle, arith_ServerIfHANDLE, associates interface information with the entry name in the name service database. The client later uses name service routines to obtain binding information by comparing the interface information in the name service database with information about its own interface. Figure 1-9, step 3 is now complete.

❺ **Register the endpoints in the local endpoint map.** The RPC runtime library assigns endpoints to the server as part of creating binding information. The *RpcEpRegister* runtime routine lets the endpoint map on the local host know that the process running at these endpoints is associated with this interface. Figure 1-9, step 4 is now complete.

❻ **Free the set of binding handles.** Memory for the binding handles was allocated with a call to the *RpcServerInqBindings* routine. When you have finished passing binding information to the other routines, release the memory using the *RpcBindingVectorFree* routine.

❼ **Listen for remote calls**. Finally, the server must wait for calls to arrive. Each system has a default for the maximum number of calls that a server can accept at one time. Microsoft RPC sets this maximum default number when you use the *RPC_C_LISTEN_MAX_CALLS_DEFAULT* argument. Figure 1-9, step 5 is now complete.

❽ Two programmer-supplied procedures—*midl_user_allocate* and *midl_user_free*—may be called by client and server stubs for certain memory management functions. Although this simple application does not require these routines, they are essential parts of many Microsoft RPC applications. Usually these are just wrapper routines for *malloc* and *free*. Chapter 4 contains more information about these procedures.

All of the server code is now complete. The compilation of the application is shown in the next section.

Producing the Application

So far we have written the interface definition, produced the stubs and header file from the interface definition with the MIDL compiler, and written the client and server portions of the application. To produce the application, compile and link the client and server separately, each on the system where you want its executable to run.

Microsoft RPC Libraries

Microsoft RPC-distributed applications must be linked with the Microsoft RPC libraries, which may vary depending on your system and vendor. This book uses the following libraries for a link on a Microsoft Windows NT system:

```
rpcrt4.lib
rpcns4.lib
libcmt.lib
kernel32.lib
```

The *rpcrt4.lib* library provides Windows runtime library functions. The *rpcns4.lib* library provides name service functions. The *libcmt.lib* library provides standard C library functions. The *kernel32.lib* library provides threads functions.

The following sections assume that your client and server files are available to the respective client and server systems.

Compile and Link the Client and Server Code

Recall that Figures 1-5 and 1-6 show the utilities used and files produced when developing a client and a server. Here, we show a portion of a makefile we use with *nmake* to compile and link the client and server code. The order in which these commands execute is:

❶ A *midl* command builds *.c* and *.h* files from the *.idl* file.

❷ The compiler generates object files for the client and server.

❸ The linker produces client and server executables.

Example 1–5: A Makefile for Building a Client and Server

```
# FILE NAME: Makefile
# Makefile for the arithmetic application
#
# definitions for this makefile
#
APPL=arith
NTRPCLIBS=rpcrt4.lib rpcns4.lib libcmt.lib kernel32.lib

# Include Windows NT macros                                  # ❶
!include <ntwin32.mak>

# NT c flags
cflags = -c -W0 -Gz -D_X86_=1 -DWIN32 -DMT /nologo           # ❷

# NT nmake inference rules
 .c.obj:                                                     # ❸
   $(cc) $(cdebug) $(cflags) $(cvarsmt) $<
   $(cvtomf)

#
# COMPLETE BUILD of the application
#
all:    client.exe server.exe                               # ❹

#
# CLIENT BUILD
#
client:     client.exe
client.exe: client.obj $(APPL)_c.obj $(APPL)_x.obj          # ❺
   $(link) $(linkdebug) $(conflags) -out:client.exe -map:client.map \
     client.obj $(APPL)_c.obj $(APPL)_x.obj \
     $(NTRPCLIBS)

#
# SERVER BUILD
#
server:     server.exe
server.exe: server.obj manager.obj $(APPL)_s.obj $(APPL)_x.obj   # ❻
   $(link) $(linkdebug) $(conflags) -out:server.exe -map:server.map \
     server.obj manager.obj $(APPL)_s.obj $(APPL)_x.obj\
     $(NTRPCLIBS)

# client and server sources                                 # ❼
client.obj:  client.c  $(APPL).h
manager.obj: manager.c $(APPL).h
server.obj:  server.c  $(APPL).h
```

Example 1-5: A Makefile for Building a Client and Server (continued)

```
# client and server stubs                                   # ❽
$(APPL)_c.obj: $(APPL)_c.c
$(APPL)_x.obj: $(APPL)_x.c
$(APPL)_s.obj : $(APPL)_s.c

# generate stubs, auxiliary and header file from the MIDL file    # ❾
$(APPL).h $(APPL)_c.c $(APPL)_x.c : $(APPL).idl
    midl $(APPL).idl
```

❶   *ntwin32.mak* contains machine specific-variables for portability.

❷   This line defines compiler options.

❸   The inference rules assign values to *nmake* options and flags.

❹   This line builds client and server executables.

❺   Link the client object files with the runtime libraries defined by $(NTRPCLIBS) to produce the executable client application.

❻   Link the server object files with the runtime libraries defined by $(NTRPCLIBS) to produce the executable server application.

❼   Compile the client and server application C source files to produce application object files. The server sources include both the remote procedure implementation and the server initialization, to create the server object files.

❽   Compile the client and server C language stub files to produce stub object files.

❾   Use the *midl* compiler to produce the client and server stub files and the header file.

Running the Application

We designed the arithmetic application for simplicity. One of our short-cuts was to let the client automatically find the server by using the name service to retrieve server binding information. The client stub obtains the binding information exported by the server to the name service database, and the client RPC runtime library completes the remote procedure call.

To run the distributed arithmetic application, follow these steps:

1.   This server exports binding information to a name service database. Make sure a Microsoft Locator is running in your Windows NT domain.

2.   Execute the server. For this example, the application-specific environment variable, ARITHMETIC_SERVER_ENTRY, is set prior to running the server. This variable represents a name for the entry that this server uses when exporting the binding information to the name service database. The usual convention for entry names is to concatenate the interface and host names. We use an

environment variable here because the name can vary depending on which host you use to invoke the server. If you do not supply a valid name, the binding information will not be placed in the name service database, and the program will fail. The prefix /.:/ (or alternatively / . . . /, represents the global portion of a name and is used for compatibility with OSF DCE naming conventions. For this example, assume that the server resides on the system *moxie.*

```
C:\SERVER> set ARITHMETIC_SERVER_ENTRY=/.:/arithmetic_moxie
C:\SERVER> server
```

3. After the server is running, execute the client on the client system:

```
C:\CLIENT> client
sums:
104
200
347
26
68
72
5
9
6
8
```

4. The server is still running and, for now, should be terminated by typing ^C (Ctrl-C). In Chapter 5 we'll show a way to gracefully terminate your server so that it removes its endpoint information from the local endpoint map.

Figure 1-12 summarizes the development of the arithmetic application.

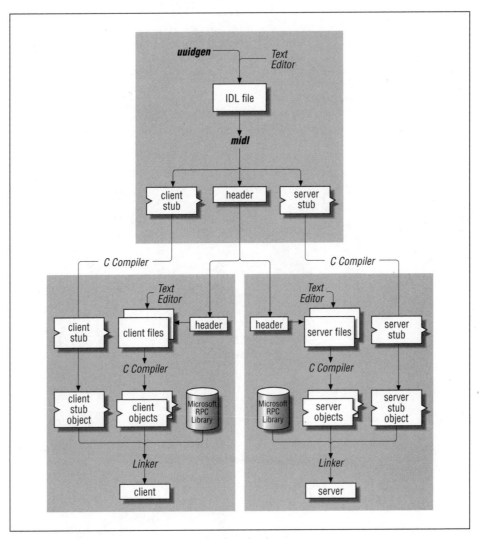

Figure 1–12. Arithmetic application: complete development

2

Using a Microsoft RPC Interface

As we discussed in Chapter 1, *Overview of an RPC Application*, the first step in creating a distributed application is to write an **interface definition**. This is also known as an IDL or MIDL file because it is written in the Microsoft Interface Definition Language and ends in the suffix *.idl*. This file contains definitions that the client and server share, and a list of all the procedures offered by the server. This chapter explains what interface definitions need to contain.

An interface definition is usually written by the person developing the server because it describes the procedures offered by that server. Client developers need to read and interpret the definition. All servers that support the interface must implement the remote procedures using the same data types and parameters. All clients must call the remote procedures consistently.

A **procedure declaration** in an interface definition specifies the procedure name, the data type of the value it returns (if any), and the number, order, and data types of its parameters (if any).

Interface definitions are compiled with the MIDL compiler (*midl*) to create the header and stub files. Use the header file with your application C code, and link the stub files with your application object code and the RPC runtime library to create a distributed application. If you make a mistake when writing an interface definition, the MIDL compiler gives useful messages to help you correct what is wrong.

Microsoft Interface Definition Language (MIDL)

Use the Microsoft Interface Definition Language (MIDL) to define the necessary data types and declare the remote procedures for an interface. Declarations in MIDL are similar to declarations in C,[*] with the addition of attributes.

Attributes

Interface definition **attributes** are special keywords that offer information to help distribute an application. They are enclosed in square brackets in the MIDL file. All of them facilitate network use in one way or another:

- Some attributes distinguish one interface from another on a network. They guarantee that a client finds the servers that implement the proper remote procedures. For example, the `uuid` attribute declares the UUID for the interface.

- Some attributes explicitly describe data transmitted over a network. Some aspects of data in C that you take for granted must be described explicitly for a distributed application. For example, a union is a data structure that allows different data types in the same area of memory. Your application uses another variable to keep track of which data type is valid. In a distributed program, this additional variable must be specified in MIDL so it is transmitted with a union parameter.

- Some attributes make data transmission more efficient. In a local application, procedures have access to both parameters and global variables so that any amount of data can be accessed efficiently. In a distributed application, all data used by the client and the remote procedure must be passed as parameters and transmitted over the network. Since most parameters are passed in only one direction, you use attributes to specify whether each parameter is used for input, output, or both.

Tables A-1 through A-8 in Appendix A, *MIDL and ACF Attributes Quick Reference*, show all MIDL attributes with brief descriptions of each. In this chapter, we discuss the MIDL attributes so you know how to write an interface definition. But to really understand how those attributes reflect your use of data in an application, you have to see them along with the application's C code—and that will appear in later chapters.

---

[*] MIDL is currently designed to work with C. However, MIDL has features such as `boolean` and `byte` data types, so that it will work in future versions for languages other than C.

Structure of an Interface Definition

An interface definition includes some or all of the following:

- The interface header
    - Interface header attributes
    - Interface name
- The interface body
    - Import ·statements
    - Constant definitions
    - Data type definitions
    - Procedure declarations

Interface Header Attributes

Interface header attributes specify RPC features that apply to an entire interface. One is the name that you have chosen, such as `arith` in the application shown in Chapter 1. But choosing a name is not enough, because someone could easily create another application called `arith`, and a client would be confused about which to use. That is where the interface UUID and the version number come in.

As we saw in Chapter 1, you generate a UUID through *uuidgen*. This distinguishes your `arith` even when someone else steals your name to create a different interface. But the creators of DCE and Microsoft RPC recognized that an interface does not stay the same forever; you are likely to update it regularly. So they also allow for a **version number** in the interface header. A complete version number consists of a major and minor version number. For example, if a version number is 2.1, the major version is 2 and the minor version is 1.

During a remote procedure call, the following rules determine whether a client can use an interface that a server supports:

- The UUID of the client and server must match.
- The major version number of the client and server must match.
- The minor version number for the client must be less than or equal to the minor version number for the server. A client minor version number that is less than the server minor version number indicates an upwardly compatible change to the interface on the server.

When you create new versions of an interface by adding new declarations and definitions, increase the minor version number. Any other changes to an interface require a major version number change, essentially creating a different interface.

The Inventory Application

The application we use in this chapter is a simple inventory: a product database is stored on the server system, and a client makes inquiries based on a part number. The complete application is shown in Appendix D, *The Inventory Application*.

Example 2-1 shows the header in the interface definition of the inventory application.

Example 2–1: Interface Header Attributes

```
/* FILE NAME: inv.idl */
[                                     /* brackets enclose attributes ❶ */
uuid(008B3C84-93A5-11C9-85B0-08002B147A61),/* universal unique identifier ❷ */
version(1.0),                         /* version of this interface ❸ */
pointer_default(unique)               /* pointer default           ❹ */
] interface  inventory                /* interface name            ❺ */

{
/* The body of an interface definition consists of import statements,     */
/* constant definitions, data type definitions, and procedure declarations. */
 .
 .
 .
}
```

❶ Brackets enclose attributes in interface definitions.

❷ The `uuid` is a required attribute that uniquely identifies an interface. All copies of this interface definition contain the same UUID.

❸ The `version` is an optional attribute used to identify different versions of an interface. In this example the major version number is 1 and the minor version number is 0.

❹ The `pointer_default` is an optional attribute needed by some interface definitions so that pointer data is efficiently transmitted.

❺ The keyword `interface` and a name are required to identify the interface. The MIDL compiler uses this name to construct data structure names. Client and server code use these data structures to access information about the interface.

Table A-1 in Appendix A lists and describes all interface header attributes.

Type Definitions, Data Attributes, and Constants

In C, a data type can map to different sizes on different systems. For example, a `long` data type in C may be 16, 32, or 64 bits, depending on the system. The size of a MIDL data type, however, must be the same on all systems so that Microsoft applications can exchange data. Consequently, you might need to change data types if you port your application code platforms with differing data type sizes.

Table 2-1 shows the basic MIDL types and the size of each in bits. You'll notice that these generally correspond to basic C data types.

Table 2–1: MIDL Basic Data Types

MIDL Data Type	Size
boolean	8 bits
byte	8 bits
char	8 bits
void	–
void *	opaque
handle_t	opaque
error_status_t	32 bits
Integers	
small	8 bits
short	16 bits
long	32 bits
Floating Point	
float	32 bits
double	64 bits
International Characters	
wchar_t	16 bits

Table 2-2 contains notes about some of the MIDL data types.

Table 2–2: Notes on MIDL Data Types

MIDL_Type	Notes
boolean	Data that is either idl_true or idl_false.
byte	Data is not automatically converted when transmitted over the network to a system with a different data format. Use this type to transmit data that is untyped or opaque so that no conversion is performed on it.
char	An unsigned, 8-bit character. C uses the char data type to represent 8-bit integers as well as characters, and it interprets them as signed on some systems and unsigned on others. Use the MIDL char data type for true character data and use small or unsigned small to represent 8-bit integers in interface definitions.
void	Indicates that a procedure does not return a value.

Table 2–2: Notes on MIDL *Data Types (continued)*

MIDL_Type	Notes
void *	Used with the `context_handle` attribute to define context handles. It refers to opaque data, the details of which are hidden from you. See Chapter 7, *Context Handles*.
handle_t	Data that denotes a binding handle. Chapter 3, *How to Write Clients*, describes how to use this data type to define binding handles in an interface definition.
error_status_t	Data that denotes an RPC communication status.
wchar_t	16-bit unsigned data element.

How do the MIDL data types help to distribute an application? The explanation lies in how the client and server stubs handle data that might need to change as it moves from one computer system to another.

During a remote procedure call, the client stub prepares input parameters for transmission, and the server stub converts the data for use by the server application. When the remote procedure completes execution on the server system, the server stub prepares the output parameters for transmission and the client stub converts the data for the client application.

Marshalling is the process during a remote procedure call that prepares data for transmission across the network. Marshalling converts data into a byte-stream format and packages it for transmission using a **Network Data Representation** (**NDR**). NDR allows successful data sharing between systems with different data formats. It handles differences like big-endian versus little-endian (byte order), ASCII characters versus EBCDIC characters, and other incompatibilities.

Data transmitted across the network undergoes a process called **unmarshalling**. If the data format of sender and receiver is different, the receiver's stub converts the data to the correct format for that system, and passes the data to the application.

Example 2-2 shows a constant and two type definitions for the inventory interface.

Example 2–2: MIDL Type Definitions

```
[
/* The header of an interface definition consists of interface header   */
/* attributes and the name of the interface.                            */
.
.
.
] interface inventory
{
    const long MAX_STRING = 30;              /* constant for string size ❶ */

    typedef long     part_num;               /* inventory part number ❷ */

    typedef [string] char part_name[MAX_STRING+1];      /* name of part ❸ */
```

Example 2-2: MIDL Type Definitions (continued)

```
.
.
.
/* The remainder of the interface definition consists of other data    */
/* type definitions and the procedure declarations.                    */
}
```

❶ Use the keyword `const` followed by a data type to declare a constant to use in type definitions and application code.

❷ Use the keyword `typedef` followed by a data type to define a new data type.

❸ A data type is not sufficient to completely describe some kinds of data. Attributes provide the necessary extra information. In this example, the `string` attribute enclosed in brackets applies to the character array `part_name`, so that it becomes a null-terminated string.

Table A-4, in Appendix A, lists and describes all the data type attributes. So far we have seen only basic MIDL data types. Now we will explain how to construct more complex data types in an interface definition.

Pointers

In a distributed application, a pointer does not provide the same convenience and efficiency that it does in a local application because there is stub overhead such as memory allocation, copying, and transmitting all the data the pointer refers to. MIDL contains three kinds of pointers to balance efficiency with more complete pointer capabilities.

A **full pointer** has all of the capabilities associated with pointers. They can be null or point to existing data. They can contain cycles or loops and they can be aliased to another pointer in the argument list. The full pointer attribute is the default pointer type. You can override this setting by using the *pointer_default* attribute.

A **unique pointer** can be null or point to existing data. But unique pointers cannot contain cycles or loops and they cannot be aliased to another pointer in the argument list. In Microsoft Extension mode, the unique pointer attribute is the default pointer type assigned to pointers that are not parameters. You can override this setting using the `pointer_default` attribute.

A **reference pointer** is a simpler pointer that refers to existing data. A reference pointer has a performance advantage, but limited capabilities compared to a unique pointer. No new memory can be allocated for the client during the remote procedure call, so memory for the data must exist in the client before the call is made.

The `unique` attribute represents a unique pointer and the `ref` attribute represents a reference pointer. Chapter 4, *Pointers, Arrays, and Memory Usage*, discusses how to use pointers.

Arrays

Array index values begin at 0 in MIDL, as in C. For example, the array `arr[10]` defined in an interface definition has elements `arr[0]`, `arr[1]`, `...`, `arr[9]` when you use it in the client or server code.

Arrays are expensive to transmit, so MIDL provides some sophisticated ways to keep down the amount of data actually sent over the network. Here are the kinds of arrays provided:

fixed array   A fixed array has constant index values for its dimensions. This is like a standard C array.

varying array   A varying array has a maximum size determined at compile time, just like a fixed array. But it also has subset bounds represented by variables. Only the portion of the array you need is transmitted in a remote procedure call.

conformant array   The size of a conformant array is represented by a dimension variable so that the actual size is determined when the application is running.

Chapter 4 discusses arrays in more detail.

Strings

In C code it is convenient to use strings to manipulate character data. C library routines, such as *strcpy*, recognize a null character as the end of a string in the character array. In MIDL, all characters in an array are transmitted, including null characters. Therefore, you must explicitly define strings with the `string` attribute, so that only the characters up to a null character are transmitted. Example 2-3 shows some string definitions.

Example 2-3: Defining Strings in MIDL

```
    const long MAX_STRING = 30;              /* a constant for string size */
    .
    .
    .

    typedef [string] char part_name[MAX_STRING+1];      /* name of part    ❶ */
    typedef [string, unique] char *paragraph;      /* description of part ❷ */
```

❶ To specify a string, apply the `string` attribute to a character or byte array. In this example, the string size is 31 in order to accommodate the terminating null byte, but the maximum string length is 30. The data type of the array elements must be a `char` or `byte`, or defined with a type definition that resolves to a `char` or `byte`. The data type can also be a structure whose fields all resolve to a `char` or `byte`.

❷ This example specifies a **conformant string** by applying the `string` attribute to a pointer to a `char` or `byte` data type.

A conformant string has the maximum length allocated in the application code. You can also specify a conformant string using array syntax. For example, the following is another way to define the conformant string paragraph:

```
typedef [string] char paragraph[];
```

When you use a conformant string as an input parameter to a remote procedure, the amount of data that is transmitted is determined from the current string length. If the string parameter is both input and output, however, apply an array attribute size_is or max_is to the string so the length can increase when the remote procedure completes. Chapter 4 discusses array attributes in greater detail.

Enumerated types

MIDL provides an enumerated type, just as modern versions of the C language do. The idea is to provide a set of symbolic names to make source code more self-documenting. These names are associated by the compiler to a set of integer values, but the values usually have no more significance than to distinguish one name from another. In Example 2-4, the keyword enum, followed by a list of identifiers, maps the identifiers to consecutive integers starting with 0. For this example, we use enumeration to specify more than one kind of measurement unit for parts in the inventory. Some parts are counted as whole items, while other parts are measured by weight.

Example 2-4: Defining an Enumerated Type in MIDL

```
typedef enum {
    ITEM, GRAM, KILOGRAM
} part_units;                           /* units of measurement */
```

Microsoft RPC extensions allow you to attach specific integer values to identifiers in an enumeration. In Example 2-5, flight numbers are attached to specific flights in an air traffic application.

Example 2-5: Attaching Specific Integer Values to Enumerators

```
typedef enum {
    BOS-CHI=716, BOS-DEN=432, BOS-SFO=510     /* flight numbers */
} flights;
```

Structures

You define structures in MIDL the same way you do in C. In Example 2-6 the struct keyword is followed by a list of typed members that define a structure. For this example, two structures are shown. The structure part_price contains a units-of-measurement member and a price-per-unit member. The part_units data type is an enumerated type. The structure part_record represents all the data for a particular part number. As in C, any user-defined types such as part_num must be defined before they are used.

Example 2-6: Defining Structures in MIDL

```
typedef struct part_price {                /* price of part */
    part_units units;
    double     per_unit;
} part_price;

.
.
.

typedef struct part_record {               /* data for each part */
    part_num       number;
    part_name      name;
    paragraph      description;
    part_price     price;
    part_quantity  quantity;
    part_list      subparts;
} part_record;
```

Discriminated unions

In C a union is a data structure that stores different types and sizes of data in the same area of memory. For example, this union stores a long integer or a double precision floating-point number:

```
typedef union {
    long int number;
    double   weight;
} quantity_t;
```

To keep track of what type is stored in the union, the application must use a discriminator variable that is separate from the union data structure. This creates a special requirement for a distributed application. If a remote procedure call includes a union parameter, the remote procedure has no way of knowing which member of the union is valid unless it receives the discriminator along with the union.

In MIDL, a **discriminated union** includes a discriminator as part of the data structure itself, so that the currently valid data type is transmitted with the union. When you define a discriminated union, it looks like a combination of a C union and a switch statement. The switch defines the discriminator, and each case of the switch defines a valid data type and member name for the union.

Example 2-7 shows how to define a discriminated union.

Example 2-7: Defining a Discriminated Union in MIDL

```
typedef enum {
    ITEM, GRAM, KILOGRAM
} part_units;                              /* units of measurement */

.
.
.
```

Example 2–7: Defining a Discriminated Union in MIDL (continued)

❶   ❷   ❸

```
   typedef union switch(part_units units) total {    /* quantity of part */
      case ITEM:     long int number;
      case GRAM:                              ❹
      case KILOGRAM: double    weight;
   } part_quantity;                           ❺
```

❶ You begin the definition of a discriminated union data type with the keywords **typedef union**.

❷ Use the keyword **switch** to specify the data type and name of the discriminator variable, **units**. The data type **part_units** is a previously defined enumerated type. A discriminator can be Boolean, character, integer, or an
enumerated type.

❸ Define the name of the union, **total**, prior to listing the union cases.

❹ Use the keyword **case** followed by a value to specify the data type and name
of each union member. The case value is the same type as the discriminator
variable. In this example, a union defines the quantity of a part in an inventory. Some parts are counted as whole items while other parts are weighed.
This union offers a choice between defining the quantity as a long integer or
as a double precision floating-point number. The union case **GRAM** has the
same data type and name as the case **KILOGRAM**.

❺ The name of the new data type is **part_quantity**, which you use in application code to allocate a discriminated union variable.

In application code, the discriminated union is a C structure. The MIDL compiler
generates a C structure with the discriminator as one member and a C union as
another member. Example 2-8 shows the structure in the generated header file for
the corresponding discriminated union in Example 2-7.

Example 2–8: A Discriminated Union Generated by the MIDL Compiler

```
   typedef struct  {
     part_units units;
     union  {
       /* case(s): 0 */
       idl_long_int number;
       /* case(s): 1, 2 */
       idl_long_float weight;
     } total;
   } part_quantity;
```

You must set the union discriminator in the application code to control which
union case is valid at any time in the application. Example 2-9 shows how you can
use the discriminated union in application code.

Example 2–9: Using a Discriminated Union in Application Code

```
    part_record part;              /* structure for all data about a part */ ❶
    .
    .

    result = order_part(part.number" "&(part.quantity), account);        ❷
    if(result > 0) {
       if(part.quantity.units == ITEM)                                   ❸
          printf("ordered %ld items\n", part.quantity.total.number);     ❹
       else if(part.quantity.units == GRAM)
          printf("ordered %10.2f grams\n", part.quantity.total.weight);
       else if(part.quantity.units == KILOGRAM)
          printf("ordered %10.2f kilos\n", part.quantity.total.weight);
    }
```

❶ In the inventory application the **part_quantity** discriminated union is a member of the **part_record** structure shown in Example 2-5.

❷ The **part.quantity** structure member is the discriminated union. In this example, you request a quantity of a part to order, and the remote procedure returns the actual quantity ordered.

❸ The **part.quantity.units** member is the discriminator for the union.

❹ The **part.quantity.total** member is the union, which contains number and weight cases.

If you omit the union name (**total** in Example 2-7), then the MIDL compiler generates the name **tagged_union** for you. You can access the structure members in application code as follows:

```
    part.quantity.units = ITEM;
    part.quantity.tagged_union.number = 1;
```

Procedure Declarations and Parameter Attributes

At the heart of an interface definition are the procedures that a server offers. The inventory application contains several remote procedures; you can find them in the interface definition in Appendix D.

Each parameter of a remote procedure is declared with its own attributes. The most important ones are the directional attributes **in** and **out**.

In the C language parameters of procedure calls are passed by value, which means a copy of each parameter is supplied to the called procedure. The variable passed is an input-only parameter because any manipulation of the procedure's copy of the variable does not alter the original variable. For a variable to be a parameter, a pointer to the variable is passed.

With a remote procedure call, we must be concerned with whether a parameter is input, output, or both. It is more efficient if the RPC runtime library can transmit data only in the relevant direction. The attributes **in** and **out** are used in an interface definition to distinguish data transmission direction for a parameter. All parameters must have at least one directional attribute. An output parameter must be a pointer or an array, as it must be in C.

Complex pointer types must have both directional attributes (in and out). This enables the client and server stubs to coordinate duplication of the unique or full pointer in the server's address space.

Example 2-10 shows procedure declarations and some associated parameter attributes.

Example 2-10: Procedure Declarations and Parameter Attributes

```
   .
   .
   .
] interface inventory
{
/* The beginning of the interface definition body usually contains   */
/* constant and type definitions (and sometimes import declarations).*/
   .
   .
   .

   /*********************** Procedure Declarations **********************/
   boolean is_part_available(          /* return true if in inventory   ❶ */
       [in] part_num number            /* input part number */
   );

   void whatis_part_name(              /* get part name from inventory  ❷ */
       [in]  part_num  number,         /* input part number */
       [in, out] part_name name        /* output part name   */
   );

   paragraph get_part_description(     /* return a pointer to a string  ❸ */
       [in]  part_num  number
   );

   void whatis_part_price(             /* get part price from inventory   */
       [in]  part_num  number,
       [out] part_price *price
   );

   void whatis_part_quantity(          /* get part quantity from inventory */
       [in]  part_num     number,
       [out] part_quantity *quantity
   );

   void whatare_subparts(              /* get list of subpart numbers     */
       [in]  part_num  number,
       [out] part_list **subparts      /* structure containing the array ❹ */
   );

   /* Order part from inventory with part number, quantity desired, and   */
   /* account number.  If inventory does not have enough, output lesser   */
   /* quantity ordered.  Return values:  1=ordered OK,                    */
   /* -1=invalid part, -2=invalid quantity, -3=invalid account.           */
```

Example 2–10: Procedure Declarations and Parameter Attributes (continued)

```
long order_part(  /* order part from inventory, return OK or error code */
    [in]      part_num       number,
    [in,out]  part_quantity  *quantity,              /* quantity ordered ❺ */
    [in]      account_num    account
  );
} /* end of interface definition */
```

❶   As in C, a MIDL procedure can return a value. In this example, the *is_part_available* procedure returns a Boolean value of idl_true if the part number is available in the inventory.

❷   Procedures defined with the void type do not return a value. Input parameters have the in directional attribute and output parameters have the out directional attribute. Here, Microsoft RPC is treating this pointer to the array element as a unique pointer because the pointer_default was set to unique (see Example 2-1). MIDL does not allow unique or full pointers to have only the [out] directional attribute because the client and server stubs need to coordinate the establishment of complex pointers in the server address space. Consequently, the directional attribute is set to [in, out]. As in C, arrays and strings are implicitly passed by reference, so the string name does not need a pointer operator.

❸   Some procedures return a data structure or a pointer to a data structure. In this example, the data type paragraph has been defined in the interface definition as a char * type. It is a full pointer to a string representing the description of the part. This remote procedure allocates new memory on the client side.

❹   Output parameters require pointers to pointers when new memory is allocated. Pointers to pointers are discussed in Chapter 4.

❺   Parameters that are changed by the remote procedure call use both in and out. In this example, a part is ordered with the part number, the quantity, and an account number. If the input quantity units are wrong or the quantity requested is more than the inventory can supply, the remote procedure changes the quantity on output.

Table A-7 in Appendix A shows all parameter attributes and Table A-8 shows all procedure attributes.

Using the MIDL Compiler

The MIDL compiler generates the header and stub files needed to incorporate the interface in a client or server. The input for a MIDL compilation is an interface definition file, ending in *.idl*. Figure 2-1 shows the utilities used and files produced during interface production.

An attribute configuration file (ACF) is an optional file, ending in *.acf*. It contains information that changes how the MIDL compiler interprets the interface definition. We'll look at the ACF file later in this chapter.

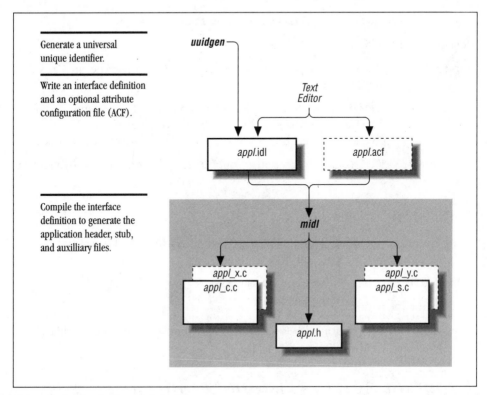

Figure 2-1. Producing an interface

Depending on which compiler options you use, the MIDL compiler produces the C language client stub, server stub, or both sets of stub files. The stub file names contain the _c suffix for clients and the _s suffix for servers. By default, the MIDL compiler also produces the header file (ending in *.h*) which will be used by both the client and server.

The MIDL compiler produces auxiliary files automatically when certain features are used. Auxiliary file names contain the _x suffix for clients and the _y suffix for servers.

Auxiliary files contain special routines required for certain complex data types, such as unique pointers, to prepare the data for transmission. You have to link the auxiliary object files with your application when these data types are used. The routines are placed in auxiliary files rather than in the stub, so that you can use the data types in other interface definitions without linking in the entire stub.

Generating Client Files

To generate the interface header file and client stub file for the inventory interface, type the following command:

```
C:\> invntry> midl inv.idl /server none /I explicit /out explicit
```

Here is an explanation of the options:

/server none   This option suppresses the generation of stub none and auxiliary files for the server.

/I explicit   The /I option causes the MIDL compiler to use the additional directory when it searches for files. For one of the clients of the inventory application an ACF in the *explicit* directory is needed.

/out explicit   This option places the output files in the chosen directory, *explicit*.

Generating Server Files

To generate the interface header file and server stub file for the inventory interface, type the following command:

```
C:\> invntry> midl inventory.idl /client none
```

Here is an explanation.

/client none   This option suppresses the generation of stub and auxiliary files for the client.

Using an ACF to Customize Interface Usage

You can control some aspects of RPC on the client side without affecting the server. The opposite is also true. These aspects should not be in the interface definition because we do not want to force them on all clients and servers. A client or server developer can use an optional attribute configuration file (ACF) to modify the way the MIDL compiler creates stubs without changing the way the stubs interact across the network. This assures that all copies of an interface behave the same when clients and servers interact.

The most significant effect an ACF has on your application code can be the addition of parameters to remote procedure calls not declared in the interface definition. For example, the explicit_handle attribute adds a binding handle as the first parameter to some or all procedures. Also, the comm_status and fault_status attributes can add status parameters to the end of a procedure's parameter list. See Table A-9 in Appendix A for a complete list of ACF attributes.

If you develop both clients and servers for an interface, you can use different ACFs (or no ACF) for the client and server. Since this can cause differences between the header files generated for the client and server, it is good development practice to separate the client and server output when using ACFs.

You do not specify an ACF when you compile an interface; instead, the MIDL compiler automatically uses an ACF if one is available in the search directories. The name of an ACF must match the name of the MIDL file it is associated with. The file extension must be *.acf*.

An ACF is useful for a number of situations: selecting binding methods, controlling errors, excluding procedures, and controlling marshalling.

Selecting a Binding Method

As will be explained in Chapter 3, three different binding methods exist. You can choose how much to let the stub do for you and how much to control binding within your own code.

The auto_handle ACF attribute selects the automatic binding method which causes the client stub to automatically select the server for your client. In the arithmetic application in Chapter 1, for instance, any server found by the client stub would be sufficient. An additional advantage offered by automatic binding is error recovery: if server communication is disrupted, the client stub can sometimes find another server, transparent to the application code.

The implicit_handle ACF attribute selects the implicit binding method which allows you to select a specific server for your remote procedure calls. For example, if many inventory servers representing different warehouses are available on the network, you may want your client to select a specific one.

The explicit_handle ACF attribute selects the explicit binding method which lets you select a specific server for each remote procedure call. For example, if your client needs data from many servers simultaneously, you need a way to control which remote procedure call uses which server.

Example 2-11 is an ACF used by the MIDL compiler to produce the header and stub files for the implicit client example of the inventory application.

Example 2–11: An Attribute Configuration File (ACF)

```
/* FILE NAME: inv.acf (implicit version)*/
/* This Attribute Configuration File is used in conjunction with the    */
/* associated MIDL file (inv.idl) when the MIDL compiler is invoked.     */
[
implicit_handle(handle_t global_binding_h)   /* implicit binding method ❶ */
]
interface inv            /* The interface name must match the MIDL file. ❷ */
{
}
```

❶   The implicit_handle attribute applies to the entire interface. A global binding handle of type handle_t is established in the client stub to refer to binding information a client uses to find a server.

❷   The interface name (inv) must match the interface name in the corresponding
      MIDL file.

Controlling Errors and Exceptions

An **exception** is a software state or condition that forces the application to go outside its normal flow of control. Such an event may be produced by hardware
(such as memory access violations) or software (such as array subscript range
checking). Microsoft RPC applications cause communication and server errors to be
raised as exceptions. Unless you design your program to handle the exceptions,
the program will exit.

An ACF can save you the trouble of writing extra layers of exception handling
code.

The comm_status and fault_status attributes apply to procedure parameters or
procedure return results of the type error_status_t. If this attribute is present
and you've added a variable of the data type error_status_t to the argument list
of your remote procedure call communication and server errors are communicated
to the client as values in the named parameter rather than raised as exceptions.
Error codes for comm_status and fault_status are different to allow correct
interpretation of the error codes. Chapter 3 discusses error and exception control
in greater detail.

Excluding Unused Procedures

The code and nocode ACF attributes allow you to define which procedures the
client stub supports. For example, if a client uses only four out of twenty remote
procedures declared in the interface, the client stub code does not need the overhead of the other procedures. However, all the procedures of an interface definition must be implemented by the server.

3

How to Write Clients

In this chapter we discuss how to develop client programs for Microsoft RPC interfaces. It is a good idea to read Chapter 1, *Overview of an RPC Application*, for a complete overview of a distributed application, and Chapter 2, *Using a Microsoft RPC Interface*, to familiarize yourself with features of interface definitions.

We discuss client development before server development because you may develop a client for an existing interface and server. We describe server development in Chapter 5, *How to Write a Server*. The code for all applications is shown in Appendices C through F.

Binding

The first question that probably comes to mind when you begin to develop a client is: How does a remote procedure call find the server it needs? Essentially, the client must create a binding, as described in Chapter 1, and load it with information that lets the RPC runtime library find the server.

Binding information mainly includes a communication protocol sequence, a host name or address, and a server process address on the host (endpoint). If you are familiar with using named pipes, these are similar to a protocol family, a computer name, and a pipe name.

Binding information can be obtained automatically and be completely invisible to your client application code. To the other extreme, you can obtain binding information by calling RPC runtime routines and using a **binding handle** as a parameter in a remote procedure call. The level of control you need depends on the needs of your client program.

A binding handle is the data structure that manages binding in applications. The handle is a reference (pointer) to information for one possible binding.

Microsoft RPC supplies the Locator as a simple and convenient name service database to store names and locations of network services. Servers use RPC runtime routines to store binding information in the name service database. Clients use other RPC runtime routines to retrieve binding information from the name service database and create binding handles for remote procedure calls.

A server's binding information can also be stored in an application-specific database or supplied to client programs by some other means, for example, as arguments when the client is invoked. If your client would not benefit from a name service (or your client system does not have a running name service), you can use RPC runtime routines in applications to convert strings of binding information to binding handles used by remote procedure calls.

Implementing a Binding Method

For each remote procedure call, the binding handle is managed in one of the following ways.

Automatic method

The client stub automatically manages bindings after the application calls a remote procedure. The client stub obtains binding information from a name service database and passes the binding handle to the RPC runtime library. If the connection is disrupted, new binding information can sometimes be automatically obtained and the call is tried again.

Implicit method

A binding handle is held in a global area of the client stub. After the application calls a remote procedure, the stub passes the binding handle to the RPC runtime library. You write application code to obtain the binding information and set the global binding handle with RPC runtime routine calls.

Explicit method

An individual remote procedure call in the application passes a binding handle explicitly as its first parameter. You write application code to obtain the binding information and set the binding handle with RPC runtime routine calls.

Figure 3-1 shows a comparison of binding methods in relation to the client code. For each method, the top portion of the box represents the client application code you write. The bottom portion of each box represents the client stub code that the MIDL compiler generates. The shading represents the portion of the client where binding handles are managed. For any given client instance, different methods may be employed for different remote procedure calls. For example, one remote procedure call can use the automatic method and another remote procedure call can use the explicit method.

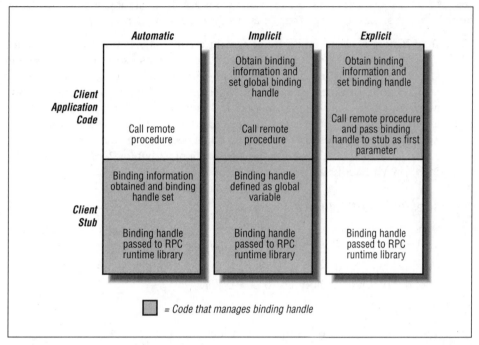

Figure 3-1. A comparison of binding management methods

The automatic and implicit methods apply to an entire interface. If you use either the automatic or implicit method for an interface, you can also use the explicit method for some or all remote procedure calls to that interface. The explicit method takes precedence over the automatic and implicit methods because the binding handle is visible as the first parameter in the procedure.

If a client uses more than one interface, you can use the automatic method for all remote procedure calls to one interface and the implicit method for all remote procedure calls to the other interface. However, a client cannot use the automatic and implicit methods simultaneously, for remote procedure calls to the same interface.

The implicit and explicit methods require that your application code obtain binding information and manage the binding handles. Binding handles need to be obtained and managed in the client application code under the following circumstances:

- The client uses a specific server.

- The client needs to set authentication and authorization information for specific binding handles.

- The server has more than one implementation of the same remote procedure. An application uses object UUIDs to distinguish between different remote procedure implementations.

Use an attribute configuration file (ACF) to establish a binding method with the attributes auto_handle, implicit_handle, or explicit_handle.

A **context handle** is a special remote procedure parameter defined in an interface definition with the context_handle attribute. Applications use a context handle in a sequence of remote procedure calls to refer to a context (state) on a specific server. We mention context handles briefly here with binding methods because they carry with them binding information and thus can act as a binding handle for remote procedure calls. When the context handle is active, it carries with it the binding information necessary to find the same server as it did before, and the server maintains the context for that particular client. (Chapter 7, *Context Handles*, describes context handle use.)

Deciding on binding methods

Automatic binding does the most work for you, so MIDL makes it the default. Another binding method is chosen in the following situations:

- The first parameter of a procedure declaration is a binding handle (in that case, the binding method has to be explicit)

- The procedure declaration has an input context handle

- An ACF establishes a different binding method

You can force explicit binding when you're sure that you want every client to specify a server when calling a particular procedure. Make a binding handle the procedure's first parameter in the MIDL file. A client cannot take away a parameter declared in the interface definition, so this remote procedure cannot use either the automatic or implicit methods. For the same reason, a context handle forces the client to use explicit binding.

The next decision is whether to use the automatic or implicit method for other procedures. If you're satisfied with using any valid server for your remote procedure calls—any server that exports the interface described in your MIDL file—the automatic method should be adequate. In particular, the automatic method works fine if the network is relatively small. However, you have no control over which server you get, so applications that use servers scattered over a wide area may be inefficient. If most of your remote procedure calls need to use a specific server, the implicit method is appropriate.

Suppose you have determined that individual remote procedure calls need control over which server each uses. For example, if you use a print server application, one call may request a server near you to print a file. Your next call may request a server in a different location to print another copy for your department manager. If you have determined that you need this kind of binding control for individual remote procedure calls, use the explicit method.

The explicit method is also necessary for clients that make multi-threaded remote procedure calls. For example, a commodity trade application may request a commodity price with remote procedure calls to many locations at the same time. This server selection control also lets you balance network load in your application. All the clients in this book are single-threaded.

Automatic Binding Management

The automatic binding management method is the simplest because you don't have to manipulate the binding handle in your interface definition, ACF, or application code. The binding handle and the complexity of its management is hidden from you in the client stub and the RPC runtime library. If you lose a server connection, the automatic method will try to rebind for you. With this method there is a relatively short learning curve to get a distributed application running.

Many applications do not require that you control binding, so it is easier to let the underlying RPC mechanism find a server. The server is selected from a set of servers that support the interface. If the particular server makes no difference, use the automatic method. For example, for a mathematics interface, the first server that supports it is probably sufficient.

The automatic method is demonstrated in the arithmetic application and shown in detail in Chapter 1. For this chapter, however, we use one of the clients for the inventory application, so you can compare client development between different methods for the same application. The application is shown in detail in Appendix D, *The Inventory Application*.

Interface development for automatic binding

There are no special requirements in the interface for automatic binding. If you wish, you can use the `auto_handle` attribute in an ACF for documentation.

Client development for automatic binding

The client requires you to:

1. Include the MIDL-generated header file with the `#include` compiler directive in the client application code:

        /* FILE NAME: client.c */
        /****** Client of the inventory application ******/
        #include <stdio.h>
        #include <stdlib.h>
        #include "inv.h" /* header file created by the MIDL compiler */
        .
        .
        .

2. Link the client application object code with the client stub, client stub auxiliary file (if available), and the following Microsoft RPC libraries:

```
rpcrt4.lib
rpcns4.lib
libcmt.lib
kernel32.lib
```

The client system must have access to a Microsoft Locator name service database on the network. Your system administrator can tell you if you have access to a name service.

The remote procedure call looks just like a local procedure call. The procedure returns a Boolean value of **true** if the part number is in the inventory or **false** if it is not:

```
case 'a': if (is_part_available(part.number)) /* Remote Procedure Call */
          puts("available: Yes");
      else
          puts("available: No");
      break;
```

If your client uses the automatic method for an interface, you can override it for specific procedures by using a binding handle as the first parameter in the call.

See Chapter 6, *Using a Name Service*, for more information on the name service.

Server development for automatic binding

For clients to use the automatic method, a server must advertise binding information to a name service entry with the *RpcNsBindingExport* runtime routine in the server initialization code.

Implicit Binding Management

Implicit binding gives you the control of binding management in the client application without a visible binding handle parameter in a remote procedure call. Use the implicit method for applications that need the same server for all or most remote procedure calls of an interface. An ACF defines the binding handle, and the MIDL compiler generates it as a client-global variable in the client stub. The client application code sets the binding handle before any remote procedure calls. During a remote procedure call, the client stub uses the global binding handle to complete the call to the RPC runtime library.

In this part of the chapter, we'll develop a client for the inventory application that uses the implicit method. The rationale is that, in this application, you may need to choose a specific server to access the right data base. Once a server is found, the rest of the remote procedure calls can use the same one.

Interface development for implicit binding

Use the implicit_handle attribute in an ACF to declare the global binding handle for the client, as shown in Example 3-1. When you compile the interface definition with the ACF available, a global binding handle is defined in the client stub. The stub uses the handle every time the client calls a remote procedure for this interface.

Example 3-1: An ACF for the Implicit Binding Method

```
/* FILE NAME: inv_i.acf (implicit version)*/
/* This Attribute Configuration File is used in conjunction with the    */
/* associated MIDL file (inv.idl) when the MIDL compiler is invoked.     */
[
implicit_handle(handle_t global_binding_h)    /* implicit binding method */
]
interface  inv           /* The interface name must match the MIDL file. */
{
}
```

The handle_t type is a MIDL data type that is used to define a binding handle named global_binding_h.

Client development for implicit binding

The client code includes the MIDL-generated header file, obtains a binding handle, and assigns the binding handle to the global binding handle. (See Example 3-2.)

Example 3-2: A Client with the Implicit Binding Method

```
/* FILE NAME: client.c */
/***** Client of the inventory application with implicit method *****/
#include <stdio.h>
#include <stdlib.h>
#include "inv.h"        /* header file created by the MIDL compiler ❶ */
   .
   .
   .
   do_import_binding("inventory_", &global_binding_h);  /* seek matching */
                                              /* uuid      ❷ */
   status = RpcBindingReset(global_binding_h);   /* remove endpoint ❸ */
   CHECK_STATUS(status, "Can't reset binding handle", ABORT);
   .
   .
   .
   case 'a': if (is_part_available(part.number))          /* ❹ */
      puts("available: Yes");
   else
      puts("available: No");
   break;
```

❶   The MIDL-generated header file must be included with the **#include** compiler directive.

❷   The client must obtain binding information and assign its handle to the global binding handle. The binding information can be obtained from the name service database as in this example, or it can be constructed from strings of binding information. The *do_import_binding* procedure is developed later in this chapter.

❸   The Microsoft Locator included with our pre-release version of Microsoft RPC unexpectedly returned server endpoints. Sometimes the endpoints were stale (left from previous server instances) and caused communication problems. We used the *RpcBindingReset* function which removes the endpoint, forcing the client to look in the server host's endpoint map for a fresh endpoint. Your application should not need this function if the Locator does not return server endpoints.

❹   A remote procedure call looks just like a local procedure call.

If your client uses the implicit method for an interface, you can override it for specific procedures by including a binding handle as the first parameter of the procedures in the MIDL file.

Server development for implicit binding

Although there are no special requirements in server development, a server must export to a name service database if the clients use a name service to find servers. The server for the inventory application exports binding information.

Explicit Binding Management

Explicit binding manages each remote procedure call separately. The first parameter of the remote procedure call is a binding handle. Use the explicit method when your application needs to make remote procedure calls to more than one server. This method is the most visible in an application because a binding handle is passed as the first parameter of the remote procedure. You completely control the binding management in the client application code.

If the procedure declaration in the interface definition file has a binding handle as the first parameter, you must use the explicit method. If the procedure declaration does not have a binding handle parameter, you can add one by using an ACF. In this case, after you compile the interface definition, the remote procedure is defined in the header file with an additional binding handle as the first parameter.

We'll use another client from the inventory application to demonstrate the explicit method.

Interface development for explicit binding

An interface definition or an ACF uses the handle_t data type to define binding handle parameters. Application code uses the rpc_binding_handle_t data type to represent and manipulate binding information.[*]

Suppose we want to use the explicit method for a remote procedure that has no explicit binding handle as the first parameter. We use an ACF with the explicit_handle attribute, making the MIDL compiler add a binding handle as the first parameter. At the time this book went to press, we were not able to completely test the use of the explicit_handle attribute. Keep in mind that the final release of Microsoft RPC Version 2.0 might differ slightly from the behavior described here.

The is_part_available procedure is defined in the interface as follows:

```
boolean is_part_available(   /* return true if in inventory */
    [in] part_num number      /* input part number */
);
```

An ACF that adds a binding handle parameter is shown in Example 3-3.

Example 3-3: Adding Binding Handles with an ACF

```
/* FILE NAME: inv.acf (explicit version)*/
/* This Attribute Configuration File is used in conjunction with the    */
/* associated MIDL file (inv.idl) when the MIDL compiler is invoked.*/
[
explicit_handle            /* explicit binding method */
]
interface  inventory     /* The interface name must match the MIDL file. */
{
}
```

When the MIDL compiler uses this ACF, all procedure declarations in the header file have a binding handle of type handle_t added as the first parameter. If you use the explicit_handle attribute this way, none of the remote procedure calls to this interface can use the automatic or implicit method for this client instance.

You can also use the explicit_handle attribute on a specific procedure in the ACF to add a binding handle as the first parameter. For example, this ACF associates a binding handle parameter only with the *is_part_available* procedure:

```
interface inventory
{
    [explicit_handle] is_part_available();
}
```

Example 3-4 defines a binding handle explicitly in the interface definition. Other clients cannot use the automatic or implicit methods of binding for the procedure.

---

[*] The handle_t and rpc_binding_handle_t data types are equivalent. The handle_t data type exists for compatibility with earlier RPC versions. The rpc_binding_handle_t data type exists for consistency in data type naming for the RPC runtime routines.

(The *is_part_available* procedure is not declared this way for the inventory interface.)

Example 3-4: Defining a Binding Handle in the Interface Definition

```
boolean is_part_available(      /* return true if in inventory */
    [in] handle_t binding_h,        /* explicit, binding handle */
    [in] part_num number            /* input part number        */
);
```

Later in this chapter we'll show how to create an application-specific, customized
binding handle in the interface definition through the handle attribute.

Client development for explicit binding

Before making the remote procedure call, the client must obtain binding information and set the binding handle. The methods of obtaining binding information for
the explicit method are almost the same as for the implicit method. For the explicit
method, you use a specific binding handle instead of assigning the binding information to the implicit global binding handle.

Example 3-5: A Client with the Explicit Binding Method

```
/* FILE NAME: client.c */
/***** Client of the inventory application with explicit method *********/
#include <stdio.h>
#include <stdlib.h>
#include "inv.h"         /* header file created by the MIDL compiler    ❶ */

    .
    .
    .
    rpc_binding_handle_t binding_h;          /* declare a binding handle ❷ */
    .
    .
    .
    do_import_binding("/.:/inventory", &binding_h);      /* find server ❸ */
    status = RpcBindingReset(global_binding_h);   /* remove endpoint    ❹ */
    CHECK_STATUS(status, "Can't reset binding handle", ABORT);
    .
    .
    .
        case 'a': if (is_part_available(binding_h, part.number))    /*  ❺ */
            puts("available: Yes");
        else
            puts("available: No");
        break;
```

❶   Include the MIDL-generated header file with the #include compiler directive.

❷   Declare binding handles of type rpc_binding_handle_t in the application.

❸   The client must obtain binding information from the name service database,
     or it can be constructed from strings of binding information. Example 3-7

shows how the application-specific procedure do_import_binding uses the name service database.

❹ The *RpcBindingReset* function fixes a problem we discovered with the Microsoft Locator. See Example 3-2 for more information.

❺ The first parameter is the binding handle.

Server development for explicit binding

To use explicit binding, the ACF must include the explicit_binding attribute or the interface definition must have a binding handle parameter for the remote procedure. Servers use the binding handle parameter to obtain client binding information for use in authentication and authorization.

Example 3-6 shows how to include a binding handle parameter in a server remote procedure.

Example 3-6: Manager Procedures with the Explicit Binding Method

```
/* FILE NAME: manager.c */
/** Implementation of the remote procedures for the inventory application. **/
#include <stdio.h>
#include <stdlib.h>
#include "inv.h"

boolean is_part_available(binding_h, number)          /* ❶ */
handle_t binding_h;                                    /* ❷ */
part_num number;
{
    part_record *part;                    /* a pointer to a part record */
    int found;

    found = read_part_record(number, &part);
    if(found)
        return(TRUE);
    else
        return(FALSE);
}
```

❶ Include a binding handle as the first parameter in a remote procedure implementation.

❷ Declare a binding handle as a parameter.

Steps in Finding Servers

Recall that Figure 1-10, in Chapter 1, shows one way to find a server. In this figure, the client stub and the RPC runtime library handle all binding management outside of the application code. The client stub automatically finds the server system binding information in a name service database. The binding handle is set and passed to the RPC runtime library, which finds the server process binding information (endpoint) in the server system's endpoint map. The RPC runtime library uses the complete binding information to bind to the server.

The key to finding a server is to obtain a protocol sequence, a server host name or address, and an endpoint. A binding handle for the remote procedure call is set to point to this binding information.

The following discussion is a generalization of what happens during the server finding process. It includes the choices you (or the RPC runtime library) have about where to obtain the necessary binding information. Where these steps are executed (client application, client stub, or RPC runtime library) depends on the kind of binding handle and binding method used.

Finding a Protocol Sequence

A client and server can communicate over a network if they both use the same network communication protocols. A protocol sequence is found in one of two ways:

- The preferred method is to use a name service database to import or look up both a host address and protocol sequence at the same time. To set the binding handle, use the RPC runtime routines that begin with *RpcNsBindingImport* or *RpcNsBindingLookup*. If your application uses the automatic method, the client stub does this for you.

- The other method is to use a protocol sequence string obtained from your application or from a call to the *RpcNetworkInqProtseqs* routine. Use the RPC runtime routines *RpcStringBindingCompose* and *RpcBindingFromString-Binding* to set the binding handle.

A **protocol sequence** is a character string containing three items that correspond to options for network communications protocols. RPC represents each valid combination of these protocols as a protocol sequence. The protocol sequence consists of a string of the options separated by underscores. The only current, valid option combinations are shown in Table 3-1.

Table 3-1: Valid Protocol Sequences

Protocol Sequence	Common Name	Description
ncacn_ip_tcp	Connection protocol sequence	Network Computing Architecture connection over an Internet Protocol with a Transmission Control Protocol for transport.
ncadg_ip_udp	Datagram protocol sequence	Network Computing Architecture datagram over an Internet Protocol with a User Datagram Protocol for transport.

Table 3-1: Valid Protocol Sequences (continued)

Protocol Sequence	Common Name	Description
ncacn_dnet_nsp	DECnet (TM)	Network Computing Architecture connection over DECnet (TM). The underlying software that implements DECnet must be purchased separately.
ncacn_nb_tcp	NetBIOS over TCP/IP	Network Computing Architecture connection using NetBIOS over TCP/IP.
ncacn_nb_nb	NetBIOS over NetBEUI	Network Computing Architecture connection using NetBIOS over the NetBEUI transport.
ncacn_np	Named pipes	Network Computing Architecture connection using named pipes.
ncacn_spx	Connection-oriented SPX	Network Computing Architecture connection using SPX.
ncalrpc	Local Windows NT communications	Network Computing Architecture using local communications only.

The three protocols of a protocol sequence are for RPC communication, network host addressing, and network transport.

1. The RPC protocol for communications has two options:

   • Network Computing Architecture connection-oriented protocol (ncacn)

   • Network Computing Architecture local interprocess communication (ncalrpc)

   The network address format used as part of the binding information has three options:

   • the Internet protocol (ip)

   • the DECnet (TM) protocol (dnet)

   • the NetBIOS (Artisoft's Network Basic Input Output System) protocol (nb)

2. The transport protocol for communications has five options:

   • Transmission control protocol (tcp)

   • Network services protocol (nsp)

   • NetBEUI (NetBIOS Extended User Interface)

- Named pipes (np)

- spx (sequenced packet exchange)

Most servers should use all available protocol sequences so clients using the interface will have every opportunity to find and use a server.

In general, your choice of protocols on the client side should not be a big concern. If most traffic on your network is TCP/IP, use that protocol. When several protocols are available to clients, you can usually just pick the one most commonly used for communications in your network.

If you want to be selective, here are some guidelines to help you choose a suitable protocol.

- Use TCP/IP or DECnet when clients and servers must communicate over a wide-area network (WAN). These protocols have long timeouts that can handle the network delays inherent in WANs. Use TCP/IP when debugging your client during remote procedure calls. Otherwise, the process could time out when the debugger stops it. Clients can control timeouts using the RPC runtime routines *RpcMgmtSetComTimeout* and *RpcMgmtInqComTimeout*.

- Use UDP/IP when clients need to bind to many servers. That's because this protocol has relatively low overhead. If a remote procedure broadcasts its call to all hosts on a local network, it must use UDP/IP. The *broadcast* attribute on the procedure declaration in the interface definition declares the broadcast capability.

- Use NetBIOS over NetBEUI for local area network (LAN) connections because it can be faster than TCP/IP or DECnet in some networks. Avoid using NetBIOS over NetBEUI when clients and servers are separated by network routers.

- Use named pipes (ncacn_np) in local area networks when you want to rely on the security built in to named pipes. Named pipes' extra security overhead can slow down remote procedure calls, so use it only when you need security.

- Use Local Windows NT RPC Communication (ncalrpc) when clients and servers reside on the same system, because it's generally faster than other protocols for interprocess communication.

Finding a Server Host

You can find a server host name or network address in two different ways:

- Use a name service database to import or look up a host address and at the same time get a protocol sequence. Use the RPC runtime routines that begin with *RpcNsBindingImport* or *RpcNsBindingLookup* to set the binding handle. If your application uses the automatic method, the client stub does this for you.

- Use a host name or host network address string obtained from your application. Use the RPC runtime routines called *RpcStringBindingCompose* and *RpcBindingFromStringBinding* to set the binding handle.

A **partially bound binding handle** is one that contains a protocol sequence and server host, but not an endpoint. This handle is what you get from the Microsoft Locator. It means you have identified the server's system, but not the server process on that system. The binding to a server cannot complete until an endpoint is found.

When a partially bound binding handle is passed to the RPC runtime library, an endpoint is automatically obtained for you from the interface or the endpoint map on the server's system.

Finding an Endpoint

A binding handle that has an endpoint as part of its binding information is called a **fully bound binding handle**. Endpoints can be well-known or dynamic. A **well-known endpoint** is a pre-assigned system address that a server process uses every time it runs. Usually a well-known endpoint is assigned by the authority responsible for a transport protocol. A **dynamic endpoint** is a system address of a server process that is requested and assigned by the RPC runtime library when a server is initialized. Most applications should use dynamic endpoints to avoid the network management needed for well-known endpoints.

You can use your application code to obtain an endpoint, but it is best to let the RPC runtime library find an endpoint for you. An endpoint is found in one of four ways:

- If the binding information obtained during an import or lookup of the protocol sequence and host in the name service database includes an endpoint, the binding handle is fully bound in one step. The name service database can be used to store well-known endpoints. But dynamic endpoints are never stored in the name service database because their temporary nature requires significant management of the database, which degrades name service performance.

- A well-known endpoint is found that was established in the interface definition with the endpoint attribute. The RPC runtime library (or your application) finds the endpoint from an interface-specific data structure.

- An endpoint is found from the endpoint map on the server system. These endpoints can be well-known or dynamic. The RPC runtime library first looks for an endpoint from the interface specification. If one is not found, the RPC runtime library looks in the server's endpoint map. When an endpoint is found, the binding to the server process completes. To obtain an endpoint from a server's endpoint map, use the *RpcEpResolveBinding* routine or routines beginning with *RpcMgmtEpEltInq* in your application.

- You can use a string from your application that represents an endpoint, and then you can use the RPC runtime routines *RpcStringBindingCompose* and *RpcBindingFromStringBinding* to set the binding handle. These endpoints can be well-known or dynamic.

Interpreting Binding Information

This section reveals what goes on in the *do_import_binding* procedure shown earlier in the chapter. When you use implicit or explicit binding, you need to interpret the binding information. To take a simple case, suppose you want to use a server on a particular host—this means you need to extract the host from the binding handles you get from CDS and isolate the host name in each handle.

Binding handles refer to the following binding information:

- Object UUID

- Protocol sequence

- Network address or host name

- Endpoint

- Network options

Object UUIDs are part of an advanced topic not discussed in this book. Network options are specific to a protocol sequence.

Example 3-7 shows how to use RPC runtime routines to interpret binding information. You use these routines in either a server or client. The *do_interpret_binding* procedure is called in the *do_import_binding* procedure.

Example 3-7: Interpreting Binding Information

```
/* FILE NAME: intbind.c */
/* Interpret binding information and return the protocol sequence. */
#include <stdio.h>
#include <rpc.h>
#include "status.h"

void do_interpret_binding(binding, protocol_seq)
rpc_binding_handle_t binding;          /* binding handle to interpret    */
char                 *protocol_seq;    /* protocol sequence to obtain    */
{
    unsigned long    status;           /* error status                   */
    unsigned char    *string_binding;  /* string of binding info.        */
    unsigned char    *protseq;         /* binding component of interest   */

    status =
    RpcBindingToStringBinding(    /* convert binding information to string ❶ */
       binding,                          /* the binding handle to convert */
       &string_binding                   /* the string of binding data    */
    );
    CHECK_STATUS(status, "Can't get string binding:", RESUME);
```

Example 3-7: Interpreting Binding Information (continued)

```
status =
RpcStringBindingParse(              /* get components of string binding ❷ */
    string_binding,         /* the string of binding data              */
    NULL,                   /* an object UUID string is not obtained   */
    &protseq,               /* a protocol sequence string IS obtained  */
    NULL,                   /* a network address string is not obtained */
    NULL,                   /* an endpoint string is not obtained      */
    NULL                    /* a network options string is not obtained */
);
CHECK_STATUS(status, "Can't parse string binding:", RESUME);

strcpy(protocol_seq, (char *)protseq);
/* free all strings allocated by other runtime routines        ❸ */
status = RpcStringFree(&string_binding);
status = RpcStringFree(&protseq      );
return;
```

❶   The *RpcBindingToStringBinding* routine converts binding information to its string representation. The binding handle is passed in and the string holding the binding information is allocated.

❷   The *RpcStringBindingParse* routine obtains the binding information items as separate allocated strings. The components include an object UUID, a protocol sequence, a network address, an endpoint, and network options. If any of the components are null on input, no data is obtained for that parameter.

❸   The *RpcStringFree* routine frees strings allocated by other RPC runtime routines.

Finding a Server from a Name Service Database

The usual way for a client to obtain binding information is from a name service database using the name service RPC runtime routines (routines beginning with *RpcNs*). This method assumes that the server you want has exported binding information to the name service database.

The name service database contains entries of information, each identified by a name used in programs, environment variables, and commands. Clients can use a name called a server entry name to begin a search for compatible binding information in the database. Entries contain binding information about specific servers. Use RPC name service runtime routines to search entries in the name service database for binding information. The example in this section does a very simple search. See Chapter 6 for a more detailed name service description.

Importing a binding handle

Since the same interface can be supported on many systems of the network, a client needs a way to select one system. The runtime import routines obtain information for one binding handle at a time from the name service database, selecting from the available list of servers supporting the interface.

Example 3-8 shows how an application obtains binding information from a name service database.

Example 3-8: Importing a Binding Handle

```
/* FILE NAME: getbind.c */
/* Get binding from name service database. */
#include <stdio.h>
#include "inv.h"
#include "status.h"

void do_import_binding(entry_name, binding_h)
char                   entry_name[];        /* entry name to begin search   */
rpc_binding_handle_t   *binding_h;          /* a binding handle             */
{
    unsigned long   status;                 /* error status                 */
    RPC_NS_HANDLE   import_context;         /* required to import           */
    char            protseq[20];            /* protocol sequence            */

    status =
    RpcNsBindingImportBegin(       /* set context to import binding handles ❶ */
        RPC_C_NS_SYNTAX_DEFAULT,           /* use default syntax            */
        (unsigned char *)entry_name,       /* begin search with this name   */
        inv_V1_0_c_ifspec,                 /* interface specification (inv.h) */
        NULL,                              /* no optional object UUID required */
        &import_context                    /* import context obtained       */
    );
    CHECK_STATUS(status, "Can't begin import:", RESUME);

    while(1) {
        status =
        RpcNsBindingImportNext(                 /* import a binding handle ❷ */
            import_context,       /* context from RpcNsBindingImportBegin */
            binding_h             /* a binding handle is obtained          */
        );
        if(status != RPC_S_OK) {
            CHECK_STATUS(status, "Can't import a binding handle:", RESUME);
            break;
        }

        /** application specific selection criteria (by protocol sequence) ❸ */
        do_interpret_binding(*binding_h ,protseq);
        if(strcmp(protseq, "ncacn_ip_tcp") == 0)  /*select connection protocol*/
            break;
        else {
            status =
            RpcBindingFree(       /* free binding information not selected ❹ */
                binding_h
            );
            CHECK_STATUS(status, "Can't free binding information:", RESUME);
        }
    } /*end while */
```

Example 3-8: Importing a Binding Handle (continued)

```
   status =
   RpcNsBindingImportDone(                      /* done with import context ❺ */
      &import_context           /* obtained from RpcNsBindingImportBegin */
   );
   return;
}
```

❶ The *RpcNsBindingImportBegin* routine establishes the beginning of a search for binding information in a name service database. An entry name syntax of RPC_C_NS_SYNTAX_DEFAULT uses the syntax in the RPC-specific environment variable DefaultSyntax.

In this example, the entry to begin the search is /.:/inventory_, which is passed as a parameter. If you use a null string for the entry name, the search begins with the name in the RPC environment variable DefaultEntry.

If you use a null string for the entry name, and the DefaultEntry is null, the Locator searches for an entry name that offers the interface UUID.

In this example, an object UUID is not required, so we use a null value. The interface handle Inv_V1_0_c_ifspec refers to the interface specification. It is generated by the MIDL compiler and defined in file *inv.h.*

Finally, the import context and error status are output. You use the import context in other import routines to select binding information from the name service database, or to free the context memory when you are done with it.

❷ The *RpcNsBindingImportNext* routine obtains binding information that supports the interface, if any exists. The routine accesses the database and does not communicate with the server. The import handle, established with the call *RpcNsBindingImportBegin,* controls the search for compatible binding handles.

❸ Once binding information is obtained, any criteria required by the application may be used to decide whether it is appropriate. In this example, the application-specific procedure, *do_interpret_binding,* shown in Example 3-6, is used to interpret binding information by returning the protocol sequence in a parameter. The *do_import_binding* procedure then selects the binding information if it contains the connection protocol.

❹ Each call to *RpcNsBindingImportNext* requires a corresponding call to the *RpcBindingFree* routine that frees memory containing the binding information and sets the binding handle to null. Free the binding handle after you finish making remote procedure calls.

❺ The *RpcNsBindingImportDone* routine signifies that a client has finished looking for a compatible server in the name service database. This routine frees the memory of the import context created by a call to *RpcNsBindingImport-Begin.* Each call to *RpcNsBindingImportBegin* must have a corresponding call to *RpcNsBindingImportDone.*

Looking up a set of binding handles

Runtime routines whose names begin with *RpcNsBindingLookup* obtain a set of binding handles from the name service database. You can then select individual binding handles from the set with the *RpcNsBindingSelect* routine or you may use your own selection criteria. Lookup routines give a client program a little more control than import routines because *RpcNsBindingImportNext* returns a random binding handle from a list of compatible binding handles. Use the lookup routines when you want to select a server or servers by more specific binding information; for example, to select a server that is running on a system in your building or to use servers supporting a specific protocol sequence.

Finding a Server from Strings of Binding Data

If you bypass the name service database, you need to construct your own binding information and binding handles. Binding information may be represented with strings. You can compose a binding handle from appropriate strings of binding information or interpret information that a binding handle refers to.

The minimum information required in your application to obtain a binding handle is:

- A protocol sequence of communication protocols

- A server network address or host name

Remember that an endpoint is required for a remote procedure call to complete, but you can let the RPC runtime library obtain one for you. To set a binding handle, obtain and present the binding information to RPC runtime routines.

Example 3-9 shows a procedure to set a binding handle from strings of binding information. The `rfile` application uses this procedure. A network address or host name is input for this procedure and the protocol sequence is obtained. This procedure creates a partially bound binding handle, so the RPC runtime library obtains the endpoint when a remote procedure uses the binding handle.

Example 3–9: Setting a Binding Handle from Strings

```
/* FILE NAME: strbind.c */
/* Find a server binding handle from strings of binding information      */
/* including protocol sequence, host address, and server process endpoint. */
#include <stdio.h>
#include "rfile.h"
#include "status.h"                    /* contains the CHECK_STATUS macro */

int do_string_binding(host, binding_h) /*return=0 if binding valid, else -1 */
char            host[];       /* server host name or network address input ❶ */
rpc_binding_handle_t *binding_h;        /* binding handle is output        */
{
    RPC_PROTSEQ_VECTOR    *protseq_vector;    /* protocol sequence list       */
    unsigned char         *string_binding;    /* string of binding information */
    unsigned long         status;             /* error status                 */
```

Example 3-9: Setting a Binding Handle from Strings (continued)

```
    int                 i, result;

    status =
    RpcNetworkInqProtseqs(     /* obtain a list of valid protocol sequences ❷ */
        &protseq_vector                /* list of protocol sequences obtained */
    );
    CHECK_STATUS(status, "Can't get protocol sequences:", ABORT);

    /* loop through protocol sequences until a binding handle is obtained */
    for(i=0; i < protseq_vector->Count; i++) {

        status =
        RpcStringBindingCompose(     /* make string binding from components ❸ */
            NULL,                         /* no object UUIDs are required      */
            protseq_vector->Protseq[i],   /* protocol sequence                 */
            (unsigned char *)host,        /* host name or network address      */
            NULL,                         /* no endpoint is required           */
            NULL,                         /* no network options are required   */
            &string_binding               /* the constructed string binding    */
        );
        CHECK_STATUS(status, "Can't compose a string binding:", RESUME);

        status =
        RpcBindingFromStringBinding(     /* convert string to binding handle ❹ */
            string_binding,               /* input string binding              */
            binding_h                     /* binding handle is obtained here */
        );
        CHECK_STATUS(status, "Can't get binding handle from string:", RESUME);
        if(status != RPC_S_OK) {
            result = -1;
            CHECK_STATUS(status, "Can't get binding handle from string:", RESUME);
        }
        else
            result = 0;

        status =
        RpcStringFree(                        /* free string binding created ❺ */
            &string_binding
        );
        CHECK_STATUS(status, "Can't free string binding:", RESUME);
        if(result == 0)  break;                    /* got a valid binding */
    }

    status =
    RpcProtseqVectorFree(             /* free the list of protocol sequences ❻ */
        &protseq_vector
    );
    CHECK_STATUS(status, "Can't free protocol sequence vector:", RESUME);
    return(result);
}
```

❶   The network address or host name on which a server is available is required binding information. For this example, the information is input as a parameter.

❷   The *RpcNetworkInqProtseqs* routine creates a list of valid protocol sequences. This example uses each protocol sequence from the list until a binding handle is created.

❸   The *RpcStringBindingCompose* routine creates a string of binding information in the argument `string_binding` from all the necessary binding information components. The component strings include an object UUID, a protocol sequence, a network address, an endpoint, and network options.

❹   The *RpcBindingFromStringBinding* routine obtains a binding handle from the string of binding information. The string of binding information comes from the *RpcStringBindingCompose* routine or from the *RpcBindingToString-Binding* routine.

When you are finished with the binding handle, use the *RpcBindingFree* routine to set the binding handle to null and to free memory referred to by the binding handle. In this example, another part of the application frees the binding handle.

❺   The *RpcStringFree* routine frees strings allocated by other RPC runtime routines. This example frees the string `string_binding` allocated by the *RpcStringBindingCompose* routine.

❻   The *RpcProtseqVectorFree* routine is called to free the list of protocol sequences. An earlier call to *RpcNetworkInqProtseqs* requires a corresponding call to *RpcProtseqVectorFree*.

Customizing a Binding Handle

The basic binding handles we have seen so far are **primitive binding handles**. A **customized binding handle** adds some information that your application wants to pass between client and server. You can use a customized binding handle when application-specific data is appropriate to use for finding a server, and the data is also needed as a procedure parameter.

For example, in an application that acts on remote files, a structure could contain a host name and a remote filename. The application creates the necessary binding information from the host name, and the filename is passed with the binding information so the server knows what data file to use. You can use a customized binding handle with the explicit or implicit binding methods, but the automatic method uses only primitive binding handles.

Figure 3-2 shows how a customized binding handle works during a remote procedure call. To define a customized binding handle, apply the `handle` attribute to a type definition in an interface definition.

You can use a customized binding handle in a client just like a primitive binding handle, but you must write special **bind** and **unbind** procedures. Your code does not call these procedures; the client stub calls them during each remote procedure

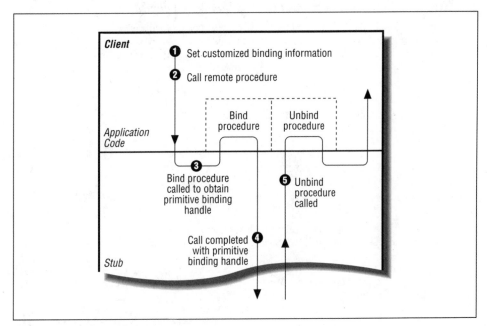

Figure 3-2. How a customized binding handle works

call. For a primitive binding handle, the client stub already has the necessary code to prepare the binding information for the call. For application-specific binding information, you must supply the code. The tasks of the bind and unbind procedures are to obtain a primitive binding handle and do application cleanup when finished with the binding handle.

Manipulate the data structure in your application the same as any structure, including passing data in the remote procedure call. However, the client stub uses the special procedures to manage the binding. The customized binding handle must be the first parameter in a remote procedure (or the global handle for the implicit method) to act as the binding handle for the call. A customized handle acts as a standard parameter if it is not the first parameter.

Example 3-10 shows how to define a customized binding handle in an interface definition.

Example 3-10: Defining a Customized Binding Handle

```
/* FILE NAME: search.idl */
[
uuid(2450F730-5170-101A-9A93-08002B2BC829),
version(1.0),
pointer_default(ref)]
interface search                    /* Search remote file for data     */
{
    const long  LINESIZE = 100;     /* Constant for maximum line size */
```

Example 3-10: Defining a Customized Binding Handle (continued)

```
    const long  FILENAME_SIZE = 100;  /* Constant for file name length */
    const long  BINDING_SIZE = 32;    /* Constant for host name size   */
    const short FILE_ERROR = -1;      /* Status for search file error  */
    const short NO_MATCH = 0;         /* Status for no match found      */

    /*
    **    Customized binding handle definition
    **    contains the file name and the string
    **    binding to use.
    */
    typedef [handle] struct {              /* customized handle type ❶ */
      unsigned char binding[BINDING_SIZE];
      unsigned char filename[FILENAME_SIZE];
    } search_spec;                                        /* ❷ */

    /*
    ** Search for a string match on the file specified
    **    in the customized binding handle above.
    */
    short searchit(                        /* search a file on the server */
      [in] search_spec custom_handle,    /* customized binding handle ❸ */
      [in,string] char search_string[LINESIZE],        /* target string */
      [out,string] char return_string[LINESIZE],              /* results */
      [out] error_status_t *error              /* comm/fault status */
    );
}
```

❶ Use the `handle` attribute in the interface definition to associate a customized binding handle with a data type.

❷ The `file_spec` data type is a structure whose members are file specifications. This is application-specific information used by the bind procedure to obtain server binding information.

❸ The customized binding handle is the first parameter of a procedure declaration. This is an example of explicit binding.

You must implement bind and unbind procedures. Example 3-11 shows how you can implement these procedures inside a client file.

Example 3-11: Bind and Unbind Procedures

```
/* FUNCTION: search_spec_bind */
handle_t __RPC_API
search_spec_bind(custom_handle)    /* bind procedure for customized handle ❶ */
search_spec custom_handle;
    rpc_binding_handle_t binding_h;

    printf("\n\t(Selecting server binding: %s)\n\n", /* Display server binding*/
        custom_handle.binding);

    status =
    RpcBindingFromStringBinding(          /* Convert the character string */
        custom_handle.binding,            /* binding into an RPC handle   */
        &binding_h,
```

Example 3-11: Bind and Unbind Procedures (continued)

```
    );
    CHECK_STATUS(status, "Invalid string binding", RESUME);
        exit (EXIT_FAILURE);
        return (binding_h);
}
/* FUNCTION: search_spec_unbind */
void __RPC_API
search_spec_unbind(                    /* unbind procedure for customized handle ❷ */
        custom_handle,
        binding_h)
search_spec custom_handle;
handle_t  binding_h;
{
    status =
    RpcBindingFree(                         /* Free the binding handle */
        &binding_h);
    CHECK_STATUS(status, "Can't free binding handle:", RESUME);
    return;
}
```

❶ The bind procedure takes an input parameter of the customized handle data type, and returns a primitive binding handle. You construct the procedure name from the data type name, *search_spec*, to which you append *_bind*. In this example *search_spec_bind* constructs a binding handle from arguments passed on the client command line to obtain a primitive binding handle.

❷ The unbind procedure takes input parameters of the customized handle data type and a primitive binding handle. You construct the procedure name from the data type name, *search_spec*, to which you append *_unbind*. In this example *search_spec_unbind* calls the RPC runtime routine, *RpcBindingFree*, to free the binding handle.

Example 3-12 shows how an application client can use a customized binding handle.

Example 3-12: A Client with a Customized Binding Handle

```
/* FILE NAME: client_send.c */
.
.
.
int
MAIN_DECL main(ac, av)
int    ac;
char *av[];
{
    short            search_status;   /* status from search        */
    idl_char         match[LINESIZE];  /* string to look for        */
    search_spec      custom_handle;    /* customized binding handle ❶ */

    match[0]  = '\0';                        /* Initialize some strings */
    custom_handle.binding[0]  = '\0';
    custom_handle.filename[0] = '\0';
```

Example 3-12: A Client with a Customized Binding Handle (continued)

```
/*
** There should be 4 parameters to searchit:
**
**     searchit <hostname> <filename> <matchstring>
**
** where
**
**     <hostname> is the hostname where the file to be searched
**                exists.
**
**     <filename> is the name of the file to be searched.
**
**     <matchstring> is the string to search <filename> for.
**
*/
if (ac != 4)             /* Exit if not the right number of parameters */
 {
 printf("\t\nUsage: searchit <hostname> <filename> <matchstring>\n\n");
 exit(EXIT_FAILURE);
 }

/*
** Set up the string binding, the filename, and the
** match string from the command line.
*/
strcpy ((char *)custom_handle.binding,  "ncacn_ip_tcp:");     /* ❷ */
strcat ((char *)custom_handle.binding,  av[1]);
strcpy ((char *)custom_handle.filename, av[2]);
strcpy ((char *)match, av[3]);

/*
** Search the given file on the given host for the
**     given string...
*/
search_status = searchit(          /* Remote procedure with input ❸ */
               custom_handle,
               match,
               result,
               &rpc_status
);
.
.
.
```

❶   The application allocates the customized binding handle.

❷   Initialize the customized binding information in the client before calling the remote procedure. For this example, when we invoke the client, we input the server host name, remote data filename, and search string as arguments.

❸   The remote procedure is called with the customized binding handle as the first parameter.

Authentication

Authentication in a distributed environment is a broad topic that is outside the scope of this book. Although we do not provide details on implementing security in Microsoft RPC applications, we will mention the major aspects and some trade-offs involved in selecting various models.

Microsoft RPC can use the security features of Microsoft Windows NT which are built into the named pipes (ncacn_np) and local RPC (ncalrpc) transports. You must restrict your application to using one of the two listed transports to use this security system.

You can use the Windows NT security features by specifying options to the endpoint parameter in a string binding. Options have names such as anonymous, identification, or impersonation, controlling which level of security to use.

Alternatively, you can use RPC security available in Microsoft RPC. This form of security is transport-independent so your application can use other transports in addition to named pipes and local RPC. Microsoft RPC security currently uses the Windows NT Security Service as the only supported security provider.

RPC security offers three kinds of protection: authentication, data integrity, and data privacy. Data integrity and data privacy involve extra encryption and decryption cycles which can be time consuming, so use these features only when necessary.

On client systems you can use RPC security by including the *RpcBindingSetAuth-Info* routine in your client program. Briefly, this routine places the client's identity information into the binding handle which is passed to the server as the first parameter in a remote procedure call.

Servers extract the client authentication information from the client binding handle using the *RpcBindingInqAuthClient* routine. Servers use this information to verify a client's authenticity.

The server system supplies its identity information to clients by registering it with the *RpcServerRegisterAuthInfo* routine. Clients or other servers can extract this information to authenticate the server's identity. Use the *RpcBindingInqAuthInfo* routine to extract server authentication information from the server binding handle.

To recap, using the transport level security built into named pipes and local RPC does not necessarily add lots of new code to an application. If you want to use security over transports other than named pipes or local RPC (for instance, TCP/IP or DECnet), you'll need to use RPC security features which can require extra programming overhead.

Error Parameters or Exceptions

Microsoft RPC client applications require special error-handling techniques to deal with errors that may occur during a remote procedure call. The following discussion pertains to both client and server development.

Server and communication errors are raised to the client as exceptions during a remote procedure call. RPC exceptions are similar to the RPC error status codes. Errors have names with S as the second component, as in RPC_S_ADDRESS_ERROR. Exceptions have X as the second component, as in RPC_X_NO_MEMORY.

Types of exceptions include the following:

- Exceptions raised on the client system, such as when the client process is out of memory (RPC_X_NO_MEMORY).

- Exceptions raised to the client application by the client stub, such as when the stub has received bad data (RPC_X_BAD_STUB_DATA).

- Exceptions raised by the client stub on behalf of the server. These errors can occur in the server stub, in the remote procedures, or in the server's RPC runtime library. The server transport layer does not return exceptions to the client.

A distributed application can have errors from a number of sources, so you will need to decide whether you want to handle errors with exception handling code or error parameters. This may simply be a matter of personal preference or consistency.

Using Exception Handlers in Clients or Servers

You can handle exceptions by writing exception handler code in the application to recover from an error or gracefully exit the application. Microsoft RPC supplies a set of macros as a framework to handle exceptions in your client or server code. (Example 5-6, in Chapter 5, uses RPC exception handling macros.) If your application is written for Win32 only, use the Win32 versions of these macros.

Using Remote Procedure Parameters to Handle Errors

In your ACF, you can add error parameters to remote procedures in order to conveniently handle communication and server errors. The RPC runtime library then stores errors values in these parameters rather than raising exceptions. You can also use a combination of exception handlers and error parameters.

When the simple arithmetic application in Chapter 1 encounters some errors, it returns a hexadecimal number. You must convert this number to a decimal error code number and then look it up to find out what happened. By making three simple changes to the arithmetic application you can get it to return the actual RPC error code:

- Add an `error_status_t` parameter to the remote procedure declaration in the MIDL file.

- Add an `error_status_t` parameter to the remote procedure implementation in the server.

- Declare the variable in the client file.

The sum_arrays procedure declaration in the following MIDL file has an [out] parameter of the type `error_status_t`.

```
void sum_arrays ( /* The sum_arrays procedure doesn't return a value */
   [in] long_array a,              /* 1st parameter is passed in  */
   [in] long_array b,              /* 2nd parameter is passed in  */
   [out] long_array c,             /* 3rd parameter is passed out */
   [out] error_status_t *rpc_status /* error parameter is passed out */
);
```

We've added the `error_status_t` parameter to the remote procedure in *manager.c*. The initialized status value can be changed by the stubs if an error occurs.

```
void sum_arrays(a, b, c, rpc_status)     /* sum_arrays implementation */
   long_array a;
   long_array b;
   long_array c;
   error_status_t *rpc_status;              /* error status parameter */
   {
      int i;

      *rpc_status = RPC_S_OK;          /* initializes the status value */
      for(i = 0; i < ARRAY_SIZE; i++)
         c[i] = a[i] + b[i]; /* array elements are added together */
   }
```

The client code declares the variable along with the rest of the variables. Then a CHECK_STATUS macro converts the RPC error code to a status message.

```
/* FILE NAME: client.c */
/* This is an arithmetic client module with error handling. */
#include <stdio.h>
#include <stdlib.h>
#include "arith.h"  /* header file created by MIDL compiler */
#include "status.h"        /* needed for CHECK_STATUS macro */

long_array a ={100,200,345,23,67,65,0,0,0,0};
long_array b ={4,0,2,3,1,7,5,9,6,8};

main ()
{
   long_array    result;
   int i;
   /* declare variable and initialize */
   error_status_t rpc_status=RPC_S_OK;

   /* remote procedure with status */
   sum_arrays(a, b, result, &rpc_status);
```

```
    /* report error and abort */
    CHECK_STATUS (rpc_status, "ERROR:", ABORT);
    puts("sums:");
    for(i = 0; i < ARRAY_SIZE; i++)
        printf("%ld\n", result[i]);
}
```

The CHECK_STATUS macro shown in Example 3-13 converts the RPC error code to
an error message.

Example 3–13: The CHECK_STATUS Macro

```
/* FILE NAME: status.h */
#include <stdio.h>
#include <stdlib.h>
#include "..\rpcerror.h"     /* maps error codes to error messages   ❶ */

#define RESUME 0
#define ABORT  1

#define CHECK_STATUS(input_status, comment, action) \
{ \
    if(input_status != RPC_S_OK) { \
        error_stat = DceErroringText(input_status, error_string); \ /* ❷ */
        fprintf(stderr, "%s %s\n", comment, error_string); \
        if(action == ABORT) \
            exit(1); \
    } \
}

static int            error_stat;
static unsigned char  error_string[DCE_C_ERROR_STRING_LEN];
```

❶   The file *rpcerror.h* is shown in Appendix C, *The Arithmetic Application*.

❷   Although Microsoft RPC does not support the DCE RPC routine
    dce_error_inq_text, we've emulated its function here.

Compiling and Linking Clients

Figure 3-3 shows the files and libraries required to produce an executable client.
When complex data types are used, the MIDL compiler produces the client stub
auxiliary file (*appl_x.c*) when the interface is compiled. Example 3-14 shows the
portion of a makefile that:

•   Compiles the C language stubs and client code along with the header file pro-
    ducing server object files

•   Links the server object files to produce the executable server file

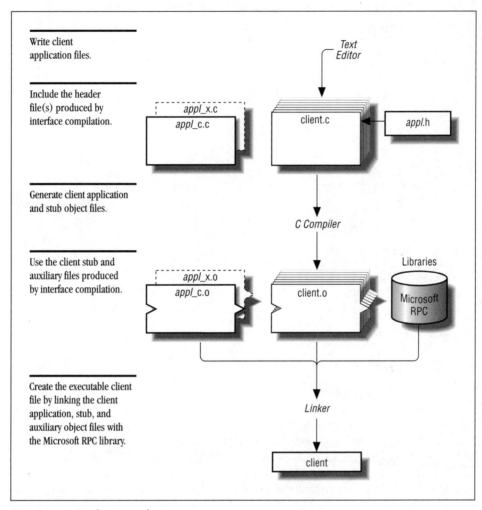

Figure 3-3. Producing a client

Example 3-14: Using a Makefile to Compile and Link a Client

```
# FILE NAME: Makefile
# Makefile for the inventory application implicit client
#
# definitions for this make file
#
APPL=inv
IDLCMD=midl
NTRPCLIBS=rpcrt4.lib rpcns4.lib libcmt.lib kernel32.lib

!include <ntwin32.mak>

## NT c flags
cflags = -c -W0 -Gz -D_X86_=1 -DWIN32 -DMT /I. /I.. /nologo
```

Example 3–14: Using a Makefile to Compile and Link a Client (continued)

```
## NT nmake inference rules
    $(cc) $(cdebug) $(cflags) $(cvarsmt) $<
    $(cvtomf)
.
.
.
#
# CLIENT BUILD
#
client:     client.exe
client.exe: client.obj getbind.obj intbind.obj $(APPL)_c.obj $(APPL)_x.obj
    $(link) $(linkdebug) $(conflags) -out:client.exe -map:client.map \
        client.obj getbind.obj intbind.obj $(APPL)_c.obj $(APPL)_x.obj \
        $(NTRPCLIBS)
.
.
.
# client and server sources
client.obj:  client.c     $(APPL).h
getbind.obj: getbind.c
intbind.obj: intbind.c
.
.
.
```

Local Testing

You can compile a local version of your client to test and debug remote procedures without using remote procedure calls. To do a local test, compile the client
object files and remote procedure implementations without the stub or auxiliary
files. The code that finds a server is also unnecessary for a local test. Applications
in this book use the compiler directive, /DLOCAL, to distinguish a test compilation
used in a local environment from a compilation used in a distributed environment.
Example 3-15 shows the portions of a makefile that produce the inventory application for local testing.

Example 3–15: Using a Makefile to Produce a Local Version of an Application

```
# FILE NAME: Makefile
# Makefile for the inventory application implicit client
#
# definitions for this make file
#
APPL=inv
IDLCMD=midl
NTRPCLIBS=rpcrt4.lib rpcns4.lib libcmt.lib kernel32.lib

!include <ntwin32.mak>

## NT c flags
cflags = -c -W0 -Gz -D_X86_=1 -DWIN32 -DMT /I. /I.. /nologo

## NT nmake inference rules
```

Example 3-15: Using a Makefile to Produce a Local Version of an Application (continued)

```
    $(cc) $(cdebug) $(cflags) $(cvarsmt) $<
    $(cvtomf)
.
.
.
#
# LOCAL BUILD of the client application to test locally
#
local:      lclient.exe
lclient.exe: lclient.obj lmanager.obj invntry.obj
    $(link) $(linkdebug) $(conflags) -out:lclient.exe -map:lclient.map \
      lclient.obj lmanager.obj invntry.obj \
      $(NTRPCLIBS)
.
.
.

# Local client sources
invntry.obj: ..\invntry.c
              $(cc) $(cdebug) $(cflags) $(cvarsmt) /DLOCAL /I. /I.. \
              /Foinvntry.obj ..\invntry.c
lclient.obj: client.c $(APPL).h
              $(cc) $(cdebug) $(cflags) $(cvarsmt) /DLOCAL /I. /I.. \
              /Folclient.obj client.c
lmanager.obj: ..\manager.c $(APPL).h
              $(cc) $(cdebug) $(cflags) $(cvarsmt) /DLOCAL /I. /I.. \
              /Folmanager.obj ..\manager.c
```

4

Pointers, Arrays, and Memory Usage

In C, pointers and arrays have a close correlation due to the way applications access the information they contain. Pointers and arrays work essentially the same in distributed and local applications. But there are a few restrictions in distributed applications because the client and server have different address spaces. In most of this chapter we discuss pointers and arrays for clients. See also Chapter 5, *How to Write a Server*, for a discussion of memory allocation for pointers and arrays in remote procedures.

To make your applications more efficient, MIDL offers several kinds of pointers and arrays to reduce network traffic and stub overhead. This chapter uses the inventory application to demonstrate the use of pointers and arrays in distributed applications.

Kinds of Pointers

A pointer is a variable containing the address of another data structure or variable. As in C, you declare a pointer in an interface definition by using an asterisk (*) followed by a variable. For example, the inventory application has the following procedure declaration:

```
void whatis_part_price(          /* get part price from inventory */
    [in] part_num   number,
    [out] part_price *price
);
```

In a distributed application, the client and server do not share the same address space. This means the data a pointer refers to in the client is not available in the remote procedure of the server. The opposite is also true. Therefore, pointer data is copied between the client and server address spaces during a remote procedure call. For the *whatis_part_price* procedure, data that the pointer argument refers to on the server is copied back to the client and placed in the memory referred to by the price pointer. This copying of pointer data does not occur during a local procedure call.

MIDL has three kinds of pointers: reference, unique, and full. We'll describe them here in order of increasing capability. Keep in mind, though, that more capabilities result in more stub overhead.

A **reference pointer** is used to refer to existing data. It is the simplest kind of pointer. Consequently, it has a performance advantage over other kinds of pointers because stub overhead is minimal. For example, the *whatis_part_price* procedure uses a reference pointer. This procedure passes by reference a pointer to an allocated part_price data structure. The remote procedure returns output data to the same memory location with the part price. Thus, for reference pointers, the data can change but not the address itself. The [ref] attribute specifies a reference pointer in an interface definition.

Sometimes you need a pointer that can do more, such as handling singly-linked lists in which the end of the list is marked with a null pointer. For this situation, a **unique pointer** might be used because it can be null. A unique pointer has many capabilities usually associated with pointers. Use unique pointers in interface definitions when a remote procedure call allocates new memory for the client. In this case, the client stub actually allocates the memory. Unique pointers cannot address data that is also addressed by other pointers in the remote procedure, so you should avoid using complex data structures with cycles (doubly-linked lists). The [unique] attribute specifies a unique pointer in the interface definition.

A **full pointer** has all of the capabilities associated with unique pointers. In addition, it allows two pointers to refer to the same address, as in a double linked list. The [ptr] attribute specifies a full pointer in the interface definition. Full pointer capability incurs significant stub overhead, so use full pointers only when necessary.

A pointer attribute must be applied where the pointer is defined with an asterisk. For instance, if you define a typedef that resolves to a pointer, you cannot apply the pointer attribute where you use the typedef.

The following sections discuss the use of pointers, and tell you when you need a reference or full pointer. Table 4-1 and Example 4-5 summarize what you need to know to declare and use pointers.

Pointers as Output Parameters

Due to the overhead of transmitting data, you have to declare MIDL parameters to be input, output, or both. In MIDL, as in C, input parameters are passed in by value, which means a copy of each input parameter is available in the procedure. Passing input parameters by value makes sense for a small amount of data. This technique offers simplicity since programmers don't have to deal with pointers or addresses. However, passing by value also means that any change to the variable in the procedure cannot reflect back to the original parameter when the call completes.

To fill in data for an output parameter (or modify an input/output parameter), both C and MIDL must pass by reference a memory address using a pointer or array parameter. During a remote procedure call, the parameter refers to existing memory, which is passed by reference to the client stub. When the remote procedure completes execution, data is sent back by the server stub to the client stub, which unmarshalls it into the memory referred to by the pointer. Therefore, the data is available to the client application when the client stub returns to the application.

Example 4-1 shows an output parameter in the *whatis_part_price* procedure declaration from the inventory interface definition. Pointer parameters (`*price`) are reference pointers by default.

Example 4–1: Defining an Output Parameter

```
void whatis_part_price(                   /* get part price from inventory */
   [in]  part_num   number,
   [out] part_price *price                       /* reference pointer */
);
```

The `part_price` structure must be allocated in the client prior to the remote procedure call, but values are assigned in the remote procedure and transmitted back. The *whatis_part_price* remote procedure call in the client looks like this:

```
part_record part;                /* structure for all data about a part */
.
.
.
   case 'p': whatis_part_price(part.number, &(part.price));
            printf("price:%10.2f\n", part.price.per_unit);
            break;
```

In the server, *whatis_part_price* reads a part record from the database for the part number input. It then assigns the values from the part record to the price structure members. Finally, the procedure returns and the price information is marshalled and transmitted by the server stub. The *whatis_part_price* remote procedure looks like this:

```
void whatis_part_price(number, price)
part_num    number;
part_price  *price;
{
   part_record *part;                  /* a pointer to a part record */

   read_part_record(number, &part);
   price->units = part->price.units;
   price->per_unit = part->price.per_unit;
   return;
}
```

You can see from the preceding explanation that an output parameter must refer to existing storage on the client, and therefore that it is always a reference pointer. In fact, the MIDL compiler refuses to let you declare an output-only parameter with the unique or ptr attribute.

Suppose we don't know how much memory should be allocated for output data, so we want a procedure to return data in a parameter as newly allocated memory. We cannot just allocate some memory and hope it's enough because if the data output is greater, data will overwrite into other memory. To solve this, we pass a pointer to a pointer. We describe how to do this later in the chapter.

A parameter used as both input and output is passed by reference. Programs commonly modify data by passing a pointer to a data structure into a procedure, which passes back the same pointer but with modified data. Optional (NULL) parameters can be used as input/output parameters. This feature is described in the following section.

Pointers as Input Parameters

Suppose our inventory interface has the following procedure declaration:

```
void store_parts(
    [in] part_record *part1,
    [in] part_record *part2
);
```

Assume this procedure adds new parts to the database. The procedure takes as parameters two pointers to structures of type **part_record**, (already defined in the interface) to store all data about a part.

The remote procedure call in a client can look like the following:

```
part_record *part1, *part2;
part1 = (part_record *)malloc(sizeof(part_record));
part2 = (part_record *)malloc(sizeof(part_record));
/* part structures are filled in */
part1->number = 123;
part2->number = 124;
    .
    .
    .

store_parts(part1, part2);
```

In this simple case, the client stub marshalls and transmits the data the pointers refer to. (This procedure is not implemented in any applications in this book, so no server code is shown.)

One reason reference pointers reduce overhead is that the stubs make certain assumptions about the use of the pointer. Since pointer parameters are reference pointers by default, one of these assumptions is that a pointer parameter points to valid data of the type specified.

Suppose we want optional parameters in our procedure definition. In this case, the client passes a null pointer value for the parameter, so the remote procedure knows to ignore it. For the stubs to know the parameter is a null value, the parameter must be a unique pointer so the stubs do not attempt to copy any data for the parameter.

Example 4-2 shows how to modify our *store_parts* procedure declaration so that both parameters are unique pointers.

Example 4–2: Defining Optional Procedure Parameters

```
void store_parts_1(                    /* ❶ */
    [in,unique] part_record *part1,
    [in,unique] part_record *part2
);
        .
        .
        .
typedef [unique] part_record *part_record_ptr;
void store_parts_2(                    /* ❷ */
    [in] part_record_ptr part1,
    [in] part_record_ptr part2
);
```

❶ To specify an optional parameter, use the unique attribute on an input (or input/output) parameter.

❷ As an alternative to method 1 for specifying an optional parameter, define a unique pointer data type and use the data type for the procedure parameter.

The client can now supply a NULL pointer:

```
store_parts_1(part1, NULL);
```

If an input/output parameter is a unique pointer with a null value on input, it is also null on output because the client does not have an address to store a return value.

Microsoft RPC allows two pointers to refer to the same data. This practice is known as **pointer aliasing**.

To minimize overhead, stubs cannot manage more than one reference pointer referring to the same data in a single remote procedure call. For example, suppose our *store_parts* procedure does something useful if we pass in the same pointer for both arguments. The following type of remote procedure call causes unpredictable behavior:

```
store_parts(part1, part1); /* WRONG--do not use ref pointer aliasing */
```

This call will *not* work as expected because the parameters (reference pointers) both point to the same address. Reference pointers and unique pointers do not allow two pointers to refer to the same data.

If *store_parts_1* were used instead of *store_parts*, the call would work correctly, because the arguments were specifically defined in the interface definition as full pointers with the `ptr` attribute.

Using Pointers to Pointers for New Output

A pointer refers to a specific amount of memory. For a procedure parameter to output newly allocated memory, we use a pointer to refer to another pointer that refers to data (or to another pointer and so on). This is also known as multiple levels of indirection.

If you use just one pointer for a procedure parameter, you would have to make two remote procedure calls to allocate new memory. The first remote procedure call obtains the size of the server's data structure. Then the client allocates memory for it. The second remote procedure call obtains data from the server and fills the previously allocated memory. In a distributed application, using two pointers allows the client and server stubs to allocate all the necessary memory in one remote procedure call. The client stub must generate a copy of the memory allocated on the server.

The *whatare_subparts* procedure in the inventory application contains a parameter with a pointer to a pointer:

```
[out] part_list **subparts
```

The procedure allocates memory for the left pointer, and the right pointer is a parameter passed by reference to return the address of the left pointer. To accomplish this, MIDL must use two kinds of pointers:

The right pointer is a reference pointer and the left pointer is a unique pointer. The reference pointer by itself cannot have new memory automatically allocated because it will point to the same address throughout the remote call. However, for the unique pointer, the amount of memory allocated by the server is allocated automatically by the client stub when the call returns.

When a pointer attribute is applied in an interface definition where there are pointers to pointers, it applies only to the right pointer and does not propagate to any other pointers.

Example 4-3 demonstrates how to return data in a parameter by using two pointers. The procedure needs to output a data structure (in this case a structure with a conformant array). The final size of the data structure is unknown when you call the remote procedure.

Example 4-3: Defining Pointers to Pointers for Memory Allocation

```
[
    .
    .
    .
pointer_default(unique)      /* the pointer default is a unique pointer ❶ */
] interface inventory
{
    .
    .
    .
    void whatare_subparts(      /* get list of subpart numbers for a part */
        [in]  part_num  number,
        [out] part_list **subparts               /* a pointer to a pointer ❷ */
    );
```

❶ Parameters or type definitions with multiple pointers use a pointer default to specify the kind of pointer for all but the right one. To establish a pointer default, use the `pointer_default` attribute in the interface definition header. In this example, the `unique` argument establishes a unique pointer default.

❷ If memory is allocated during remote procedure execution, output parameters require multiple pointers. By default, the right pointer of a procedure parameter is a reference pointer. The left pointer must be a unique pointer. This is accomplished through the `pointer_default` attribute.

The `part_list` structure is allocated during the remote procedure call. On the server, the remote procedure allocates memory and assigns data. The server stub marshalls and transmits the data back to the client. The server stub then frees the memory allocated in the remote procedure. The client stub allocates memory and unmarshalls the transmitted data into the new memory. The remote procedure call in a client for *whatare_subparts* looks like:

```
    part_record part;       /* structure for all data about a part  */
    part_list   *subparts;  /* pointer to parts list data structure */
    .
    .
    case 's': whatare_subparts(part.number, &subparts);
            for(i = 0; i < subparts->size; i++)
                printf("%ld  ", subparts->numbers[i]);
            printf("\ntotal number of subparts:%ld\n", subparts->size);
```

When you finish with the data, free the memory allocated by unique pointers:

```
free(subparts);
break;
```

See Example 5-9 in Chapter 5 for the server implementation of the remote procedure *whatare_subparts*.

Pointers as Procedure Return Values

As we have described previously, the client must allocate memory for reference pointer data before it is used in a remote procedure call. This simplifies the client stub by giving unmarshalling code a place to put data after the server sends it. Now consider the following remote procedure call in client application code:

```
unsigned long *a;
a = proc();
```

The address of the procedure assignment, a, is available only when the procedure returns, and not during its execution. Therefore, we cannot use the method just described for a reference pointer to allocate memory in the client prior to the call, and expect the stub to complete the assignment for us. Procedures that return pointer results always return full pointers, so that the stub allocates any necessary memory and unmarshalls data into it for us. Example 4-4 shows a procedure that returns a pointer.

Example 4-4: Defining a Procedure that Returns a Pointer

```
typedef [string, unique] char *paragraph;        /* description of part ❶ */
.
.
.
paragraph get_part_description(        /* return a pointer to a string ❷ */
    [in]  part_num  number
);
```

❶   A pointer attribute (unique) on a pointer data type (char *paragraph) specifies the kind of pointer for that data type wherever it is used in the interface. (If a pointer data type does not have a pointer attribute, the pointer specified with the pointer_default attribute applies.) To specify a pointer to a string, apply the string attribute as well.

❷   Procedures that return a pointer result always return a full pointer. A procedure result cannot be a reference pointer because new storage is always allocated by the client stub, which copies data into it when the call returns.

The call to get_part_description looks like:

```
part_record part;              /* structure for all data about a part */
.
.
.
```

```
case 'd': part.description = get_part_description(part.number);
          printf("description:\n%s\n", part.description);
```

When you finish with the data, free the memory allocated by unique pointers:

```
if(part.description != NULL)
    free(part.description);     /* free memory allocated */
```

On the server, the remote procedure allocates memory that the server stub copies and transmits back to the client. The server stub then frees the memory allocated. Example 5-8 shows how to allocate memory in the *get_part_description* remote procedure.

Pointer Summary

As reference pointers, unique pointers, and full pointers represent increases in capability, they also require increases in stub overhead needed to manage them. Therefore, you must differentiate among reference, unique, and full pointers in the interface definition. Table 4-1 summarizes and compares pointer types. Example 4-5 shows how to recognize which kind of pointer applies in an interface definition. A visible ref or unique pointer attribute overrides a default.

Table 4-1: A Summary of Reference and Unique Pointers

	Reference Pointer	Unique Pointer	Full Pointer
Attribute name	ref	unique	ptr
Characteristics	Provides indirection where the value is always the address of valid data	Multiple levels of indirection	Indirection and full pointer capabilities
Stub overhead	Minimum	Moderate	Maximum
Value of NULL	Cannot be NULL	Can be NULL	Can be NULL
Address value	Never changes when a call returns	May change when a call returns	May change when a call returns
Storage	Storage exists prior to the call	Storage is allocated automatically if needed	Storage is allocated automatically if needed
Input and output parameter	Data is written into existing storage when the call returns	The storage location of data on output may be different from the storage location on input. If the input value is NULL, the output value is also NULL.	The storage location of data on output may be different from the storage location on input. If the input value is NULL, the output value is also NULL.

Table 4–1: A Summary of Reference and Unique Pointers (continued)

	Reference Pointer	Unique Pointer	Full Pointer
Output parameter	Parameter is a reference pointer by default	Not allowed	Not allowed
Input parameter	Data is read from existing storage	Data is read from existing storage; if the value is NULL, no data is read	Data is read from existing storage; if the value is NULL, no data is read
Pointer aliasing	Not allowed	Not allowed	Allowed

Example 4–5: How to Determine Kinds of Pointers

```
[

    .

    .

    .

pointer_default(unique);                    /* ❶ */
] inventory interface
{

    .

    .

    .

typedef [string, unique] char *paragraph;/* ❷ */
    .

    .

    .

paragraph get_part_description(             /* ❸ */
    [in] part_num number,
);

    .

    .

    .

void whatis_part_price(
    [in]  part_num    number,
    [out] part_price *price              /* ❹ */
);

    .

    .

    .

void whatare_subparts(
    [in]  part_num   number,
    [out] part_list **subparts           /* ❺ */
);

    .

    .

    .

typedef struct {                            /* ❻ */
    [ref] part_num      *number;
```

Example 4-5: How to Determine Kinds of Pointers (continued)

```
    [ref] part_quantity *quantity;
    [ref] account_num    *account;
} part_order;
    .
    .
    .
void store_parts_1(                        /* ❼ */
    [in,unique] part_record *part1,
    [in,unique] part_record *part2
);
}
```

❶ The MIDL compiler attempts to assign the appropriate kind of pointer to pointers without a full, unique, or ref attribute. The pointer_default interface header attribute specifies which kind of pointer applies when one cannot be automatically determined. You can give the pointer_default attribute an argument of ref, unique, or full. If a pointer attribute is not specified for the data type, the interface requires a pointer default to specify the kind of pointer for the following cases:

- Pointers in typedefs (see callout 2)

- Multiple pointers other than the right pointer (see callout 5)

- Pointers that are members of structures or cases of discriminated unions (see callout 6)

❷ A pointer type attribute specifies the kind of pointer used. In this example, all occurrences that use the **paragraph** data type are unique pointers. If none of the pointer attributes—ref, unique or full—is present in the typedef, the pointer_default attribute specifies the kind of pointer.

❸ A pointer return value of a procedure is always a unique pointer because new memory is allocated. The **paragraph** data structure is a pointer to a string.

❹ A pointer parameter of a procedure is a reference pointer by default. Parameter reference pointers must always point to valid storage (never null). (See also callout 7.)

❺ With multiple pointers, the pointer_default attribute specifies all pointers except the right-most pointer. In this example, the right pointer is a reference pointer because it is a parameter pointer. The left pointer is determined by the pointer default. In this procedure, the left pointer must be a unique pointer so the array of parts in the **subparts** structure is automatically allocated by the client stub when the call returns.

❻ When a structure member or discriminated union case is a pointer, you must assign it a unique or ref attribute, either explicitly or through the attribute pointer_default. This interface definition specifies the structure members as reference pointers in order to override the unique pointer default. Unique or full pointers are unnecessary for these structure members; therefore, it is more efficient to use reference pointers to minimize the overhead associated with unique pointers.

❼   An input or input/output pointer parameter can be made an optional procedure parameter by applying the unique attribute. An attribute of either unique or ptr is required if you pass a value of NULL in a call.

Kinds of Arrays

You can use the following kinds of arrays in RPC applications:

* **Fixed arrays** contain a specific number of elements defined in the interface definition. They are defined just like standard C declarations.

* **Varying arrays** have a fixed size but clients and servers select a portion to transmit during a remote procedure call. The interface definition specifies subset bound variables used by the clients and servers to set the bounds.

* **Conformant arrays** have their size determined in the application code. The interface definition specifies an array size variable that the clients and servers use to control the amount of memory allocated and data transmitted.

Selecting a Portion of a Varying Array

For some clients or servers you need to use only a portion of an array in a remote procedure call. If this is the case, it is more efficient to transmit only the needed portion of the array. Procedures or structures that use varying arrays with data limit variables allow you to select the portion of an array that is processed by a remote procedure call.

A varying array has a fixed size when the application is compiled, but the portion of the array that contains the relevant, transmissible data is determined at runtime. For example, given the varying array arr[100], you can specify any index values in the range $0 \leq L \leq U \leq 99$, where L represents the lower data limit of the array and U represents the upper data limit.

An array is varying if you declare it in your interface definition with two extra attributes: first_is to indicate where transmission starts (L), and either length_is or last_is to indicated where transmission stops (U). Whether you use length_is or last_is depends on convenience.

Suppose that the following procedure appears in an interface definition:

```
const long SIZE = 100;

void proc(
    [in] long first,
    [in] long length,
```

```
        [in, first_is(first), length_is(length)] data_t arr[SIZE]
    );
```

To select a portion of the array to transmit, assign values to the variables `first` and `length`. For input parameters, the client sets them prior to the remote procedure call. Be sure the upper data limit value does not exceed the size of the array, for example:

```
    long first = 23;
    long length = 54;
    data_t arr[SIZE];

    proc(first, length, arr);
```

The transmitted array portion is represented by the indices $\boxed{23}$ . . . $\boxed{76}$ (23 + 54 - 1). The entire array is available in the client and the server, but only the portion represented by the data limit variables is transmitted and meaningful for the given remote procedure call. If the data limit parameters are also output, the remote procedure can set them to control the portion of the array transmitted back to the client.

A structure is an alternate way to define a varying array in an interface definition; for example:

```
    typedef struct varray_t {
        long first;
        long length;
        [first_is(first), length_is(length)] data_t arr[SIZE];
    } varray_t;

    proc([in] varray_t varray);
```

Managing the Size of a Conformant Array

Conformant arrays are defined in an interface definition with empty brackets or an asterisk (*) in place of the first dimension value.

```
    . . . c1[*] . . .
    . . . c2[][10] . . .
```

The conformant array `c1[*]` has index values $\boxed{0}$ . . . $\boxed{M}$ in which the dimension variable, M, represents the upper bound of the array. The dimension variable is specified in the interface definition and used in the application code at runtime to establish the array's actual size.

To specify an array size variable or a maximum upper bound variable, use one of the array size attributes, `size_is` or `max_is`, in an interface definition. These variables are used in the application to represent the size of the array. You can use either one, depending on which you find most convenient. Example 4-6 shows how a conformant array is defined in a structure.

Example 4-6: A Conformant Array in an Interface Definition

```
      .
      .
      .
   typedef struct part_list{                   /* list of part numbers */
      long                   size;        /* number of parts in array ❶ */
      [size_is(size)] part_num numbers[*];  /* conformant array of parts ❷ */
   } part_list;

   typedef struct part_record {                   /* data for each part */
      part_num      number;
      part_name     name;
      paragraph     description;
      part_price    price;
      part_quantity quantity;
      part_list     subparts; /* Conformant array or struct must be last ❸ */
   } part_record;
      .
      .
      .
void whatare_subparts(        /* get list of subparts numbers for a part */
   [in]  part_num  number,
   [out] part_list **subparts                              /* ❹ */
);
      .
      .
      .
```

❶   When an array member of a structure (numbers[*]) has an array attribute, the
    dimension variable (size) must also be a structure member. This assures that
    the dimension information is always available with the array when it is trans-
    mitted. The dimension variable member must be, or must resolve to, an inte-
    ger.

❷   The size_is attribute specifies a variable (size) that represents the number
    of elements the array dimension contains. In the application, the array indices
    are [0] . . . [size-1] . For example, if size is equal to 8 in the application code,
    then the array indices are [0] [1] [2] [3] [4] [5] [6] [7].

❸   If a conformant array is a member of a structure, it must be last so that your
    application can allocate any amount of memory needed. A conformant struc-
    ture (structure containing a conformant array member) must also be the last
    member of a structure containing it.

❹   Use a conformant structure and multiple levels of indirection for remote pro-
    cedures that allocate a conformant array. Chapter 5 implements this proce-
    dure.

To specify a variable that represents the highest index value for the first dimension
of the array rather than the array size, use the max_is attribute instead of the
size_is attribute. For example, the conformant structure defined in Example 4-6
can also be defined as follows:

```
typedef struct part_list{
   long  max;
   [max_is(max)] part_num numbers[*];
} part_list;
```

The variable **max** defines the maximum index value of the first dimension of the array. In the application, the array indices are $\boxed{0}$ . . . $\boxed{\text{max}}$. For example, if max is equal to 7 in the application code, then the array indices are $\boxed{0}$ $\boxed{1}$ $\boxed{2}$ $\boxed{3}$ $\boxed{4}$ $\boxed{5}$ $\boxed{6}$ $\boxed{7}$.

To avoid making mistakes in application development, be consistent in the interface definitions you write. Use either the **size_is** attribute or the **max_is** attribute for all your conformant arrays.

Conformant arrays as procedure parameters

When you call a remote procedure that contains a conformant array, you must pass the number of elements that are contained by the array. When a client calls the *whatare_subparts* remote procedure of Example 4-3, the dimension information is available in the **part_list** structure. However, if an array is passed as a parameter, the dimension information must also be an **in** parameter of the procedure.

For example, instead of obtaining an array of all the subparts for a part (as the *whatare_subparts* procedure does) you may want only the first five subparts. This procedure is defined as follows:

```
void get_n_subparts(            /* get n subpart numbers for a part */
   [in]  part_num   number,
   [in]  long       n,
   [out,size_is(n)] part_num subparts[]
);
```

In the client, the input includes the part number, a **5** representing the number of subparts desired, and a previously allocated array, large enough for the five subpart numbers. The output is the array with the first five subpart numbers. (The *get_n_subparts* procedure is not defined in the inventory interface definition.)

Dynamic memory allocation for conformant arrays

Suppose the following procedures appear in interface definitions:

```
proc1([in] long size, [in, size_is(size)] data_t arr[]);
proc2([in] long max,  [in, max_is(max)]   data_t arr[]);
```

You have to allocate memory for each array needed in the application. To allocate dynamic memory for conformant arrays, use a scheme such as the following:

```
unsigned long s,m;
data_t       *s_arr, *m_arr; /* pointers to some data structures  */

   /* some application specific constants */
s = SIZE;
m = MAX;
```

```
    /* allocation of the arrays */
s_arr = (data_t *)malloc( (s)   * sizeof(data_t) );
m_arr = (data_t *)malloc( (m+1) * sizeof(data_t) );

    /* the remote procedure calls */
proc1(s, s_arr);
proc2(m, m_arr);
```

In this example, SIZE is defined in the client to represent an array size and MAX is defined to represent the maximum index value of an array. Notice an array that has the max_is attribute in its interface definition must have an extra array element allocated because arrays begin with an index value of 0.

Memory allocation for conformant structures

Structures containing a conformant array require memory allocation in the client before they are input to a remote procedure call, because a statically allocated conformant structure has storage for only one array element. For example, the following is the part_list structure of the inventory interface:

```
typedef struct part_list{
    long                    size;
    [size_is(size)] part_num numbers[*]
} part_list;
```

The structure in the header file generated by the MIDL compiler has an array size of only one, as follows:

```
    typedef struct part_list {
        unsigned long size;
        part_num numbers[1];
    } part_list;
```

The application is responsible for allocating memory for as much of the array as it needs. Use a scheme such as the following to allocate more memory for a conformant structure:

```
part_list *c;       /* a pointer to the conformant structure */
long s;
s = 33;             /* the application specific array size    */

c = (part_list *)malloc(sizeof(part_list) + (sizeof(part_num)*(s-1)));
```

Notice that since the declared structure's size contains an array of one element representing the conformant array, the new memory allocated needs one array element less than the requested array size.

Memory Usage

Distributed applications usually involve more complicated memory management than single-system applications because the address spaces are on separate machines. Fortunately, for many programming situations, Microsoft RPC's default memory usage method can automate most of the memory management details, freeing programmers to concentrate on the application itself. In the default method, memory on clients and servers is allocated automatically by the stub code for each part of the data structure being stored.

However, while this automation is certainly convenient, it can sometimes result in large stub code and slower performance, especially when the data structures being managed are complex. Consequently, Microsoft RPC offers alternative memory usage methods which can help optimize performance, decrease stub size, or let you tailor your application to specific programming circumstances.

Before we look at specific methods, let's look at the kind of data structures that are passed between clients and servers. Sizeable amounts of data are usually passed between clients and servers as pointers. Simple pointer data can usually be handled by the stub code using the default memory management scheme. But more complex data structures such as linked lists might benefit from the use of alternative memory management methods. Linked lists can be made up of many nodes connected with pointers. The size of a linked list is often variable and members need to be inserted or deleted in the middle easily.

A two-dimensional linked list could represent a sparse array which your application sends to a compute server to be multiplied. Tree structures are a natural form for parsed language data. For example, you might call a "parse server" with a filename and it could return a syntax tree of the data broken down according to grammar rules. Arithmetic expressions are often represented internally in tree form. Graphs of nodes are used in resource allocation problems, usually representing networks of computers, of cities, and so on.

In any case, linked lists consist of multiple nodes which must be allocated storage space in both clients and servers. By default, the client and server stub code which marshalls and unmarshalls data uses a crude but effective algorithm to manage the pointers. It makes separate calls to *midl_user_allocate* and *midl_user_free* to allocate and deallocate each individual node in the data structure. While this approach can add stub overhead to the application, it relieves you from having to concern yourself with memory management details.

In addition to the default method, there are three other memory usage methods which you can use by including ACF attributes or by making slight changes to the IDL file. The methods together, are:

- node-by-node allocation and deallocation (the default)

- single buffer allocation

- client application allocated buffers

- persistent storage on the server

Of the four methods, the first two rely solely on the stubs to allocate and free memory while the last two involve the application. In previous chapters we explained that you must include user-written versions of *midl_user_allocate* and *midl_user_free* in both the client and server parts of your application. The reason for this is that the client and server stubs or, in some cases, your application code, calls these procedures to allocate and deallocate memory used by application parameters.

Table 4-2 shows whether the stub code or the application is responsible for memory management in each method.

Table 4–2: What Allocates Memory

	Client		Server	
	Stub Code	Application	Stub Code	Application
Node by node allocation and deallocation				
midl_user_allocate	✓		✓	
midl_user_free	✓		✓	
Single buffer allocation				
midl_user_allocate	✓		✓	
midl_user_free	✓		✓	
Client application-allocated buffers				
midl_user_allocate		✓	✓	
midl_user_free		✓	✓	
Persistent storage on the server				
midl_user_allocate	✓		✓	
midl_user_free	✓			✓

The following sections examine the reasoning behind each memory usage method. The sections also describe how to use ACF attributes to select a method for use with a given situation. All of the alternative (non-default) memory usage methods use attributes that are extensions of DCE IDL. The use of these attributes requires the **/ext** MIDL compiler switch at compile time.

Node-By-Node Allocation and Deallocation

When you are passing simple pointers back and forth between a client and a server, you needn't worry about choosing a particular memory usage method. The stub code, which marshalls and unmarshalls parameters, will allocate and deallocate memory for you on both the client and the server.

On the other hand, separate stub calls to *midl_user_allocate* for each node in a complex linked list can add unnecessary stub overhead to the application. If you are worried about the overhead, perhaps you could use this method to get your application up and running and then choose another method if you think memory usage is a bottleneck.

Using Contiguous Server Memory

When memory on the server is contiguous, as it ordinarily is with Microsoft Windows NT, you might increase performance by directing the stub to allocate a single linear buffer for the entire tree or graph.

In this case, the client stub determines the size of the buffer needed by chasing all of the pointers in the structure. This approach relieves the server stubs from making separate calls to *midl_user_allocate* for each node in the data structure. Because data can be accessed sequentially, memory performance might also be improved by using this technique.

To use this technique, apply the ACF attribute `allocate(all_nodes)` to the pointer type in a typedef in the ACF file.

```
/* ACF fragment */
typedef [allocate(all_nodes)] pointer_name;
```

Allocating Buffers with the Client Application

When you know how big a data structure is, you can specify the buffer size in the client application and pass it to the server as a parameter to the remote procedure. This technique can help minimize the stub size on clients and servers and improve the performance of the affected remote procedure call because the client stub doesn't have to chase pointers. The server stub allocates the buffer space with one call to *midl_user_allocate*, using the size parameter taken from the remote procedure call. The runtime library will raise an exception if insufficient memory is allocated, however. After the call completes, the server stub frees the memory with one call to *midl_user_free*.

The client side can benefit from this technique, too. For instance, say your application has a multiplication interface that multiplies matrixes as in `multiply_matrix (matrix *m1 *m2)`. Now let's say that the client makes many calls to this same interface. In this case, it's probably more efficient for the client application to allocate and control memory directly, reusing the memory that is allocated only once, rather than have the client stubs allocate and free memory with each call.

Even when you know the buffer size, you might not want to take the time to use this technique. But if memory allocation causes a bottleneck in your application, the technique may help.

This method requires two steps. First, add a size parameter to the procedure declaration in the IDL file, as illustrated in the following IDL file fragment in which we include the parameter *cBytes*.

```
/* IDL file function declaration (fragment) */

void GetEmployeeRecord(
    [in,string] char EmployeeName[NAMESIZE],
    [in] short cBytes,
    [out, ref] P_RECORD_TYPE pRecord   /* record for named employee */
);
```

Second, in the ACF file, apply the ACF **byte_count** attribute to the parameter that will store the size of the buffer.

```
/* ACF file (fragment */

GetEmployeeRecord ([byte_count(cBytes)] pRecord );
```

Now the server stub will make a single call to *midl_user_allocate* using the *cBytes* size parameter to allocate memory for this buffer.

Persistent Storage on the Server

Persistent state, or "context," offers a way to manage data on the server so that you can reuse it from call to call, and clean it up properly after you're done with it. One example of persistent state might be a dictionary server or a symbol table server. You pass the server a tree which it saves away, and then you make queries against it later. This technique can save time because your application does not need to copy the same data into a buffer each time it's needed.

To use this method, apply the **allocate(dont_free)** attribute to the ACF typedef declaration in the ACF file, as in the following usage example.

```
/* ACF fragment */
typedef [allocate(all_nodes, dont_free)] pointer_name;
```

Using this method, the server stub does not call *midl_user_free* when the remote procedure call completes. Instead, the server application must call *midl_user_free* when its procedures are finished using the data structure. To make the parameters available for use by other remote procedure calls on the server, you must copy the pointers to global variables.

In Chapter 7, *Context Handles*, we'll see a different way of managing server context through the use of context handle types. While context handles require more programming than the simpler persistent data technique mentioned here, they offer more automatic functions which you may want to use. For instance, context handles track and free memory resources automatically and they can associate server contexts with specific clients.

5

How to Write a Server

RPC servers are more complicated than clients—at least at this introductory stage—because the servers have a more complicated role: they have to be continuously active and be prepared to handle multiple calls in any order. This chapter uses the inventory example as the basis for showing the various issues required by servers.

Before reading this chapter, it's a good idea to read Chapter 1, *Overview of an RPC Application*, for an overview of a distributed application, and Chapter 2, *Using a Microsoft RPC Interface*, for features of interface definitions. You should also read Chapter 3, *How to Write Clients*, to understand how clients use servers.

You write the following two distinct portions of code for all servers:

- Server **initialization** includes most of the RPC-specific details including RPC runtime routines. This code is executed when the server begins, before it processes any remote procedure calls.

- The **manager** portion, or remote procedure implementations, include special techniques for memory management.

Some Background on Call Processing

Chapter 1 describes how a typical distributed application works:

- Figure 1-9 shows the initialization steps to prepare a server before it processes remote procedure calls.

- Figure 1-10 shows how a client finds a server using the automatic binding method.

- Figure 1-11 shows the basic steps during a remote procedure call after the client finds the server.

To understand server initialization, it is useful at this point to explain how the RPC runtime library handles an incoming call. Figure 5-1 shows how the server system and RPC runtime library handle a client request.

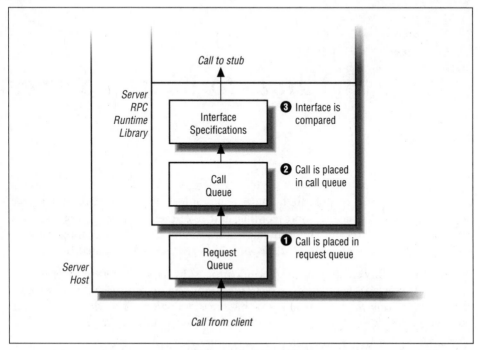

Figure 5-1. How the server runtime library handles a call

❶ A call request for the server comes in over the network. The request is placed in a request queue for the endpoint. (The server initialization can select more than one protocol sequence on which to listen for calls, and each protocol sequence can have more than one endpoint associated with it.) Request queues temporarily store all requests, thus allowing multiple requests on an endpoint. If a request queue fills, however, the next request is rejected.

❷ The RPC runtime library dequeues requests one at a time from all request queues and places them in a single call queue. The server can process remote procedures concurrently, using threads. If a thread is available, a call is immediately assigned to it. (Server initialization can select the number of threads for processing remote procedure calls.) In this figure, only one thread is executing. If all threads are in use, the call remains in the call queue until a thread is available. If the call queue is full, the next request is rejected.

❸ After a call is assigned to a thread, the **interface specification** of the client call is compared with the interface specifications of the server. An interface specification is an opaque data structure containing information (including the UUID and version number) that identifies the interface. **Opaque** simply means the details are hidden from you. If the server supports the client's interface, processing goes to the stub code. If the server does not support the client's interface, the call is rejected.

When the call finally gets to the stub, it unmarshalls the input data. Unmarshalling involves memory allocation (if needed), copying the data from the RPC runtime library, and converting data to the correct representation for the server system.

Initializing the Server

The server initialization code includes a sequence of runtime calls that prepare the server to receive remote procedure calls. The initialization code typically includes the following steps:

1. Register the interface with the RPC runtime library.

2. Create server binding information by selecting one or more protocol sequences for the RPC runtime library to use in your network environment.

3. Advertise the server location so the clients have a way to find it. A client uses binding information to establish a relationship with a server. Advertising the server usually includes storing binding information in a name service database. Occasionally an application stores server binding information in an application-specific database, or displays it, or prints it.

4. Manage endpoints in a local endpoint map.

5. Listen for remote procedure calls.

During server execution, no remote procedure calls are processed until the initialization code completes execution. RPC runtime routines are used for server initialization. (Table B-2 in Appendix B, *RPC Runtime Routines Quick Reference*, lists all the RPC runtime routines for servers.)

Example 5-1 shows the necessary header files and data structures for server initialization of the inventory application.

Example 5–1: Server Header Files and Data Structures

```
/* FILE NAME: server.c */
#include <stdio.h>
#include <stdlib.h>
#include <ctype.h>
#include "inv.h"              /* header created by the MIDL compiler  ❶ */
#include "status.h"           /* contains the CHECK_STATUS macro       */
#define STRINGLEN 50

main (argc, argv)
int argc;
char *argv[];
{
    error_status_t       status;      /* error status (nbase.h)       ❷ */
                                      /* RPC vectors                   ❸ */
```

Example 5–1: Server Header Files and Data Structures (continued)

```
rpc_binding_vector_t *binding_vector; /* binding handle list (rpcdce.h)   */
rpc_protseq_vector_t *protseq_vector; /*protocol sequence list(rpcdce.h) */

char entry_name[STRINGLEN];             /* name service entry name          */
char annotation[STRINGLEN];             /* annotation for endpoint map      */
char hostname[STRINGLEN];               /* used to store the computer name */
DWORD hostname_size=STRINGLEN;          /* required by GetComputerName      */
 .
 .
 .
/* For the rest of the server initialization, register interfaces,   */
/* create server binding information, advertise the server,          */
/* manage endpoints, and listen for remote procedure calls.          */
```

❶   Always include the C language header file (created by the MIDL compiler) from all interfaces the server uses. This file contains the definitions of data types and structures that are needed by the RPC runtime routines.

❷   An **unsigned32** variable is needed to report errors that may occur when an RPC runtime routine is called.

❸   Some RPC runtime routines use a data structure called a vector. A **vector** in RPC applications contains a list (array) of other data structures and a count of elements in the list. Vectors are necessary because the number of elements on the list is often unknown until runtime. The **rpc_binding_vector_t** is a list of binding handles in which each handle refers to some binding information. The list in **rpc_protseq_vector_t** contains protocol sequence information representing the communication protocols available to a server. RPC runtime routines create vectors, use vectors as input, and free the memory of vectors.

Many header files such as *rpc.h* and *rpcndr.h* are included in the interface header *inv.h*. The *rpc.h* file in turn has included within it header files such as *rpcdce.h*, *rpcnsi.h*, and *rpcnterr.h*. Many of these header files are associated with RPC-specific interface definitions. These interface definitions contain data structure definitions you may need to refer to in order to access structure members and make runtime calls.

Object UUIDs are scattered throughout the RPC runtime routines as parameters for developing certain kinds of applications. You do not need to use object UUIDs to develop many applications so they are not covered in this book.

Registering Interfaces

All servers must register their interfaces so that their information is available to the RPC runtime library. This information is used when a call from a client comes in, so the client is sure the server supports the interface, and the call can be correctly dispatched to the stub.

Before a client makes a call, it checks its interface against the one advertised in the server's binding information. But that does not guarantee that the server supports the client's interface. For example, it is possible for a complex server to temporarily suspend support for a specific interface. Therefore, when a remote procedure call arrives, a comparison is made between the client's and server's interface specifications. If the server supports the client's interface, the RPC runtime library can dispatch the call to the stub.

Use an interface handle to refer to the interface specification in application code. An **interface handle** is a pointer defined in the C language header file and generated by *midl*. For example, the server interface handle for the inventory application is inv_V1_0_s_ifspec. The interface handle name contains the following:

- The interface name given in the interface definition header (inv).

- The version numbers in the **version** attribute (v1_0). If the interface definition has no version declared, version 0.0 is assumed.

- The letter s or c depending on whether the handle is for the server or client portion of the application.

- The word ifspec.

The default style of interface names generated by the **midl** version 2.0 compiler is compatible with names generated by the OSF DCE IDL compiler. Note that the **midl** version 1.0 compiler generates another form of interface handle name such as inv_ClientIfHandle and inv_ServerIfHandle. To generate older names that are compatible with **midl** version 1.0 interface names, you must use the **/oldnames** option with a **midl** version 2.0 compiler.

Example 5-2 is a portion of C code that registers one interface.

Example 5–2: Registering an Interface with the Runtime Library

```
/* The header files and data structures precede registering interfaces. */
    .
    .
    .

    /*********************** REGISTER INTERFACE ***********************/
    status =
    RpcServerRegisterIf(                                     /* ❶ */
        inv_V1_0_s_ifspec,              /* interface specification (inv.h) */
        NULL,
        NULL
    );
    CHECK_STATUS(status, "Can't register interface:", ABORT);     /* ❷ */
    .
    .
    .

/* For the rest of the server initialization, create server binding    */
/* information, advertise the server, manage endpoints, and listen for  */
/* remote procedure calls.                                              */
```

❶ The *RpcServerRegisterIf* routine is a required call to register each interface the server supports. The interface handle, inv_V1_0_s_ifspec, refers to the interface specification.

❷ The CHECK_STATUS macro is defined in the *status.h* file. It is an application-specific macro used in this book to process status values returned from RPC runtime calls (see Example 3-12).

Multiple interfaces may be registered from a single server by calling the *RpcServerRegisterIf* routine with a different interface handle.

The second and third arguments to the *RpcServerRegisterIf* call are used in complex applications to register more than one implementation for the set of remote procedures. When only one implementation exists, these arguments are set to NULL. Also, in the event of a symbol name conflict between the remote procedure names of an interface and other symbols in your server (such as procedure names), you can use these arguments to assign different names to the server code's remote procedures.

Creating Server Binding Information

Server binding information is created when you select protocol sequences during server initialization. RPC uses protocol sequences (described in Chapter 3, *How to Write Clients*) to identify the combinations of communications protocols that RPC supports. Most servers offer all available protocol sequences so that you do not limit the opportunities for clients to communicate with the server.

Recall that besides a protocol sequence, binding information includes a host network address. A server process runs on only one host at a time, so this binding information is obtained from the system and not controlled in your server code.

When a protocol sequence is selected, an endpoint is also obtained. You have several choices when obtaining endpoints.

Using dynamic endpoints

Chapter 3 describes the difference between dynamic and well-known endpoints. Most servers use dynamic endpoints for their flexibility and to avoid the problem of two servers using the same endpoints. Dynamic endpoints are selected for you by the RPC runtime library and vary from one invocation of the server to the next. When the server stops running, dynamic endpoints are released and may be reused by the server system.

Example 5-3 is a portion of the inventory server initialization showing the selection of one or all protocol sequences and dynamic endpoints. For this example, invoke the server with a protocol sequence argument to select a specific protocol sequence. If you invoke this server without an argument, the server uses all available protocols.

Example 5-3: Creating Server Binding Information

```
/* Registering interfaces precedes creating server binding information. */
.
.
.
    /****************** CREATING SERVER BINDING INFORMATION ******************/
    if(argc > 1) {
        status =
        RpcServerUseProtseq(              /* use a protocol sequence    ❶ */
            (unsigned char *)argv[1],     /* the input protocol sequence   */
            RPC_C_PROTSEQ_MAX_REQS_DEFAULT,  /* (rpcdce.h)                    */
            NULL                          /* security descriptor (not reqd)*/
        );
        CHECK_STATUS(status, "Can't use this protocol sequence:", ABORT);
    }
    else {
        puts("You can invoke the server with a protocol sequence argument.");
        status =
        RpcServerUseAllProtseqs(          /* use all protocol sequences ❷ */
            RPC_C_PROTSEQ_MAX_REQS_DEFAULT,  /* (rpcdce.h)                    */
            NULL                          /* security descriptor (not reqd) */
        );
        CHECK_STATUS(status, "Can't register protocol sequences:", ABORT);
    }

    status =
    RpcServerInqBindings(                 /* get binding information for server ❸ */
        &binding_vector
    );
    CHECK_STATUS(status, "Can't get binding information:", ABORT);
.
.
.

/* For the rest of the server initialization, advertise the server,    */
/* manage endpoints, and listen for remote procedure calls.            */
```

❶ The *RpcServerUseProtseq* routine is called with the chosen protocol sequence string. This call selects one protocol sequence on which the server listens for remote procedure calls. For this example, when the server is invoked, argc is the number of arguments on the command line, and argv[1] is the protocol sequence string argument. The constant RPC_C_PROTSEQ_MAX_CALLS_DEFAULT sets the request queue size for the number of calls an endpoint can receive at any given moment.

❷ The *RpcServerUseAllProtseqs* routine is called to select all available protocol sequences on which the RPC runtime library listens for remote procedure calls.

❸ The *RpcServerInqBindings* routine is a required call to obtain the set of binding handles referring to all of this server's binding information.

Dynamic endpoints must be registered with the server system's local endpoint map using the *RpcEpRegister* routine, so that clients can look them up when they try to find a server.

Using well-known endpoints

An endpoint is well-known if it is specifically selected and assigned to a single server every time it runs. Well-known endpoints are more restrictive than dynamic endpoints because, in order to prevent your servers from using the same endpoints as someone else, you need to register well-known endpoints with the authority responsible for a given transport protocol. For example, the ARPANET Network Information Center controls the use of well-known endpoint values for the Internet Protocols.

Well-known endpoints are often employed for widely-used applications. One server that needs well-known endpoints is the RPC service. This service runs on each system hosting RPC servers, maintaining the database that maps servers to endpoints. When a client has a partially bound handle, and it needs to obtain an endpoint for its application's server, the client RPC runtime library contacts the server system's RPC service. In short, the RPC service is required for finding dynamic endpoints. For clients to contact it, the RPC service itself must have a well-known endpoint.

Although you do not need to register well-known endpoints in the server system's endpoint map, you are encouraged to, so that clients are unrestricted in finding your servers. Use the *RpcEpRegister* routine to register endpoints in the endpoint map.

Table 5-1 shows the RPC runtime routines that create server binding information with well-known endpoints.

Table 5-1: Creating Binding Information with Well-known Endpoints

RPC Runtime Routine	Description
RpcServerUseProtseqEp	Uses a specified protocol sequence and well-known endpoint, supplied in application code, to establish server binding information. Even though the endpoint is not dynamically generated, clients do not have an obvious way to get it. So the server must register the endpoint in the server system's endpoint map.
RpcServerUseProtseqIf	Uses a specified protocol sequence, but well-known endpoints are specified in the interface definition with the endpoint attribute. Both clients and servers know the endpoints through the interface definition.

Table 5-1: Creating Binding Information with Well-known Endpoints (continued)

RPC Runtime Routine	Description
RpcServerUseAllProtseqsIf	Uses all supported protocol sequences, but well-known endpoints are specified in the interface definition with the endpoint attribute. Both clients and servers know the endpoints through the interface definition.

Advertising the Server

Advertising the server means that you make the binding information available for clients to find this server. You can advertise the server by one of the following methods:

- Export to a name service database.

- Store binding information in an application-specific database.

- Print or display binding information for clients.

The method you use depends on the application, but the most common way is through a name service database. Binding information and the interface specification are first exported to a server entry in the database. The information is associated with a recognizable name appropriate for the application. This information can now be retrieved by a client using this name. When the client imports binding information, the RPC runtime library compares the interface specifications of the client and the name service entries, to be sure the client and server are compatible.

Conventions for naming RPC server entries rely on associating a host computer name with the server entry name, thereby creating a unique server entry name. Unique server entry names allow multiple instances of a server to coexist in one NT domain. Although it's possible for multiple servers to share use of a single server entry, problems arise if the true owner of the entry removes the entry from the name service; binding information for all other servers is removed as well.

Using this convention means that clients that use server entry names to find servers will need to know which computer a server is running on. Automatic clients usually seek servers based on the interface UUID so they are freed from having to know the server's computer name. When NT domains do not contain multiple instances of servers, you don't need to use the convention.

If you plan to store your entry names in DCE CDS, you can also export a group entry name that is not associated with a computer name. The convention for naming RPC group entries includes the interface name. The server entry name is added as a member of the group. When the client imports binding information using the group name, the group members are searched until a compatible server entry is found. Microsoft RPC includes the API functions that control group and profile operations for use with DCE CDS. Note, however, that the Microsoft Locator version 1.0 does not fully support group or profile operations.

Example 5-4 is a portion of the inventory initialization code that uses the name service database to advertise the server.

Example 5-4: Advertising the Server to Clients

```
/* Registering interfaces and creating server binding information    */
/* precede advertising the server.                                   */
    .
    .
    .

    /************************* ADVERTISE SERVER ***************************/
    strcpy(entry_name, "/.:/inventory_");
    GetComputerName(&hostname, &hostname_size);
    strcat(entry_name, hostname);
    status =
    RpcNsBindingExport(               /* export to a name service database ❶ */
        RPC_C_NS_SYNTAX_DEFAULT,      /* syntax of entry name (rpcdce.h)      */
        (unsigned char *)entry_name,  /* name of entry in name service        */
        inv_V1_0_s_ifspec,            /* interface specification (inv.h)      */
        binding_vector,               /* binding information                  */
        NULL                          /* no object UUIDs exported             */
    );
    CHECK_STATUS(status, "Can't export to name service database:", RESUME);
    .
    .
    .

/* For the rest of the server initialization, manage endpoints and   */
/* listen for remote procedure calls.                                */
```

❶ The *RpcNsBindingExport* routine exports the server binding information to a name service database. The constant RPC_C_NS_SYNTAX_DEFAULT establishes the syntax the RPC runtime library uses to interpret an entry name. (Microsoft RPC currently has only one syntax.) The entry name is the recognizable name used in the database for this binding information.

The interface handle (inv_V1_0_s_ifspec) is needed so interface information is associated with the binding information in the name service database. The binding vector is the list of binding handles that represents the binding information exported. (The NULL value represents an object UUID vector. For this application, no object UUIDs are used.)

The *RpcNsBindingExport* routine exports well-known endpoints to the name service database along with other binding information, but, because of their temporary nature, dynamic endpoints are not exported. Performance of the name service will degrade if it becomes filled with obsolete endpoints generated when servers restart. Also, clients will fail more often trying to bind to servers of nonexistent endpoints. Since dynamic endpoints are not in a name service database, clients need to find them from another source. The next section discusses how to manage endpoints.

Managing Server Endpoints

When the server uses dynamic endpoints, clients need a way to find them, because neither the name service database nor the interface specification store dynamic endpoints. The **endpoint map** is a database on each RPC server system that associates endpoints with other server binding information. As a general rule, have your server store all endpoints (dynamic and well-known) in the endpoint map. If all endpoints are placed in the endpoint map, system administrators have an easier time monitoring and managing all RPC servers on a host system.

When a client uses a partially bound binding handle for a remote procedure call, the RPC runtime library obtains an endpoint from the server system's endpoint map. (However, if a well-known endpoint is available in the interface specification, the server's endpoint map is not used.) To find a valid endpoint, the client's interface specification and binding information (protocol sequence, host, and object UUID) are compared to the information in the endpoint map. When an endpoint of an appropriate server is finally obtained, the resulting fully bound binding handle is used to complete the connection at that endpoint. Example 5-5 shows how a server registers its endpoints in the endpoint map.

Example 5–5: Managing Endpoints in an Endpoint Map

```
/* Registering interfaces, creating server binding information, and     */
/* advertising the server precede managing endpoints.                   */
    .
    .
    .

    /************************** MANAGE ENDPOINTS ***************************/
    strcpy(annotation, "Inventory interface");
    status =
    RpcEpRegister(                     /* add endpoints to local endpoint map ❶ */
        inv_V1_0_s_ifspec,            /* interface specification (inv.h)        */
        binding_vector,               /* vector of server binding handles       */
        NULL,                         /* no object UUIDs to register            */
        (unsigned char *)annotation   /* annotation supplied (not required)     */
    );
    CHECK_STATUS(status, "Can't add endpoints to local endpoint map:", RESUME);

    status =
    RpcBindingVectorFree(              /* free server binding handles ❷ */
        &binding_vector
    );
    CHECK_STATUS(status, "Can't free server binding handles:", RESUME);

    open_inventory();                  /* application specific procedure */
    .
    .
    .
```

Example 5–5: Managing Endpoints in an Endpoint Map (continued)

```
/* For the rest of the server initialization, listen for remote    */
/* procedure calls.                                                 */
```

❶   The *RpcEpRegister* routine registers the server endpoints in the local endpoint map. Use the same interface handle, binding vector, and object UUID vector as you used in the *RpcNsBindingExport* routine (see Example 5-4). An annotation argument is not needed because Microsoft RPC provides no way to retrieve this information from the endpoint map.

❷   The *RpcBindingVectorFree* routine is a required call that frees the memory of the binding vector and all binding handles in it. Each call to *RpcServerInq-Bindings* (see Example 5-3) requires a corresponding call to *RpcBinding-VectorFree*. Make this call prior to listening for remote procedure calls, so the memory is available when remote procedure calls are processed.

The *RpcEpRegister* call is required if dynamic endpoints are established with the *RpcServerUseProtseq* or *RpcServerUseAllProtseqs* runtime routines, because each time the server is started, new endpoints are created (see Example 5-3). If well-known endpoints are established with the *RpcServerUseProtseqEp* runtime routine, you should use the *RpcEpRegister* routine, because even though the endpoint may always be the same, a client needs to find the value. If well-known endpoints are established with the *RpcServerUseProtseqIf* or *RpcServerUseAllProtseqsIf* call, they need not be registered, because the client has access to the endpoint values through the interface specification.

When a server stops running, endpoints registered in the endpoint map become outdated. The RPC service maintains the endpoint map by removing outdated endpoints. However, an unpredictable amount of time exists in which a client can obtain an outdated endpoint. If a remote procedure call uses an outdated endpoint, it will not find the server and the call will fail. To prevent clients from receiving outdated endpoints, use the *RpcEpUnregister* routine before a server stops executing.

The only way to actively manage endpoints in the endpoint map is by using *RpcEpRegister* and other RPC runtime routines in the server initialization code (see Example 5-5).

Listening for Remote Procedure Calls

The final requirement for server initialization code is to listen for remote procedure calls.

Many of the RPC runtime routines used in this book have an error status variable, used to determine whether the routine executed successfully. However, when the server is ready to process remote procedure calls, the *RpcServerListen* runtime routine is called. The *RpcServerListen* runtime routine does not return unless the server is requested to stop listening by one of its own remote procedures using the *RpcMgmtStopServerListening* routine.

Any errors occurring during stub code or remote procedure execution are reported as exceptions, and, unless your code is written to handle exceptions, it will abruptly exit. You can use a set of RPC macros to help process some system exceptions that occur outside the application code. The macros RpcTryExcept, RpcExcept, and RpcEndExcept delineate code sections in which exceptions are controlled. If an exception occurs during the RpcTryExcept section, code in the RpcExcept section is executed to handle any necessary error recovery or cleanup such as removing outdated endpoints from the endpoint map.

These macros are not likely to be invoked when exceptions occur within the server application code itself; exceptions within a server usually cause the server to abort before the exceptions are reported back to the application.

The RpcExcept section contains clean-up code that does such things as remove outdated endpoints from the endpoint map. The RpcTryExcept and RpcExcept sections end with the RpcEndExcept macro.

Example 5-6 is a portion of C code that shows how the inventory server listens for remote procedure calls and handles exceptions.

Example 5-6: Listening for Remote Procedure Calls

```
/* Registering interfaces, creating server binding information,     */
/* managing endpoints, and advertising the server precede listening */
/* for remote procedure calls.                                      */
   /***************** LISTEN FOR REMOTE PROCEDURE CALLS ***************/
   RpcTryExcept                         /* thread exception handling macro    ❶ */
   {
      status =
      RpcServerListen(                                             /* ❷ */
         1,               /* process one remote procedure call at a time */
         RPC_C_LISTEN_MAX_CALLS_DEFAULT,
         NULL
      );
      CHECK_STATUS(status, "rpc listen failed:", RESUME);
   }
   RpcExcept (RpcExceptionCode())        /* error recovery and cleanup */
   {
      close_inventory();           /* application specific procedure */
      status =
      RpcServerInqBindings(              /* get binding information   ❸ */
         &binding_vector
      );
      CHECK_STATUS(status, "Can't get binding information:", RESUME);

      status =
      RpcEpUnregister(     /* remove endpoints from local endpoint map  ❹ */
         inv_V1_0_s_ifspec,    /* interface specification (inventory.h) */
         binding_vector,           /* vector of server binding handles */
         NULL                                      /* no object UUIDs */
```

Example 5–6: Listening for Remote Procedure Calls (continued)

```
    );
    CHECK_STATUS(status, "Can't remove endpoints from endpoint map:", RESUME);

    status =
    RpcBindingVectorFree(              /* free server binding handles ❺ */
        &binding_vector
    );
    CHECK_STATUS(status, "Can't free server binding handles:", RESUME);

    puts("\nServer quit!");
  }
  RpcEndExcept;
} /* END SERVER INITIALIZATION */
```

❶   The RpcTryExcept macro begins a section of code in which you expect exceptions to occur. For this example, the RpcTryExcept section contains only the *RpcServerListen* routine. If an exception occurs during the remote procedure execution, the code section beginning with the RpcExcept macro is executed to handle application-specific cleanup.

❷   The *RpcServerListen* routine is a required call that causes the runtime to listen for remote procedure calls. The first argument sets the number of threads the RPC runtime library uses to process remote procedure calls. In this example, the RPC runtime library can process one remote procedure call at a time. If your remote procedures are not thread safe, set this value to 1.

❸   The *RpcServerInqBindings* routine obtains a set of binding handles referring to all of the server's binding information.

❹   The *RpcEpUnregister* routine removes the server endpoints from the local end-point map. If the server registered endpoints with a call to *RpcEpRegister*, this call is recommended before the process is removed (see Example 5-5).

❺   The *RpcBindingVectorFree* routine is called to free the memory of a binding vector and all binding handles in it. Each call to *RpcServerInqBindings* requires a corresponding call to *RpcBindingVectorFree*.

The server initialization code for the inventory application is now complete. All of the server initialization code is shown in Example D-5. Table B-2 lists all the run-time routines that servers can use.

Writing Remote Procedures

When writing your remote procedures, consider the issues of memory management, threads, and client binding handles.

Remote procedures require special memory management techniques. Suppose a procedure allocates memory for data that it returns to the calling procedure. In a local application, the calling procedure can free allocated memory because the procedure and calling procedure are in the same address space. However, the client (calling procedure) is not in the same address space as the server (remote procedure), so the client cannot free memory on the server. Repeated calls to a remote procedure that allocates memory, without some way to free the memory, will obviously waste the server's resources.

You must manage memory for remote procedures by calling programmer-supplied wrapper routines for *malloc* and *free* in remote procedures. These routines enable the server stub to free memory allocated in remote procedures, after the remote procedure completes execution.

Recall that the *RpcServerListen* routine in server initialization determines the number of threads a server uses to process remote procedure calls. If the server listens on more than one thread, the remote procedures need to be thread safe. For example, the remote procedures should not use server global data unless locks are used to control thread access. In the inventory application, when reading from or writing to the inventory application database, a lock may be needed so data is not changed by one thread while another thread is reading it. The topic of multi-threaded application development is beyond the scope of this book.

So far, we have used server binding handles and server binding information to allow clients to find servers. When a server receives a call from a client, the client RPC runtime library supplies information about the client side of the binding to the server RPC runtime library. **Client binding information** is used in server code to inquire about the client. This client binding information includes:

- The RPC protocol sequence used by the client for the call.

- The network address of the client.

- The object UUID requested by the client. This can be simply a nil UUID.

To access client binding information in remote procedures use a **client binding handle**. If the client binding handle is available, it is the first parameter of the remote procedure. If you require client binding information, the procedure declarations in the interface definition must have a binding handle as the first parameter. No further details of client binding information are described in this book.

Managing Memory in Remote Procedures

In typical applications, you use the C library routines, *malloc* and *free*, or your own allocation scheme, to allocate and free memory that pointers must refer to. In RPC servers, when implementing a remote procedure that returns a pointer to newly allocated memory to the client, use programmer-supplied wrapper routines to *malloc* and *free* to manage memory in the remote procedures. The routines, which are named *midl_user_allocate* and *midl_user_free*, are also called by the stub code to allocate and free memory.

Example 5-7 shows how you can write the wrapper routines for *malloc* and *free*.

Example 5-7: Programmer-Supplied Wrapper Routines for malloc and free

```
/**************************************************************************/
/***                  midl_user_allocate / midl_user_free          ***/
/**************************************************************************/
void * __RPC_API
midl_user_allocate
           (
             size
           )
size_t size;
{
    unsigned char * ptr;
    ptr = malloc( size );
    return ( (void *)ptr );
}
void __RPC_API
midl_user_free
           (
             object
           )
void * object;
{
    free (object);
}
```

Use the *midl_user_allocate* routine instead of the C library routine *malloc*, so bookkeeping is maintained for memory management. This also ensures that memory on the server is automatically freed by the server stub after the remote procedure has completed execution. Memory allocation will not accumulate on the server and get out of control.

For reference pointers, memory on the client side must already exist, so no memory management is required for remote procedures whose output parameters are reference pointers. After you make the remote procedure call, first the server stub automatically allocates necessary memory and copies the data for the reference pointer into the new memory. Then it calls the implementation of the remote procedure. Finally, the remote procedure completes, output data is transmitted back to the client stub and the server stub frees the memory it allocated.

On both the client and server, more complex memory management occurs for unique pointers than for reference pointers. If a remote procedure allocates memory for an output parameter, the server stub copies and marshalls the data, then the stub frees the memory that was allocated in the remote procedure. When the client receives the data, the client stub allocates memory and copies the data into the new memory. It is the client application's responsibility to free the memory allocated by the client stub.

Example 5-8 shows how to use the *midl_user_allocate* routine to allocate memory for unique pointers. The procedure *get_part_description* of the inventory application returns a string of characters representing the description of a part in the inventory. The call in the client is as follows:

```
part_record part; /* structure for all data about a part  */
    .
    .
    .
part.description = get_part_description(part.number);
```

Example 5-8: Memory Management in Remote Procedures

```
paragraph get_part_description(number)
part_num  number;
{
    part_record *part;                      /* a pointer to a part record */
    paragraph description;
    int size;
    char *strcpy();

    if( read_part_record(number, &part) ) {
        /* Allocated data that is returned to the client must be allocated */
        /* with the midl_user_allocate routine.                */
        size = strlen((char *)part->description) + 1;          /* ❶ */
        description = (paragraph)midl_user_allocate((unsigned)size);  /* ❷ */
        strcpy((char *)description, (char *)part->description);
    }
    else
        description = NULL;
    return(description);
}
```

❶   An additional character is allocated for the null terminator of a string.

❷   The remote procedure calls the *midl_user_allocate* stub support routine to allocate memory in the remote procedure.

When the procedure completes, the server stub automatically frees the memory allocated by *midl_user_allocate* calls. When the remote procedure call returns, the client stub automatically allocates memory for the returned string. When the client application code is finished with the data, it frees the memory allocated by the client stub as follows:

```
if(part.description != NULL)
    free(part.description);
```

For more complex memory management, there is a programmer-supplied counterpart to the C library routine *free* called *midl_user_free*.

The only time you don't use the *midl_user_allocate* and *midl_user_free* routines for memory management is when you use context handles. Memory allocated for context on the server must not use these routines because subsequent calls by the client must have access to the same context as previous calls. See Chapter 7 for more information on context handles.

Allocating Memory for Conformant Arrays

The *whatare_subparts* procedure of the inventory application allocates memory for a conformant array in a structure, and returns a copy of the conformant structure to the client. The *whatare_subparts* procedure is declared in the interface definition as follows:

```
typedef struct part_list{                /* list of part numbers    */
    long                    size;         /* number of parts in array */
    [size_is(size)] part_num numbers[*];  /* conformant array of parts */
} part_list;
    .
    .
    .
void whatare_subparts(     /* get list of subpart numbers for a part */
    [in]  part_num number,
    [out] part_list **subparts  /* the structure containing the array */
);
```

Output pointer parameters are reference pointers, which must have memory allocated in the client prior to the call. Therefore, you need a unique pointer in order for new memory to be automatically allocated by the client stub for the **subparts structure when the *whatare_subparts* procedure returns. A pointer to a pointer is required so that the reference pointer points to a full pointer, which in turn points to the structure.

Example 5-9 shows how to allocate memory in the remote procedure for a conformant structure. The call in the client is as follows:

```
part_record part;          /* structure for all data about a part  */
part_list   *subparts;     /* pointer to parts list data structure */
    .
    .
    .
    whatare_subparts(part.number, &subparts);
```

Example 5-9: Conformant Array Allocation in a Remote Procedure

```
void whatare_subparts(number, subpart_ptr)
part_num  number;
part_list **subpart_ptr;
{
    part_record *part;                        /* pointer to a part record */
    int i;
    int size;

    read_part_record(number, &part);

    /* Allocated data that is output to the client must be allocated with  */
    /* the midl_user_allocate stub support routine.  Allocate for a part_list */
    /* struct plus the array of subpart numbers.  Remember the part_list   */
    /* struct already has an array with one element, hence the -1.         */
    size = sizeof(part_list)
        + (sizeof(part_num) * (part->subparts.size-1));           /* ❶ */
```

Example 5-9: Conformant Array Allocation in a Remote Procedure (continued)

```
    *subpart_ptr = (part_list *)midl_user_allocate((unsigned)size);      /* ❷ */

    /* fill in the values */
    (*subpart_ptr)->size = part->subparts.size;
    for(i = 0; i < (*subpart_ptr)->size; i++)
        (*subpart_ptr)->numbers[i] = part->subparts.numbers[i];
    return;
}
```

❶   The allocated memory includes the size of the conformant structure plus enough memory for all the elements of the conformant array. The conformant structure generated by the MIDL compiler already has an array of one element, so the new memory allocated for the array elements is one less than the number in the array.

❷   Use the RPC stub support routine *midl_user_allocate* to allocate memory so bookkeeping is maintained for memory management, and so the server stub automatically frees memory on the server after the remote procedure completes execution.

When the data for the conformant structure is returned to the client, the client stub allocates memory and copies the data into the new memory. The client application code uses the data and frees the memory allocated, as follows:

```
    for(i = 0; i < subparts->size; i++)
        printf("%ld  ", subparts->numbers[i]);
    printf("\nTotal number of subparts:%ld\n", subparts->size);
    free(subparts); /* free memory allocated for conformant structure */
```

Compiling and Linking Servers

Figure 5-2 shows the files and libraries required to produce an executable server. When complex data types are used, the MIDL compiler produces the server stub auxiliary file (*appl_y.c*) when the interface is compiled. The auxiliary file contains data marshalling procedures that can be used by other interfaces. No stub auxiliary files are produced for the inventory application. Example 5-10 shows the portion of a makefile that:

• Compiles the C language stubs and server code along with the header file producing server object files.

• Links the server object files to produce the executable server file.

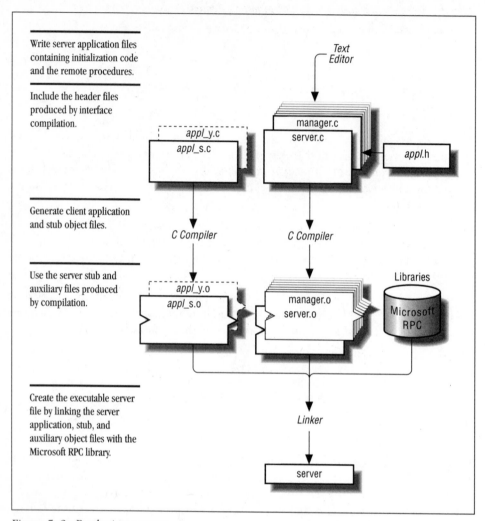

Figure 5–2. Producing a server

Example 5–10: Using a Makefile to Compile and Link a Server

```
# FILE NAME: Makefile
# Makefile for the inventory application
#
# definitions for this make file
#
APPL=inv
NTRPCLIBS=rpcrt4.lib rpcns4.lib libcmt.lib kernel32.lib

!include <ntwin32.mak>

## NT c flags
cflags = -c -W0 -Gz -D_X86_=1 -DWIN32 -DMT /nologo
```

Example 5-10: Using a Makefile to Compile and Link a Server (continued)

```
## NT nmake inference rules
    $(cc) $(cdebug) $(cflags) $(cvarsmt) $<
    $(cvtomf)
.
.
.
#
# SERVER BUILD
#
server:     server.exe
server.exe: server.obj manager.obj invntry.obj $(APPL)_s.obj $(APPL)_x.obj
    $(link) $(linkdebug) $(conflags) -out:server.exe -map:server.map \
      server.obj manager.obj invntry.obj $(APPL)_s.obj $(APPL)_x.obj\
      $(NTRPCLIBS)
.
.
.
# client and server sources
client.obj:  client.c  $(APPL).h
manager.obj: manager.c $(APPL).h
server.obj:  server.c  $(APPL).h
invntry.obj: invntry.c $(APPL).h
.
.
.
```

6

Using a Name Service

We have seen in earlier chapters that clients query a name service to find a host where a server is running. We have set up our environment in a simplistic, if not inconvenient, manner so that we could avoid discussing details about the name service. For instance, in Chapter 1, *Overview of an RPC Application*, our arithmetic server used a simple server entry name. While this simple name is easy to create and use, it makes it difficult for an NT domain to accommodate other identical servers because they'll all be exporting their binding information to the same entry name in the name service.

In a production environment, you don't want to restrict the number of servers you can have in a domain. That would defeat the purpose of the name service, which is to allow servers to be moved, added, and removed without affecting end-users.

In this chapter, we discuss how to use a name service to provide multiple servers in your domain, which increases reliability and availability. You accomplish this by giving a server different names when it runs on different hosts. This is necessary because each server should be uniquely identified in the name service. Towards the end, we discuss some rules and caveats for using the Microsoft Locator.

In DCE, the Cell Directory Service uses group entries and profile entries as a way to organize servers and control a client's search for server entries. The Microsoft Locator Version 1.0 does not support the use of CDS group entries or profile entries. However, Microsoft RPC includes group and profile routines in its runtime library for compatibility with DCE, for situations when you are running on a network where other machines have DCE and you want to store binding information in CDS.

Naming

Microsoft RPC supplies the Locator as the name service used by Microsoft RPC applications to locate servers. Servers store their binding information in the Locator's RPC name service database where it can be retrieved by clients. Clients then use the binding information to connect to servers.

Because so many servers can exist in a Locator's domain, the collection of names is hierarchically organized. In DCE, this hierarchy really corresponds to the way that the name service stores the entries in its distributed database. But with the Microsoft Locator, the names are simply strings. The hierarchy is merely an appearance, just for the convenience of the users—for instance, so that related servers can have similar names. But it is still useful.

Here are examples of entry names in the Locator:

```
/.../manufacturing/services/graphics/servers/gif_server
/.:/services/graphics/servers/gif_server
```

Names like those in the example can help organize servers logically so clients can find them by using consistent naming patterns.

The above example shows two ways to name a server. The first example includes the name of the domain, manufacturing, as part of the name. The second example avoids using the /.../manufacturing prefix by beginning the name with /.:. The domain name prefix is implicit because a Locator maintains entry names only from its own domain—in this case, the manufacturing domain. The second example allows server portability across domains that use similar naming conventions.

When a server starts, it can export its name to the Locator database along with its protocol sequence and host address. Unlike DCE, Microsoft RPC does not provide independent tools for administrators to manage the entries. Consequently, your applications must do any needed entry management.

DefaultEntry

Recall that if you use automatic binding, the client stub finds a server for you. By default, a client searches the Locator for a server offering an interface with a matching interface UUID. You can override this behavior by setting the Default-Entry Windows NT registry value to a valid server entry name.

You can set the DefaultEntry on Windows NT client using the *regedt32* program. In the HKEY_LOCAL_MACHINE on Local Machine window, you should select SOFTWARE/Microsoft/Rpc/NameService.

If the DefaultEntry value exists in the right portion of the window, double click on it to invoke a dialog box for typing in the server entry name. Type in the name and then click on **OK**.

If the `DefaultEntry` value does not exist, you can add it by pulling down the **Edit** menu and clicking on **Add Value** . . . . In the **Value Name** field, type `DefaultEntry`. Then click on **OK**. In the resulting String dialog box, type in the server entry name and then click on **OK**.

You can set the `DefaultEntry` on Microsoft DOS and Windows 3.1 clients by using a text editor to add a line like the following to the `C:\RPCREG.DAT` configuration file.

```
\Root\Software\Microsoft\Rpc\NameService\DefaultEntry=/.:/arithmetic_RIGEL.
```

Server Entries

A name service **server entry** stores binding information for an RPC server. Figure 6-1 depicts server entries in the name service database.

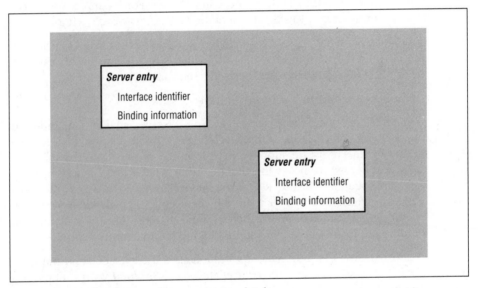

Figure 6-1. Server entries in the name service database

A server entry contains the following information:

- An **interface identifier** consists of an interface UUID and a version number. During the search for binding information, RPC name service routines use this identifier to determine if a compatible interface is found.

- **Binding information** is the information a client needs to find a server. It includes one or more sets of protocol sequence and host address combinations. Well-known endpoints can also be part of the binding information, but dynamic endpoints cannot.

- Some applications use optional **object UUIDs** to identify application-specific objects or resources.

A reasonable naming scheme for server entries combines the host system name and a meaningful definition of what the server offers. For example, the arithmetic interface on a host system named **RIGEL** can have the following name service entry:

```
/.:/arithmetic_RIGEL
```

In this way, using a simple convention that all servers can follow, you are assured that each server at your site has a unique name—as long as you have only one server per host. Normally, a host should only provide one server for an interface. You can increase the number of clients a server handles by increasing the number of threads a server can spawn. In the unusual case in which your system has multiple servers offering the same interface, you need to distinguish each server with separate name service entries and unique entry names. For example, one server might be /.:/arithmetic1_RIGEL, and another /.:/arithmetic2_RIGEL.

If you structure your entry names to included embedded host names, using the host name again in the right-most part of the name is redundant. In this case, the arithmetic application might have the following entry name:

```
/.:/product_development/test_servers/host_RIGEL/arithmetic
```

When your client uses the name service to find a server, it does an **import** or **lookup** for binding information, starting at an entry name known to be in the database. Entry names must be supplied to you in one of two ways: by the name service administrator who knows the name service database organization, or by the server administrator. You use RPC name service routines to search the name service database. These routines compare the client's interface identifier with interface identifiers in the database. When there is a match and the entry contains compatible binding information, the compatible binding information is returned.

Figure 6-2 shows how the arithmetic application uses a server entry in the name service database. The arithmetic server uses the *RpcNsBindingExport* runtime routine to export binding information to the /.:/arithmetic_RIGEL server entry. The arithmetic server's use of *RpcNsBindingExport* is shown in Example 1-4 in Chapter 1.

The arithmetic client uses the automatic binding method, so the client stub finds the server without using the server entry name. Instead, the automatic client requests a binding for an interface with a matching interface UUID. When client application code assists the search, as when using implicit or explicit binding methods, you can set a programmer-supplied environment variable such as ARITHMETIC_SERVER_ENTRY, to something like /.:/arithmetic_RIGEL on the client system **SIRIUS**, so the client stub has a name to search for in the name service. In this example, the name service simply searches for the server entry name

`/.:/arithmetic_RIGEL`. The server entry's binding information is returned, and the remote procedure call is completed.

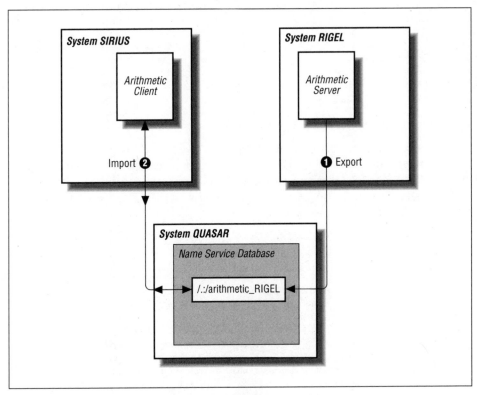

Figure 6–2. A simple use of a name service database

Creating a Server Entry and Exporting Binding Information

Microsoft RPC offers flexible ways for servers to construct server entry names. A name can be hard-coded in the server itself, but this method makes it difficult to change a server name because the server must be recompiled. To make your server more portable, you can specify a server name outside the program by setting an environment variable used by the server. For instance, you can use a batch file to set a server-specific environment variable and then start the server.

```
@REM FILE NAME: arith.bat
@ECHO OFF
set ARITHMETIC_SERVER_ENTRY=/.:/arithmetic_rigel
server
```

The server constructs the entry name using the WIN32 API *getenv* routine to read in the environment variable. The server then uses the NSI routine *RpcNsBinding-*

Export to export binding information to the name service entry. If an entry does not already exist, the Locator creates one for you.

```
entry_name = (unsigned char *)getenv("ARITHMETIC_SERVER_ENTRY");
status =
RpcNsBindingExport(            /* export entry to name service database  */
    RPC_C_NS_SYNTAX_DEFAULT,   /* syntax of the entry name (rpcdce.h)    */
    entry_name,                /* entry name for name service            */
    arith_ServerIfHandle,      /* interface specification (arith.h)      */
    binding_vector,            /* the set of server binding handles      */
    NULL
);
CHECK_STATUS(status, "Can't export to name service database", ABORT);
```

Alternatively your server can use the WIN32 API *getcomputername* routine to read the computer name and append it to a string that is associated with the ARITH-METIC_SERVER_ENTRY environment variable. This method can make servers even more portable because you don't have to modify the .BAT file if you move the server to a different host.

```
DWORD hostname_size=STRINGLEN;        /* required by GetComputerName     */
    .
    .
    .
strcpy(entry_name, "ARITHMETIC_SERVER_ENTRY");
GetComputerName(&hostname, &hostname_size);
strcat(entry_name, hostname);
status =
RpcNsBindingExport(            /* export to a name service database       */
    RPC_C_NS_SYNTAX_DEFAULT,      /* syntax of entry name (rpcdce.h)      */
    (unsigned char *)entry_name, /* name of entry in name service        */
    inv_ServerIfHandle,          /* interface specification (inv.h)      */
    binding_vector,              /* binding information                  */
    NULL                         /* no object UUIDs exported             */
);
CHECK_STATUS(status, "Can't export to name service database:", RESUME);
```

If you expect the server to be removed from service for a long period of time or even permanently, you should remove the server binding information from the name service using the *RpcNsBindingUnexport* runtime routine.

Some Rules for Using the Microsoft Locator

When your Windows NT domain is large and contains several Advanced Servers, the Locator does not always work smoothly. Changes to the database can sometimes result in inconsistencies.

A Windows NT domain is a group of users and their systems sharing common security and administration. A domain consists of one domain controller which maintains the master copy of the domain's user and group database. The controller also stores the master copy of the Microsoft Locator.

Domains should also contain one or more Windows NT Advanced Servers which maintain copies of the master databases stored on the domain controller. The Windows NT Advanced Servers in the domain query the domain controller every five minutes asking whether changes have been made. The controller sends just the changes to the requesting server, minimizing network traffic. If the domain controller becomes unavailable for some reason, for example it crashes, a Windows NT Advanced Server in the domain is promoted to be the new domain controller. If the new controller's RPC name service database is not up-to-date, missing entries must be re-exported by their servers to the new controller. Consequently, out-of-date data tends to stay out of date.

Domain controllers also maintain group entry information while Windows NT Advanced Servers do not. When a server is promoted to be the new domain controller, group entries that existed before the promotion are lost. Consequently, Microsoft encourages users to rely on server entries rather than group entries.

The domain controller and Windows NT Advanced Servers maintain the RPC name service database in transient memory rather than in a file. This model cannot guarantee the integrity of the database structure. If the domain controller crashes, all unpropagated server entries and all group entries must be reconstructed.

7

Context Handles

Some applications require that a server maintain information between remote procedure calls. This is called **maintaining context** (or maintaining state). Global data is one way a local application can maintain information between procedure calls. In a distributed application, however, the client and server are in different address spaces, so the only data common to each are passed as parameters. Even if a set of remote procedures use server global data, there is nothing to prevent more than one client from making calls that modify the data. A **context handle** is the mechanism that maintains information on a particular server for a particular client. An **active context handle** refers to valid (non-null) context, and includes binding information because a specific server maintains information for a particular client.

The Remote_file Application

The `rfile` application is a simple file transfer example that copies text from the client to the server. A client uses a context handle to refer to server context. The server context is the file handle used by remote procedures to open, write, and close the file. In this application, the filename on the server may be the same or different from the filename on the client, but the server does not overwrite an existing file on the server system.

If you do not select any filenames, this application uses standard input (*stdin*) of the client and standard output (*stdout*) of the server to transfer a message from the client to the server. The complete `rfile` application is shown in Appendix E, *The Rfile Application*.

Declaring Context in an Interface Definition

A file handle in a local application is analogous to a context handle in a distributed application. The information a file handle refers to is maintained by the C library and the operating system, not your application. You call some library routines to open or close the file, and other routines to read from or write to the file.

A context handle is maintained by the stubs and RPC runtime library, not by your application code. What you have to write is a remote procedure that returns an active context handle, and one that frees the context when you are finished with it. Other remote procedures can access or manipulate the active context.

Example 7-1 shows how to define context handles in the `rfile` interface definition.

Example 7-1: Defining Context Handles

```
/* FILE NAME: rfile.idl */
[
uuid(A61E4024-A53F-101A-B1AF-08002B2E5B76),
version(1.0),
pointer_default(unique)
]
interface rfile              /* file manipulation on a remote system  */
{
    typedef [context_handle] void *filehandle;  /* ❶ */
    typedef              byte buffer[];

filehandle remote_open(       /* open for write ❷ */
    [in] handle_t binding_h,   /* explicit primitive binding handle     */
    [in, string] char name[],  /* if name is null, use stdout in server */
    [in, string] char mode[]   /* values can be "r", "w", or "a"        */
);

long remote_send(
    [in] filehandle fh,                    /* ❸ */
    [in, max_is(max)] buffer buf,
    [in] long max
);

void remote_close(
    [in,out] filehandle *fh                /* ❹ */
);
}
```

❶ To define a context handle data type, apply the `context_handle` attribute to a void * type (or a type that resolves to void *) in a type definition. If the client-server communication breaks down or the client fails, a context handle data type allows the server to automatically clean up the user-defined context with a call to a **context rundown procedure**. If a context handle is applied in a type definition, then the server application developer must write a context rundown procedure.

❷   At least one remote procedure initializes the context handle and returns it to the client for later use. A procedure returning a context handle result always returns a new active context handle. Also, if a parameter is an out-only context handle, the procedure creates a new active context handle.

❸   A procedure with a context handle parameter that is input only must use an active context handle.

❹   When the client application is finished with the server context, the context must be freed.

If the context handle is null upon return from a procedure, the remote procedure on the server has freed the context and the client stub has freed the context handle. A remote procedure that frees a context handle requires the parameter to have the in directional attribute so the server can free the context, and the out directional attribute so the client stub can also free the client's copy of the context handle.

Using a Context Handle in a Client

The client uses a context handle to refer to the server context through the remote procedure calls. In the client, the context handle refers to an **opaque structure**. This means that the data is hidden and cannot be manipulated by the client application code. The context handle can be tested for null, but not assigned any values by the client application. The server code accomplishes all context modification, but the status of the context is communicated to the client through the context handle. The client stub manipulates the context handle in the client on behalf of the server. Example 7-2 shows a typical sequence of remote procedure calls when using context handles.

Example 7-2: Using a Context Handle in a Client

```
/* FILE NAME: client.c */
#include <stdio.h>
#include <stdlib.h>
#include <string.h>
#include "rfile.h"
#define MAX 200          /* maximum line length for a file */

main(argc, argv)
int argc;
char *argv[];
{
    FILE            *local_fh;              /* file handle for client file input */
    char            host[100];        /* name or network address of remote host */
    char            remote_name[100];              /* name of remote file */
    rpc_binding_handle_t binding_h;                 /* binding handle */
    filehandle      remote_fh;                      /* context handle */
    buffer          *buf_ptr;            /* buffer pointer for data sent */
    int             size;                    /* size of data buffer */

    get_args(argc, argv, &local_fh, host, (char *)remote_name);
```

Example 7–2: Using a Context Handle in a Client (continued)

```
#ifndef LOCAL
    if(do_string_binding(host, &binding_h) < 0) {                    /* ❶ */
        fprintf(stderr, "Cannot get binding\n");
        exit(1);
    }
#endif
    remote_fh = remote_open(binding_h, remote_name, (char *)"w");    /* ❷ */
    if(remote_fh == NULL) {
        fprintf(stderr, "Cannot open remote file\n");
        exit(1);
    }

    /* The buffer data type is a conformant array of bytes; */
    /* memory must be allocated for a conformant array.     */
    buf_ptr = (buffer *)malloc((MAX+1) * sizeof(buffer));

    while( fgets((char *)buf_ptr, MAX, local_fh) != NULL) {
        size = (int)strlen((char *)buf_ptr); /* data sent will not include \0 */
        if( remote_send(remote_fh, (*buf_ptr), size) < 1) {         /* ❸ */
            fprintf(stderr, "Cannot write to remote file\n");
            exit(1);
        }
    }
    remote_close(&remote_fh);                                        /* ❹ */
}
```

❶   Before a context handle becomes valid, a client must establish a binding with the server that will maintain the context. For the explicit or implicit binding methods, your application has to perform this step. For the automatic binding method, binding occurs in the client stub during the first remote procedure call. Then, to find the server after the context handle is established, subsequent calls use it instead of a binding handle. The *do_string_binding* procedure is an application-specific procedure that creates a binding handle from a host input and a generated protocol sequence. It is shown in Chapter 3, *How to Write Clients*.

The symbol LOCAL is used in applications in this book, to distinguish compiling this client to test in a local environment, from compiling to run in a distributed environment.

❷   To establish an active context handle, a procedure must either return the context handle as the procedure result or have only the out directional attribute on a context handle parameter. The context handle cannot be used by any other procedure until it is active. For the *remote_open* procedure, an explicit binding handle is the first parameter.

❸   Procedures using only an active context handle can be employed in any way the application requires. Note that for a procedure to use the context handle, a context handle parameter must have at least the in attribute. The *remote_send* procedure sends a buffer of text data to the server, where the remote procedure writes the data to the file referred to by the context handle.

❹ When you have finished with the context, free the context handle to release resources.

Binding Handles and Context Handles

A procedure can use a binding handle and one or more context handles. However, make sure all handles in the parameter list refer to the same server because a remote procedure call cannot directly refer to more than one server at a time.

Table 7-1 shows how to determine whether a binding handle or a context handle directs the remote procedure call to the server.

Table 7–1: Binding Handles and Context Handles in a Call

Procedure Format	Other Parameters	Handle that Directs Call
proc(. . .)	No binding or context handles	The interface-wide automatic or implicit binding handle directs the call.
proc([in] bh . . .)	May include context handles	The explicit binding handle, bh, directs the call.
proc(. . . [in]ch . . .)	May include other context handles but no binding handles	The first context handle that is an input-only parameter directs the call. If it is null, the call will fail.
proc(. . . [in,out]ch . . .)	May include other input/output or output-only context handles but no binding handles or input-only context handles	The first non-null context handle that is an input/output parameter directs the call. If all are null, the call will fail.

Managing Context in a Server

When more than one remote procedure call from a particular client needs context on a server, the server stub and server application maintain the context. This section describes how to implement the procedures that manipulate context in a server.

A **server context handle** refers to context in the server code. It communicates the status of the context back to the client. From the perspective of the server developer, a server context handle is an untyped pointer that can be tested for null, assigned null, or assigned any value.

Once the server context handle is active (non-null), the server maintains the context for the particular client until one of the following occurs:

- The client performs a remote procedure call that frees the context.

- The client terminates while context is being maintained.

- Communication breaks between the client and server.

If the client terminates or the client-server communication breaks while the server maintains context, the server's RPC runtime library may invoke a context rundown procedure to clean up user data.

Writing Procedures That Use a Context Handle

Example 7-3 shows how to implement a procedure that obtains an active context handle, one that uses the active context handle, and one that frees the context handle.

Example 7-3: Procedures That Use Context Handles

```
/* FILE NAME: manager.c */
#include <stdio.h>
#include <string.h>
#include <io.h>
#include <errno.h>
#include "rfile.h"

filehandle remote_open(binding_h, name, mode)   /* ❶ */
rpc_binding_handle_t binding_h;
char                 name[];
char                 mode[];
{
    FILE *FILEh;

    if(strlen((char *)name) == 0)                       /* no file name given */
        if(strcmp((char *)mode, "r") == 0)
            FILEh = NULL;                        /* cannot read nonexistent file */
        else FILEh = stdout;                            /* use server stdout */

    else if(access((char *)name, 0) == 0)                    /* file exists */
        if(strcmp((char *)mode, "w") == 0)
            FILEh = NULL;                        /* do not overwrite existing file */
        else FILEh = fopen((char *)name, (char *)mode);   /* open read/append */

    else                                            /* file does not exist */
        if(strcmp((char *)mode, "r") == 0)
            FILEh = NULL;                        /* cannot read nonexistent file */
        else FILEh = fopen((char *)name, (char *)mode);  /* open write/append */

    return( (filehandle)FILEh );        /* cast FILE handle to context handle */
}
```

Example 7-3: Procedures That Use Context Handles (continued)

```
long int remote_send(fh, buf, max)          /* ❷ */
filehandle fh;
buffer buf;
long int max;
{
    /* write data to the file (context), which is cast as a FILE pointer */
    return( fwrite(buf, max, 1, fh) );
}


void remote_close(fh)                        /* ❸ */
filehandle *fh;   /* the client stub needs the changed value upon return */
{
    if( (FILE *)(*fh) != stdout )
      fclose( (FILE *)(*fh) );
    (*fh) = NULL;        /* assign NULL to the context handle to free it */
    return;
}
```

❶ Initialize data as required by later calls, and assign the application context to the server context handle. In this example, a file handle is obtained and assigned to the context handle when the procedure returns. Outside of the server process this file handle is meaningless, but when the client makes subsequent calls, the server uses this file handle to write data or close the file.

❷ Use the server context handle parameter defined with the in directional attribute. This procedure must have an active context handle as input. For this example, the buffer (buf) of max number of items is written to the file. Cast the server context handle to the context's data type (FILE *).

❸ Free the context by using a procedure whose context handle parameter is defined with the in and out directional attributes. This procedure must have an active context handle as input. To free the context, assign null to the server context handle and use the C library procedure *free* or a corresponding method to clean up your application. In this example, before freeing the file handle, the context is tested to be sure it does not refer to *stdout*. The server context handle is cast to the context's data type.

When this procedure returns to the client, the client stub automatically frees the context handle on the client side if the server context handle is set to NULL.

If memory must be allocated for the context, use the C library procedure *malloc* or another method. Do *not* use the stub support procedure *midl_user_allocate* because you do not want the allocated memory to be automatically freed by the server stub after the procedure completes.

Writing a Context Rundown Procedure

A context rundown procedure allows orderly cleanup of the server context. The server RPC runtime library automatically calls it when a context is maintained for a client, and either of the following occurs:

- The client terminates without requesting that the server free the context.

- Communication breaks between the client and server.

In our example, the interface definition defines the following type as a context handle:

```
typedef [context_handle] void *filehandle;
```

Example 7-4 shows the context rundown procedure to implement in the server code. The procedure name is created by appending _rundown_ to the type name (*filehandle*). The procedure does not return a value and the only parameter is the context handle. In this example, when the context rundown procedure executes, it closes the file that represents the context.

Example 7-4: A Context Rundown Procedure

```
/* FILE NAME: crndwn.c */
#include <stdio.h>
#include "rfile.h"

void filehandle_rundown(remote_fh)
filehandle remote_fh;                /* the context handle is passed in  */
{
   fprintf(stderr, "Server executing context rundown\n");
   if( (FILE *)remote_fh != stdout )
     fclose( (FILE *)remote_fh );  /* file is closed if client is gone */
   remote_fh = NULL;              /* must set context handle to NULL  */
   return;
}
```

The context handle must be defined as a type in the interface definition in order for the server runtime to automatically call the context rundown procedure. And if you define the context handle as a type, then you must implement a context rundown procedure in the server.

MIDL and ACF Attributes
Quick Reference

All MIDL attributes are shown in Tables A-1 through A-8, and all ACF attributes are shown in Table A-9, but not all are demonstrated in this book.

Table A-1: MIDL Interface Header Attributes

Attribute	Description
uuid(*uuid_string*)	A universal unique identifier is generated by the *uuidgen* utility and assigned to the interface to distinguish it from other interfaces. This attribute is required unless the local attribute is used.
version(*major.minor*)	A particular version of a remote interface is identified when more than one version exists.
pointer_default(*kind*)	The default treatment for pointers is specified. Kinds of pointers include reference (ref) and unique (unique).
endpoint(*string*)	An endpoint is a number representing the transport-layer address of a server process. This attribute specifies a well-known endpoint on which servers will listen for remote procedure calls. Well-known endpoints are usually established by the authority responsible for a particular transport protocol.
local	The MIDL compiler can be used as a C language header file generator. When this attribute is used, all other interface header attributes are ignored and no stub files are generated by the MIDL compiler.

Table A–2: MIDL Array Attributes

Attribute	Description
string	An array is specified to have the properties of a string.
Conformant Array Attributes	
size_is(*size*)	A variable is defined in the interface definition and used at runtime to establish the array size.
max_is(*max*)	A variable is defined in the interface definition and used at runtime to establish the maximum index value.
Varying Array Attributes	
first_is(*first*)	A variable is defined in the interface definition and used at runtime to establish the lowest index value of transmitted data. The value is not necessarily the lowest bound of the array.
last_is(*last*)	A variable is defined in the interface definition and used at runtime to establish the highest index value of transmitted data. The value is not necessarily the highest bound of the array.
length_is(*length*)	A variable is defined in the interface definition and used at runtime to establish the number of elements transmitted for a portion of the array.

Table A–3: MIDL Pointer Type Attributes

Attribute	Description
unique	A pointer is specified as a unique pointer with the unique attribute. Unique pointers provide basic indirection and they can be null. Unique pointers cannot contain cycles or loops.
ref	A pointer is specified as a reference pointer with the ref attribute. This attribute gives basic indirection without the implementation overhead associated with unique pointers.
string	A pointer is specified as pointing to a string.

Table A-4: MIDL Data Type Attributes

Attribute	Description
pointer type attributes	A data type with a visible pointer operator may be specified with a pointer type attribute (See Table A-3).
context_handle	A state is maintained on a particular server between remote procedure calls from a specific client by maintaining a context handle as a data type. The context handle identifies the state.
handle	A defined data type is specified as a customized handle so that the client-server binding information is associated with it.
transmit_as(*type*)	A data type that is manipulated by clients and servers may be specified so that it is converted to a different data type for transmission over the network.

Table A-5: MIDL Structure Member Attributes

Attribute	Description
array attributes	A structure member can have array attributes if it has array dimensions or a visible pointer operator. A structure member that has a visible pointer operator and the size_is or max_is attribute defines a pointer to a conformant array, not an array structure member (see Table A-2).
pointer type attributes	A structure member can have a pointer type attribute if it has a visible pointer operator (see Table A-3).
ignore	Do not transfer the data in this structure member (a pointer) during a remote procedure call. This can save the overhead of copying and transmitting data to which the pointer refers.

Table A-6: MIDL Union Case Attributes

Attribute	Description
pointer type attributes	A union case can have a pointer type attribute if it has a visible pointer operator. See Table A-3.

Table A–7: MIDL *Procedure Parameter Attributes*

Attribute	Description
in	The parameter is input when the remote procedure is called.
out	The parameter is output when the remote procedure returns.
array attributes	A parameter with array dimensions can have array attributes. A conformant array is a procedure parameter with a visible pointer operator and the size_is or max_is attribute (see Table A-2).
pointer type attributes	A parameter with a visible pointer operator can have a pointer type attribute. See Table A-3.
context_handle	A parameter that is a void * type can have the context handle attribute.

Table A–8: MIDL *Procedure Attributes*

Attribute	Description
	Procedure Result Attributes
string	A procedure result is specified to have the properties of a string with the string attribute.
ptr	A procedure that returns a pointer result always returns a full pointer. It may be specified with the ptr attribute but this is not necessary. Full pointers provide basic indirection and they can be null. They can also contain cycles or loops.
unique	Unique pointers provide basic indirection and they can be null. Unique pointers cannot contain cycles or loops. Unique pointers can be specified with the unique attribute.
context_handle	A procedure returns a context handle result in order to indicate a state on a particular server, which is then referred to in successive remote procedure calls from a specific client.

Table A–9: ACF *Attributes*

Attribute	Description
	Binding Methods
auto_handle	The automatic binding method is selected.
implicit_handle(*type name*)	The implicit binding method is selected.
explicit_handle(*type name*)	The explicit binding method is selected.

Table A-9: ACF Attributes (continued)

Exceptions as Parameters	
comm_status	Names a parameter or the procedure result to which a status code is written if a communication error is reported by the client runtime to the client stub. The client remote procedure call must include the error_status_t data type in its argument list. If an error is reported and this attribute and error_status_t data type are not used, the client stub raises an exception.
fault_status	Names a parameter or the procedure result to which a status code is written if an error is reported by the server runtime to the server stub, an exception occurs in the server stub, or an exception occurs in the remote procedure. If an error is reported and this attribute is not used, the client stub raises an exception.
Excluding Unused Procedures	
code	All or selected procedures from the interface have the associated client stub code generated by the MIDL compiler.
nocode	All or selected procedures from the interface do not have the associated client stub code generated by the MIDL compiler.

B

RPC Runtime Routines Quick Reference

The following tables organize the RPC runtime routines. Table B-1 shows all the routines that client applications can use, and Table B-2 shows all the routines that server applications can use. The following abbreviations are used in RPC runtime routine names:

Auth	authentication, authorization
Elt	element
Ep	endpoint
Exp	expiration
Id	identifier
If	interface
Inq	inquire
Mbr	member
Mgmt	management
Ns	name service
Protseq	protocol sequence
Rpc	remote procedure call
Stats	statistics

Numbers next to the calls have the following meaning:

[1] Function is limited to using Windows NT Security.

[2] Function is supported on Microsoft Windows NT systems only.

[3] Function acts on only the local process with Microsoft RPC Version 1.0.

[4] Function provided for compatibility with DCE CDS. Not supported by the Microsoft Locator Version 1.0.

Table B-1 Client RPC Runtime Routines

Manage Binding Handles	Manage UUIDs
RpcBindingCopy	UuidCreate
RpcBindingFree	UuidFromString
RpcBindingReset	UuidToString
RpcEpResolveBinding	UuidCompare
RpcBindingInqObject	UuidEqual
RpcBindingSetObject	UuidHash
RpcBindingInqAuthInfo[1]	UuidIsNil
RpcBindingSetAuthInfo[1]	**General Utility**
RpcBindingVectorFree	RpcStringFree
RpcStringBindingCompose	**Manage Name Service Entries**
RpcBindingFromStringBinding	RpcNsMgmtEntryCreate[4]
RpcBindingToStringBinding	RpcNsEntryObjectInqBegin
RpcSsDestroyClientContext	RpcNsEntryObjectInqNext
RpcStringBindingParse	RpcNsEntryObjectInqDone
Find Servers from a Name Service	RpcNsEntryExpandName
RpcNsBindingImportBegin	RpcNsMgmtEntryInqIfIds
RpcNsBindingImportNext	RpcNsMgmtBindingUnexport
RpcNsBindingImportDone	RpcNsMgmtEntryDelete
RpcNsBindingInqEntryName	**Manage Name Service Groups**
RpcNsBindingLookupBegin	RpcNsGroupMbrAdd[4]
RpcNsBindingLookupNext	RpcNsGroupMbrInqBegin[4]
RpcNsBindingSelect	RpcNsGroupMbrInqNext[4]
RpcNsBindingLookupDone	RpcNsGroupMbrInqDone[4]
Manage Name Service Expirations	RpcNsGroupMbrRemove[4]
RpcNsMgmtInqExpAge	RpcNsGroupDelete[4]
RpcNsMgmtSetExpAge	**Manage Endpoints**
RpcNsMgmtHandleSetExpAge	RpcEpUnregister

Table B-1　Client RPC Runtime Routines　(continued)

Manage Name Service Profiles	Handle Exceptions
RpcNsProfileEltAdd[4] RpcNsProfileEltInqBegin[4] RpcNsProfileEltInqNext[4] RpcNsProfileEltInqDone[4] RpcNsProfileEltRemove[4] RpcNsProfileDelete[4]	RpcAbnormalTermination RpcEndExcept RpcEndFinally RpcExcept RpcFinally RpcExceptionCode RpcRaiseException RpcTryExcept RpcTryFinally
Manage the Client	
RpcMgmtEnableIdleCleanup RpcMgmtInqComTimeout RpcMgmtSetComTimeout RpcMgmtSetCancelTimeout RpcWinSetYieldInfo YieldFunctionName	**Manage Memory**
	RpcSmAllocate RpcSmClientFree RpcSmDestroyClientContext RpcSmDisableAllocate RpcSmEnableAllocate RpcSmFree RpcSmGetThreadHandle RpcSmSetClientAllocFree RpcSmSetThreadHandle RpcSmSwapClientAllocFree RpcSsAllocate RpcSsDestroyClientContext RpcSsDisableAllocate RpcSsEnableAllocate RpcSsFree RpcSsGetThreadHandle RpcSsSetClientAllocFree RpcSsSetThreadHandle RpcSsSwapClientAllocFree
Manage Local or Remote Applications	
RpcMgmtIsServerListening[3] RpcMgmtStopServerListening[3] RpcMgmtInqStats[3]	
Inquire of Protocol Sequences	
RpcNetworkIsProtseqValid	
Manage Interface Information	
RpcIfInqId RpcIfRegisterAuthInfo RpcIfIdVectorFree	

Table B-2 Server RPC Runtime Routines

Manage Binding Handles	Manage UUIDs
RpcServerInqBindings RpcBindingToStringBinding RpcStringBindingParse RpcStringBindingCompose RpcBindingInqAuthClient[1] RpcBindingInqObject RpcBindingServerFromClient RpcBindingVectorFree	UuidCreate UuidFromString UuidToString UuidCompare UuidEqual UuidHash UuidIsNil
Manage Interfaces	**Manage Name Service Entries**
RpcServerRegisterIf RpcServerInqIf RpcServerUnregisterIf RpcIfInqId RpcIfIdVectorFree	RpcNsMgmtEntryCreate RpcNsEntryObjectInqBegin RpcNsEntryObjectInqNext RpcNsEntryObjectInqDone RpcNsEntryExpandName[4] RpcNsMgmtEntryInqIfIds RpcNsMgmtBindingUnexport RpcNsMgmtEntryDelete
Manage Name Service Expirations	
RpcNsMgmtInqExpAge RpcNsMgmtSetExpAge RpcNsMgmtHandleSetExpAge	**Manage Name Service Groups**
Create Binding Information	RpcNsGroupMbrAdd[4] RpcNsGroupMbrInqBegin[4] RpcNsGroupMbrInqNext[4] RpcNsGroupMbrInqDone[4] RpcNsGroupMbrRemove[4] RpcNsGroupDelete[4]
RpcImpersonateClient[2] RpcRevertToSelf[2] RpcServerUseProtseq RpcServerUseAllProtseqs RpcServerUseProtseqEp RpcServerUseProtseqIf RpcServerUseAllProtseqsIf RpcNetworkInqProtseqs RpcProtseqVectorFree	**Manage Endpoints**
	RpcEpRegister RpcEpRegisterNoReplace RpcEpResolveBinding RpcEpUnregister

Table B-2 Server RPC Runtime Routines (continued)

Manage Name Service Profiles	Manage the Server
RpcNsProfileEltAdd[4] RpcNsProfileEltInqBegin[4] RpcNsProfileEltInqNext[4] RpcNsProfileEltInqDone[4] RpcNsProfileEltRemove[4] RpcNsProfileDelete[4]	RpcMgmtSetServerStackSize RpcMgmtWaitServerListen
	Handle Exceptions
	RpcAbnormalTermination RpcEndExcept
Listen for RPCs	RpcEndFinally RpcExcept
RpcServerListen	RpcFinally
General Utility	RpcExceptionCode RpcRaiseException
RpcStringFree	RpcTryExcept
Manage Local or Remote Applications	RpcTryFinally
	Manage Memory
RpcMgmtIsServerListening[3] RpcMgmtStopServerListening[3] RpcMgmtInqStats[3] RpcMgmtStatsVectorFree	RpcSmAllocate RpcSmClientFree RpcSmDisableAllocate RpcSmEnableAllocate
Manage Object Types	RpcSmFree RpcSmGetThreadHandle
RpcObjectSetType RpcObjectSetInqFn RpcObjectInqType	RpcSmSetThreadHandle RpcSsAllocate RpcSsDisableAllocate
Manage Authentication	RpcSsEnableAllocate RpcSsFree
RpcServerRegisterAuthInfo[1] RpcBindingInqAuthClient[1]	RpcSsGetThreadHandle RpcSsSetThreadHandle
Export Servers to a Name Service	
RpcNsBindingExport RpcNsBindingUnexport	

The Arithmetic Application

The arithmetic application makes a remote procedure call to a procedure named *sum_arrays*, which adds together the values for the same array index in two long integer arrays, and returns the sums in another long integer array.

The application demonstrates the basics of a distributed application with a remote procedure call and includes these features:

- Defining a simple array in an interface definition

- Using the automatic binding method

- Exporting a server to the name service

- Checking the error status of RPC runtime calls

How to Build and Run the Application

To build the server of the distributed application, type the following:

        C:\SERVER> nmake server

To run the server of the distributed application, type the following:

        C:\SERVER> arith

To build the client of the distributed application, type the following:

        C:\CLIENT> nmake client

To run the client of the distributed application, type the following:

        C:\CLIENT> client

Application Files

Makefile contains descriptions of how the application is compiled. Use the compilation make all to create all the executable files for the application. See Example C-1.

arith.bat is a batch file that sets the environment and executes the server. See Example C-2.

arith.idl contains the description of the constants, data types, and procedures for the interface. See Example C-3.

client.c initializes two arrays, calls the remote procedure *sum_arrays*, and displays the results of the returned array. See Example C-4.

manager.c is the remote procedure implementation. See Example C-5.

server.c initializes the server with a series of Microsoft RPC runtime calls. See Example C-6.

status.h defines the CHECK_STATUS macro, which interprets error status codes that may return from Microsoft RPC runtime calls. See Example C-7.

Example C-1: The Makefile for the Arithmetic Application

```
# FILE NAME: Makefile
# Makefile for the arithmetic application
#
# definitions for this make file
#
APPL=arith
IDLCMD=midl
NTRPCLIBS=rpcrt4.lib rpcns4.lib libcmt.lib kernel32.lib

# Include Windows NT macros
!include <ntwin32.mak>

# NT c flags
cflags = -c -W0 -Gz -D_X86_=1 -DWIN32 -DMT /nologo

# NT nmake inference rules
   $(cc) $(cdebug) $(cflags) $(cvarsmt) $<
   $(cvtomf)

#
# COMPLETE BUILD of the application
#
#all:   local interface client server
all:    lclient.exe interface client.exe server.exe

#
# INTERFACE BUILD
#
interface: $(APPL).h $(APPL)_c.obj $(APPL)_s.obj
```

Example C-1: The Makefile for the Arithmetic Application (continued)

```
#
# LOCAL BUILD of the client application to test locally
#
local:      lclient.exe
lclient.exe: lclient.obj lmanager.obj
    $(link) $(linkdebug) $(conflags) -out:lclient.exe -map:lclient.map \
      lclient.obj lmanager.obj \
      $(NTRPCLIBS)

#
# CLIENT BUILD
#
client: client.exe
client.exe: client.obj $(APPL)_c.obj
    $(link) $(linkdebug) $(conflags) -out:client.exe -map:client.map \
      client.obj $(APPL)_c.obj \
      $(NTRPCLIBS)


#
# SERVER BUILD
#
server:      server.exe
server.exe: server.obj manager.obj $(APPL)_s.obj
    $(link) $(linkdebug) $(conflags) -out:server.exe -map:server.map \
      server.obj manager.obj $(APPL)_s.obj \
      $(NTRPCLIBS)

# client and server sources
client.obj:  client.c  $(APPL).h
manager.obj: manager.c $(APPL).h
server.obj:  server.c  $(APPL).h

# Local client sources
lclient.obj: client.c $(APPL).h
    $(cc) $(cdebug) $(cflags) $(cvarsmt) /DLOCAL /Folclient.obj client.c
lmanager.obj: manager.c $(APPL).h
    $(cc) $(cdebug) $(cflags) $(cvarsmt) /DLOCAL /Folmanager.obj manager.c

# client stubs
$(APPL)_c.obj: $(APPL)_c.c
$(APPL)_x.obj: $(APPL)_x.c

# compile the server stub
$(APPL)_s.obj : $(APPL)_s.c

# generate stubs, auxiliary and header file from the IDL file
$(APPL).h $(APPL)_c.c $(APPL)_x.c : $(APPL).idl
    $(IDLCMD) $(APPL).idl

# clean up for fresh build
clean:
    del $(APPL)_?.c
    del *.obj
    del $(APPL).h
    del *.map
```

Example C-1: The Makefile for the Arithmetic Application (continued)

```
    del *.pdb

clobber: clean
    if exist client.exe  del client.exe
    if exist lclient.exe del lclient.exe
    if exist server.exe  del server.exe
```

Example C-2: The Server Batch File for the Arithmetic Application

```
@ECHO OFF
@REM FILE NAME: arith.bat
set ARITHMETIC_SERVER_ENTRY=/.:/arithmetic_serverhost
server
```

Example C-3: The MIDL File of the Arithmetic Application

```
/* FILE NAME: arith.idl */
/* This Interface Definition Language file represents a basic arithmetic   */
/* procedure that a remote procedure call application can use.             */
[
uuid(6AF85260-A3A4-101A-B1AE-08002B2E5B76),          /* Universal Unique ID   */
pointer_default(ref)                      /* default pointer type is reference */
]
interface arith                                /* interface name is arith    */
{
    const unsigned short ARRAY_SIZE = 10;/* an unsigned integer constant     */
    typedef long long_array[ARRAY_SIZE]; /* an array type of long integers   */

    void sum_arrays ( /* The sum_arrays procedure does not return a value   */
        [in] long_array a,                    /* 1st parameter is passed in  */
        [in] long_array b,                    /* 2nd parameter is passed in  */
        [out] long_array c                    /* 3rd parameter is passed out */
    );
}
```

Example C-4: The Client File of the Arithmetic Application

```
/* FILE NAME: client.c */
/* This is the client module of the arithmetic example. */
#include <stdio.h>
#include <stdlib.h>
#include "arith.h"          /* header file created by IDL compiler      */

long_array a ={100,200,345,23,67,65,0,0,0,0};
long_array b ={4,0,2,3,1,7,5,9,6,8};

main ()
{
    long_array    result;
    int i;

    sum_arrays(a, b, result);              /* A Remote Procedure Call      */
    puts("sums:");
    for(i = 0; i < ARRAY_SIZE; i++)
        printf("%ld\n", result[i]);
}
```

Example C-4: The Client File of the Arithmetic Application (continued)

```
/****************************************************************************/
/***                    MIDL_user_allocate / MIDL_user_free            ***/
/****************************************************************************/

void * __RPC_API
MIDL_user_allocate
            (
             size
             )
size_t size;
{

    unsigned char * ptr;
    ptr = malloc( size );
    return ( (void *)ptr );

}

void __RPC_API
MIDL_user_free
            (
             object
             )
void * object;
{
    free (object);
}
```

Example C-5: Remote Procedure of the Arithmetic Application

```
/* FILE NAME: manager.c */
/* An implementation of the procedure defined in the arithmetic interface. */
#include <stdio.h>
#include "arith.h"                 /* header file produced by IDL compiler    */

void sum_arrays(a, b, c)     /* implementation of the sum_arrays procedure    */
    long_array a;
    long_array b;
    long_array c;
    {
       int i;

       for(i = 0; i < ARRAY_SIZE; i++)
          c[i] = a[i] + b[i];    /* array elements are each added together   */
    }
```

Example C-6: Server Initialization of the Arithmetic Application

```
/* FILE NAME: server.c */
#include <stdio.h>
#include "arith.h"                      /* header created by the idl compiler */
#include "status.h"                     /* header with the CHECK_STATUS macro */

main ()
{
    unsigned long         status;                         /* error status */
    rpc_binding_vector_t *binding_vector;        /* set of binding handles */
```

Example C-6: Server Initialization of the Arithmetic Application (continued)

```
unsigned char        *entry_name;           /* entry name for name service */

status =                                              /* error status */
RpcServerRegisterIf(        /* register interface with the RPC runtime   */
    arith_v0_0_s_ifspec,            /* interface specification (arith.h) */
    NULL,
    NULL
);
CHECK_STATUS(status, "Can't register interface", ABORT);

status =
RpcServerUseAllProtseqs(                     /* create binding information */
    RPC_C_PROTSEQ_MAX_REQS_DEFAULT,              /* queue size for calls  */
    NULL                             /* no security descriptor is used   */
);
CHECK_STATUS(status, "Can't create binding information", ABORT);

status =
RpcServerInqBindings(      /* obtain this server's binding information    */
    &binding_vector
);
CHECK_STATUS(status, "Can't get binding information", ABORT);

entry_name = (unsigned char *)getenv("ARITHMETIC_SERVER_ENTRY");
status =
RpcNsBindingExport(        /* export entry to name service database      */
    RPC_C_NS_SYNTAX_DEFAULT,              /* syntax of the entry name     */
    entry_name,                  /* entry name for name service          */
    arith_v0_0_s_ifspec,             /* interface specification (arith.h)*/
    binding_vector,              /* the set of server binding handles    */
    NULL
);
CHECK_STATUS(status, "Can't export to name service database", ABORT);

status =
RpcEpRegister(             /* register endpoints in local endpoint map   */
    arith_v0_0_s_ifspec,             /* interface specification (arith.h) */
    binding_vector,              /* the set of server binding handles    */
    NULL,
    NULL
);
CHECK_STATUS(status, "Can't add address to the endpoint map", ABORT);

status =
RpcBindingVectorFree(             /* free set of server binding handles   */
    &binding_vector
);
CHECK_STATUS(status, "Can't free binding handles and vector", ABORT);

puts("Listening for remote procedure calls...");
status =
RpcServerListen(                          /* listen for remote calls    */
    1,                                    /* minimum number of threads */
    RPC_C_LISTEN_MAX_CALLS_DEFAULT,       /*concurrent calls to server */
    NULL               /* continue listening until explicitly stopped */
```

Example C-6: Server Initialization of the Arithmetic Application (continued)

```
    );
    CHECK_STATUS(status, "rpc listen failed", ABORT);
}

/***************************************************************************/
/***                MIDL_user_allocate / MIDL_user_free          ***/
/***************************************************************************/

void * __RPC_API
MIDL_user_allocate
            (
                size
            )
size_t size;
{

    unsigned char * ptr;
    ptr = malloc( size );
    return ( (void *)ptr );

}

void __RPC_API
MIDL_user_free
            (
                object
            )
void * object;
{
    free (object);
}
```

Example C-7: The Check Error Status Macro

```
/* FILE NAME: status.h */
#include <stdio.h>
#include <stdlib.h>

#define RESUME 0
#define ABORT  1
#define ERROR_TEXT_SIZE 1025

#define CHECK_STATUS(input_status, comment, action) \
{ \
    if(input_status != RPC_S_OK) { \
        error_stat = FormatMessage( FORMAT_MESSAGE_FROM_SYSTEM \
                                    ,NULL                      \
                                    ,input_status              \
                                    ,0                         \
                                    ,error_string              \
                                    ,ERROR_TEXT_SIZE           \
                                    ,NULL);                    \
        fprintf(stderr, "%s %s\n", comment, error_string);     \
        if(action == ABORT) \
            exit(1); \
    } \
```

Example C-7: The Check Error Status Macro (continued)

```
}

static int          error_stat;
static unsigned char  error_string[ERROR_TEXT_SIZE];
```

The Inventory Application

The inventory application allows a user to inquire about, and order from, a simple inventory. Data structures are defined for the following items:

- Part number (to identify a part)

- Part name

- Part description

- Part price

- Quantity of part

- Part list

- Account number (to identify a user)

Procedures are also defined in the interface definition to do the following:

- Confirm if a part is available

- Obtain a part name

- Obtain a part description

- Obtain a part price

- Obtain the quantity of parts available

- Obtain a list of subpart numbers

- Order a part

The application demonstrates many features of Microsoft RPC application development including:

- Using strings, pointers, structures, a union, and a conformant array.

- Allocating new memory in a remote procedure for data returned to the client using stub support routines. The *get_part_description* and *whatare_subparts* remote procedures demonstrate server allocation of a string and a conformant structure.

- Managing protocol sequences, interpreting binding information, selecting binding information, and using exception handler macros.

- Variations on a client using ACFs and the automatic, implicit, and explicit binding methods.

- Finding a server by importing from a name service database.

How to Run the Application

To run the local test of the client, type the following:

```
C:\> nmake local
C:\> lclient.exe
```

To run the server of the distributed application, type the following:

```
C:\SERVER> nmake server
C:\SERVER> server.exe
```

To run the client that uses the automatic binding method, type the following:

```
C:\CLIENT> nmake client
C:\CLIENT> client.exe
```

To run a nondistributed local test of the implicit client, type the following in the *implicit* subdirectory:

```
C:\> nmake local
C:\> lclient.exe
```

To run the implicit client of the distributed application using the automatic server, type the following in the *implicit* subdirectory:

```
C:\CLIENT> nmake client
C:\CLIENT> client.exe
```

To run the explicit server of the distributed application, type the following in the *explicit* subdirectory:

```
C:\SERVER> nmake server
C:\SERVER> server.exe
```

To run the explicit client of the distributed application using the explicit server, type the following in the *explicit* subdirectory:

```
C:\CLIENT> nmake client
C:\CLIENT> client.exe
```

Application Files

Makefile contains descriptions of how the application is compiled. Some files depend on the header file *status.h* from the arithmetic application for the CHECK_STATUS macro. See Example D-1.

inv.idl contains the description of the constants, data types, and procedures for the interface. See Example D-2.

manager.c is the implementation of all the remote procedures defined in this interface. See Example D-3.

invntry.c is the implementation of the inventory database. For simplicity, only three inventory items are included. The part numbers for these are printed when the inventory is opened. See Example D-4.

server.c initializes the server with a series of runtime calls prior to servicing remote procedure calls. In addition to the required calls, this server also selects a specific protocol sequence, uses exception handling macros, and does some basic cleanup when the server quits. See Example D-5.

client.c displays the instructions for the user and processes user input in a loop until exit is selected. Each remote procedure is exercised depending on the input from the user. See Example D-6.

implicit\Makefile contains descriptions of how the implicit client is compiled. Some files depend on the header file *status.h* from the arithmetic application for the CHECK_STATUS macro. See Example D-7.

implicit\inv_i.acf customizes how you use an interface. In this application it is used to select the implicit binding method. See Example D-8.

implicit\client.c imports a binding handle from the name service database. See Example D-9.

implicit\getbind.c contains the *do_import_binding* procedure, which shows how to import a binding handle from the name service database. See Example D-10.

implicit\intbind.c contains the *do_interpret_binding* procedure, which shows how to obtain the binding information to which a binding handle refers. See Example D-11.

The server for the implicit client is the same as the one for the automatic client.

explicit\Makefile contains descriptions of how the explicit client is compiled. The compilation depends on some files from the implicit client development. See Example D-12.

explicit\inv.idl contains the description of the constants, data types, and procedures for the interface. All procedure declarations include a binding handle as the first parameter. See Example D-13.

explicit\manager.c is the implementation of all the remote procedures defined in this interface. All procedure implementations include a binding handle as the first parameter. See Example D-14.

explicit\client.c imports a binding handle from the name service database. All procedures have a binding handle as the first parameter. See Example D-15.

The server's main program for the explicit client is the same as the one for the automatic and implicit clients.

Example D-1: The Makefile for the Inventory Application

```
# FILE NAME: Makefile
# Makefile for the inventory application
#
# definitions for this make file
#
APPL=inv
NTRPCLIBS=rpcrt4.lib rpcns4.lib libcmt.lib kernel32.lib

!include <ntwin32.mak>

## NT c flags
cflags = -c -W0 -Gz -D_X86_=1 -DWIN32 -DMT /nologo

## NT nmake inference rules
    $(cc) $(cdebug) $(cflags) $(cvarsmt) $<
    $(cvtomf)

#
# COMPLETE BUILD of the application
#
all:    local interface client server

#
# INTERFACE BUILD
#
interface: $(APPL).h $(APPL)_c.obj $(APPL)_s.obj

#
# LOCAL BUILD of the client application to test locally
#
local:        lclient.exe
lclient.exe: lclient.obj lmanager.obj invntry.obj
    $(link) $(linkdebug) $(conflags) -out:lclient.exe -map:lclient.map \
        lclient.obj lmanager.obj invntry.obj\
        $(NTRPCLIBS)

#
# CLIENT BUILD
#
client:       client.exe
client.exe: client.obj $(APPL)_c.obj
    $(link) $(linkdebug) $(conflags) -out:client.exe -map:client.map \
        client.obj $(APPL)_c.obj  \
        $(NTRPCLIBS)

#
```

Example D-1: The Makefile for the Inventory Application (continued)

```
# SERVER BUILD
#
server:      server.exe
server.exe: server.obj manager.obj invntry.obj $(APPL)_s.obj
    $(link) $(linkdebug) $(conflags) -out:server.exe -map:server.map \
        server.obj manager.obj invntry.obj $(APPL)_s.obj\
        $(NTRPCLIBS)


# client and server sources
client.obj:  client.c  $(APPL).h
manager.obj: manager.c $(APPL).h
server.obj:  server.c  $(APPL).h
invntry.obj: invntry.c $(APPL).h

# Local client sources
lclient.obj: client.c $(APPL).h
              $(cc) $(cdebug) $(cflags) $(cvarsmt) /DLOCAL\
                 /Folclient.obj client.c
lmanager.obj: manager.c $(APPL).h
              $(cc) $(cdebug) $(cflags) $(cvarsmt) /DLOCAL \
                 /Folmanager.obj manager.c

# client stubs
$(APPL)_c.obj: $(APPL)_c.c
$(APPL)_x.obj: $(APPL)_x.c
$(APPL)_s.obj : $(APPL)_s.c

# generate stubs, auxiliary and header file from the IDL file
$(APPL).h $(APPL)_c.c $(APPL)_x.c : $(APPL).idl
    midl $(APPL).idl

# clean up for fresh build
clean:
    del $(APPL)_?.c
    del *.obj
    del $(APPL).h
    del *.map
    del *.pdb

clobber: clean
    if exist client.exe  del client.exe
    if exist lclient.exe del lclient.exe
    if exist server.exe  del server.exe
```

Example D-2: The MIDL File of the Inventory Application

```
/* FILE NAME: inv.idl */
[                                       /* brackets enclose attributes  */
uuid(A61E3FC0-A53F-101A-B1AF-08002B2E5B76), /* universal unique identifier  */
version(1.0),                           /* version of this interface    */
pointer_default(unique)                 /* pointer default              */
] interface  inv                        /* interface name               */
{
    const long MAX_STRING = 30;             /* constant for string size */

    typedef long     part_num;              /* inventory part number    */
```

Example D-2: The MIDL File of the Inventory Application (continued)

```
typedef [string] char part_name[MAX_STRING+1];           /* name of part    */

typedef [string, unique] char *paragraph;        /* description of part    */

typedef enum {
    ITEM, GRAM, KILOGRAM
} part_units;                                    /* units of measurement    */

typedef struct part_price {                              /* price of part    */
    part_units units;
    double      per_unit;
} part_price;

typedef union switch(part_units units) total {      /* quantity of part    */
    case ITEM:      long int number;
    case GRAM:
    case KILOGRAM: double   weight;
} part_quantity;

typedef struct part_list{                        /* list of part numbers    */
    long                    size;                /* number of parts in array */
    [size_is(size)] part_num numbers[*];         /* conformant array of parts */
} part_list;

typedef struct part_record {                        /* data for each part */
    part_num      number;
    part_name     name;
    paragraph     description;
    part_price    price;
    part_quantity quantity;
    part_list     subparts;
} part_record;

typedef long account_num;                        /* user account number */

/*********************** Procedure Declarations ************************/
boolean is_part_available(              /* return true if in inventory      */
    [in] part_num number                /* input part number */
);

void whatis_part_name(                  /* get part name from inventory     */
    [in]  part_num  number,             /* input part number */
    [in, out] part_name name            /* output part name   */
);

paragraph get_part_description(         /* return a pointer to a string     */
    [in]  part_num  number
);

void whatis_part_price(                 /* get part price from inventory    */
    [in]  part_num   number,
    [out] part_price *price
);

void whatis_part_quantity(              /* get part quantity from inventory */
    [in]  part_num       number,
    [out] part_quantity *quantity
```

Example D-2: The MIDL File of the Inventory Application (continued)

```
    );

    void whatare_subparts(                  /* get list of subpart numbers    */
        [in]  part_num  number,
        [out] part_list **subparts          /* structure containing the array */
    );

    /* Order part from inventory with part number, quantity desired, and  */
    /* account number.  If inventory does not have enough, output lesser  */
    /* quantity ordered.  Return values:  1=ordered OK,                   */
    /* -1=invalid part, -2=invalid quantity, -3=invalid account.          */

    long order_part(   /* order part from inventory, return OK or error code */
        [in]      part_num       number,
        [in,out]  part_quantity *quantity,                /* quantity ordered */
        [in]      account_num   account
    );
} /* end of interface definition */
```

Example D-3: Remote Procedures of the Inventory Application

```
/* FILE NAME: manager.c */
/** Implementation of the remote procedures for the inventory application. **/
#include <stdio.h>
#include <stdlib.h>
#include "inv.h"

boolean is_part_available(number)
part_num number;
{
    part_record *part;                  /* a pointer to a part record */
    int found;

    found = read_part_record(number, &part);
    if(found)
        return(TRUE);
    else
        return(FALSE);
}


void whatis_part_name(number, name)
part_num  number;
part_name name;
{
    part_record *part;                  /* a pointer to a part record */

    read_part_record(number, &part);
    strncpy((char *)name, (char *)part->name, MAX_STRING);
    return;
}


paragraph get_part_description(number)
part_num  number;
{
    part_record *part;                  /* a pointer to a part record */
```

Example D-3: Remote Procedures of the Inventory Application (continued)

```
    paragraph description;
    int size;

    if( read_part_record(number, &part) ) {
       /* Allocated data that is returned to the client must be allocated */
       /* with the MIDL_user_allocate stub support routine.              */
       size = strlen((char *)part->description) + 1;
       description = (paragraph)MIDL_user_allocate((unsigned)size);
       strcpy((char *)description, (char *)part->description);
    }
    else
       description = NULL;
    return(description);
}


void whatis_part_price(number, price)
part_num    number;
part_price  *price;
{
    part_record *part;                    /* a pointer to a part record */

    read_part_record(number, &part);
    price->units = part->price.units;
    price->per_unit = part->price.per_unit;
    return;
}


void whatis_part_quantity(number, quantity)
part_num        number;
part_quantity *quantity;
{
    part_record *part;                    /* a pointer to a part record */

    read_part_record(number, &part);
    quantity->units = part->quantity.units;
    switch(quantity->units) {
       case ITEM: quantity->total.number = part->quantity.total.number;
                break;
       case KILOGRAM:
       case GRAM: quantity->total.weight = part->quantity.total.weight;
                break;
    }
    return;
}


void whatare_subparts(number, subpart_ptr)
part_num number;
part_list **subpart_ptr;
{
    part_record *part;                             /* pointer to a part record */
    int i;
    int size;

    read_part_record(number, &part);
```

Example D-3: Remote Procedures of the Inventory Application (continued)

```
    /* Allocated data that is output to the client must be allocated with    */
    /* the MIDL_user_allocate stub support routine.  Allocate for a          */
    /* part_list struct plus the array of subpart numbers.  Remember the     */
    /* part_list struct already has an array with one element, hence the -1. */
    size = sizeof(part_list) + (sizeof(part_num) * (part->subparts.size-1));
    *subpart_ptr = (part_list *)MIDL_user_allocate((unsigned)size);

    /* fill in the values */
    (*subpart_ptr)->size = part->subparts.size;
    for(i = 0; i < (*subpart_ptr)->size; i++)
        (*subpart_ptr)->numbers[i] = part->subparts.numbers[i];
    return;
}


long int order_part(number, quantity, account)
part_num        number;
part_quantity *quantity;
account_num     account;
{
    part_record *part;              /* pointer to a part record */

    long error = 1;   /* assume no error to start */
    /* Test for valid input */
    if( !read_part_record(number, &part) ) /* invalid part number input */
        error = -1;
    else if(quantity->units == ITEM)          /* invalid quantity input    */
        error = (quantity->total.number <= 0) ? -2 : error;
    else if(quantity->units == GRAM || quantity->units == KILOGRAM)
        error = (quantity->total.weight <= 0.0) ? -2 : error;
    /* else if()   invalid account, not implemented */
    /*     error = -3;                              */
    if(error < 0)
        return(error);

    /* convert input quantity & units if units are not correct for part */
    if(quantity->units != part->quantity.units) {
        if(part->quantity.units == ITEM)        /* convert weight to items  */
            quantity->total.number = (long int)quantity->total.weight;
        else if(quantity->units == ITEM)        /* convert items to weight  */
            quantity->total.weight = (long float)quantity->total.number;
        else if(quantity->units == GRAM && part->quantity.units == KILOGRAM)
            quantity->total.weight /= 1000.0; /* convert grams to kilograms */
        else if(quantity->units == KILOGRAM && part->quantity.units == GRAM)
            quantity->total.weight *= 1000.0; /* convert kilograms to grams */
        quantity->units = part->quantity.units;
    }

    /* check if enough in inventory for this order */
    switch(part->quantity.units) {
    case ITEM:
        if(part->quantity.total.number > quantity->total.number)
            /* reduce quantity in inventory by amount ordered */
            part->quantity.total.number -= quantity->total.number;
        else {
```

Example D-3: Remote Procedures of the Inventory Application (continued)

```
        /* order all available and reduce quantity in inventory to 0 */
        quantity->total.number = part->quantity.total.number;
        part->quantity.total.number = 0;
      }
      break;
  case KILOGRAM:
  case GRAM:
    if(part->quantity.total.weight > quantity->total.weight)
        /* reduce quantity in inventory by amount ordered */
        part->quantity.total.weight -= quantity->total.weight;
    else {
        /* order all available and reduce quantity in inventory to 0.0 */
        quantity->total.weight = part->quantity.total.weight;
        part->quantity.total.weight = 0.0;
      }
      break;
  }

  write_part_record(part);    /* update inventory */

  return(1); /* order ok */
}
```

Example D-4: The Inventory Implementation

```
/* FILE NAME: invntry.c */
/* A sample implementation of an inventory.                            */
/* For simplicity, a few inventory items are maintained in the inventory.  */
/* The valid numbers are printed when the open_inventory() procedure is    */
/* called so the user knows what numbers to test.                     */
#include <stdio.h>
#include <stdlib.h>
#include "inv.h"
#define MAX_PARTS    10      /* maximum number of parts in this inventory */
#define MAX_SUBPARTS 5       /* maximum number of subparts for a part     */

static part_record *rec[MAX_PARTS]; /* array of pointers for this inventory */
static inventory_is_open = 0;        /* flag is reset to non-zero when open  */

/* Data for empty record or unknown part number */
static part_record no_part = {0,"UNKNOWN"};
static part_num    no_subparts[MAX_SUBPARTS];


void open_inventory()  /***** setup inventory ******************************/
{
  int i,j;
  unsigned size;

  /* Allocate memory for the inventory array.  Each part gets the size of  */
  /* a part_record plus enough memory for a subpart list.  Since the       */
  /* subpart list is already defined in the part_record as an array of 1,  */
  /* the new array memory only needs to be MAX_SUBPARTS-1 in size.         */
  for(i = 0; i < MAX_PARTS; i++) {
      size = sizeof(part_record) + (sizeof(part_num) * (MAX_SUBPARTS-1));
      rec[i] = (part_record *)malloc(size);
```

Example D-4: The Inventory Implementation (continued)

```
   }
   /* assign some data to the inventory array (part of an exercise machine) */
   rec[0]->number             = 102;
   strncpy((char *)rec[0]->name, "electronics display module", MAX_STRING);
   rec[0]->description = (paragraph)malloc(1000);
   strcpy((char *)rec[0]->description,
       "The electronics display module is a liquid crystal display containing\n\
a timer, counter, metronome, and calorie counter.");
   rec[0]->price.units        = ITEM;
   rec[0]->price.per_unit      = 7.00;
   rec[0]->quantity.units     = rec[0]->price.units;
   rec[0]->quantity.total.number = 432;
   rec[0]->subparts.size      = 4;  /* cannot be greater than MAX_SUBPARTS */
   for(i = 0; i < rec[0]->subparts.size; i++) /* values used are not relevant */
       rec[0]->subparts.numbers[i] = rec[0]->number + 1 + i;

   rec[1]->number             = 203;
   strncpy((char *)rec[1]->name, "base assembly", MAX_STRING);
   rec[1]->description = (paragraph)malloc(1000);
   strcpy((char *)rec[1]->description,
       "The base assembly rests on the floor to stabilize the machine.\n\
The arm and bench assemblies are attached to it.");
   rec[1]->price.units        = ITEM;
   rec[1]->price.per_unit      = 85.00;
   rec[1]->quantity.units     = rec[1]->price.units;
   rec[1]->quantity.total.number = 1078;
   rec[1]->subparts.size      = 5;  /* cannot be greater than MAX_SUBPARTS */
   for(i = 0; i < rec[1]->subparts.size; i++) /* values used are not relevant */
       rec[1]->subparts.numbers[i] = rec[1]->number + 17 + i;

   rec[2]->number             = 444;
   strncpy((char *)rec[2]->name, "ballast", MAX_STRING);
   rec[2]->description = (paragraph)malloc(1000);
   strcpy((char *)rec[2]->description,
       "The ballast is used to counterbalance the force exerted by the user.");
   rec[2]->price.units        = KILOGRAM;
   rec[2]->price.per_unit      = 1.59;
   rec[2]->quantity.units     = rec[2]->price.units;
   rec[2]->quantity.total.weight = 13456.2;
   rec[2]->subparts.size      = 0;  /* cannot be greater than MAX_SUBPARTS */
   for(i = 0; i < MAX_SUBPARTS; i++)  /* zero out subpart array */
       rec[2]->subparts.numbers[i] = no_subparts[i];

   /* fill in rest of inventory as "empty" data */
   for(i = 3; i < MAX_PARTS; i++) {
      rec[i] = &no_part;
      for(j = 0; j < MAX_SUBPARTS; j++)
         rec[i]->subparts.numbers[j] = no_subparts[j];
   }
   puts("Part numbers in inventory:");
   for(i = 0; i < MAX_PARTS; i++)
      if(rec[i]->number > 0)
         printf("%ld\n", rec[i]->number);
   inventory_is_open = 1;
```

Example D-4: The Inventory Implementation (continued)

```
    return;
}

void close_inventory()  /**** close inventory ******************************/
{
    /* Undo whatever is done in open_inventory.  Free memory and so forth.   */
    /* (not implemented) */
    return;
}


int read_part_record(number, part_ptr) /** get record for this part number **/
part_num number;
part_record **part_ptr;
{
    int i;

    if(inventory_is_open == 0)
        open_inventory();
    *part_ptr = &no_part;                       /* initialize assuming no part */
    for(i = 0; i < MAX_PARTS; i++)              /* search the inventory        */
        if(rec[i]->number == number) {         /* found the part              */
            *part_ptr = rec[i];
            break;
        }
    if( (*part_ptr)->number > 0)
        return(1);
    else                                        /* not a valid part           */
        return(0);
}


int write_part_record(part)  /*** update inventory for this part number *****/
part_record *part;
{
    int i;

    if(inventory_is_open == 0)
        open_inventory();
    for(i = 0; i < MAX_PARTS; i++)
        if(rec[i]->number == part->number) {
            rec[i] = part;   /* overwrite inventory with new data */
            return(1);
        }
    return(0);
}

/* dump the part data to the screen.
static dump_part_record(index)
int index;
{
    printf("number input:%ld  part number:%ld\n", number, rec[index]->number);
    printf("part name:%s\n", rec[index]->name);
    printf("description:%s\n", rec[index]->description);
    printf("price:%f per %s\n", rec[index]->price.per_unit,
```

Example D-4: The Inventory Implementation (continued)

```
            (rec[index]->price.units == ITEM) ? "item" : "gram");
    printf("quantity:");
    switch(rec[index]->quantity.units) {
    case ITEM: printf("%ld items\n", rec[index]->quantity.total.number); break;
    case GRAM: printf("%f grams\n", rec[index]->quantity.total.weight); break;
    case KILOGRAM: printf("%f kilos\n", rec[index]->quantity.total.weight);
            break;
    }
    printf("subparts: ");
    for(i = 0; i < rec[index]->subparts.size; i++)
        printf("%ld  ", rec[index]->subparts.numbers[i]);
    printf("\n");
}*/
```

Example D-5: Server Initialization of the Inventory Application

```
/* FILE NAME: server.c */
#include <stdio.h>
#include <stdlib.h>
#include <ctype.h>
#include "inv.h"                        /* header created by the IDL compiler   */
#include "status.h"                     /* contains the CHECK_STATUS macro       */
#define STRINGLEN 50

main (argc, argv)
int argc;
char *argv[];
{
    error_status_t          status;          /* error status                    */
                                             /* RPC vectors                     */
    rpc_binding_vector_t *binding_vector;    /* binding handle list             */
    RPC_PROTSEQ_VECTOR   *protseq_vector;    /*protocol sequence list           */

    char entry_name[STRINGLEN];              /* name service entry name         */
    char group_name[STRINGLEN];              /* name service group name         */
    char annotation[STRINGLEN];              /* annotation for endpoint map     */
    char hostname[STRINGLEN];                /* used to store the computer name */
    DWORD hostname_size=STRINGLEN;           /* required by GetComputerName      */
    /************************* REGISTER INTERFACE ************************/
    status =
    RpcServerRegisterIf(
        inv_v1_0_s_ifspec,               /* interface specification (inv.h) */
        NULL,
        NULL
    );
    CHECK_STATUS(status, "Can't register interface:", ABORT);

    /***************** CREATING SERVER BINDING INFORMATION *****************/
    if(argc > 1) {
        status =
        RpcServerUseProtseq(                       /* use a protocol sequence       */
            (unsigned char *)argv[1],              /* the input protocol sequence   */
            RPC_C_PROTSEQ_MAX_REQS_DEFAULT,        /* the default number of requests*/
            NULL                                   /* security descriptor (not reqd)*/
        );
```

Example D–5: Server Initialization of the Inventory Application (continued)

```
        CHECK_STATUS(status, "Can't use this protocol sequence:", ABORT);
    }
    else {
        puts("You can invoke the server with a protocol sequence argument.");
        status =
        RpcServerUseAllProtseqs(                 /* use all protocol sequences    */
            RPC_C_PROTSEQ_MAX_REQS_DEFAULT,  /* the default number of requests */
            NULL                             /* security descriptor (not reqd) */
        );
        CHECK_STATUS(status, "Can't register protocol sequences:", ABORT);
    }

    status =
    RpcServerInqBindings(           /* get binding information for server    */
        &binding_vector
    );
    CHECK_STATUS(status, "Can't get binding information:", ABORT);

    /*************************** ADVERTISE SERVER ***************************/

    strcpy(entry_name, "/.:/inventory_");
    GetComputerName(&hostname, &hostname_size);
    strcat(entry_name, hostname);
    status =
    RpcNsBindingExport(             /* export to a name service database     */
        RPC_C_NS_SYNTAX_DEFAULT,    /* syntax of entry name                  */
        (unsigned char *)entry_name, /* name of entry in name service        */
        inv_v1_0_s_ifspec,          /* interface specification (inv.h)       */
        binding_vector,             /* binding information                   */
        NULL                        /* no object UUIDs exported              */
    );
    CHECK_STATUS(status, "Can't export to name service database:", RESUME);

    /*************************** MANAGE ENDPOINTS ***************************/
    strcpy(annotation, "Inventory interface");
    status =
    RpcEpRegister(                  /* add endpoints to local endpoint map   */
        inv_v1_0_s_ifspec,          /* interface specification (inv.h)       */
        binding_vector,             /* vector of server binding handles      */
        NULL,                       /* no object UUIDs to register           */
        (unsigned char *)annotation /* annotation supplied (not required)    */
    );
    CHECK_STATUS(status, "Can't add endpoints to local endpoint map:", RESUME);

    status =
    RpcBindingVectorFree(                    /* free server binding handles   */
        &binding_vector
    );
    CHECK_STATUS(status, "Can't free server binding handles:", RESUME);

    open_inventory();                        /* application specific procedure */

    /****************** LISTEN FOR REMOTE PROCEDURE CALLS ******************/
    RpcTryExcept                    /* thread exception handling macro       */
    {
```

Example D-5: Server Initialization of the Inventory Application (continued)

```
        status =
        RpcServerListen(
            1,                      /* process one remote procedure call at a time */
            RPC_C_LISTEN_MAX_CALLS_DEFAULT,
            NULL
        );
        CHECK_STATUS(status, "rpc listen failed:", RESUME);
    }
    RpcExcept (RpcExceptionCode())                  /* error recovery and cleanup */
    {
        close_inventory();                      /* application specific procedure */
        status =
        RpcServerInqBindings(                       /* get binding information   */
            &binding_vector
        );
        CHECK_STATUS(status, "Can't get binding information:", RESUME);

        status =
        RpcEpUnregister(        /* remove endpoints from local endpoint map  */
            inv_v1_0_s_ifspec,  /* interface specification (inv.h)           */
            binding_vector,     /* vector of server binding handles          */
            NULL                /* no object UUIDs                           */
        );
        CHECK_STATUS(status, "Can't remove endpoints from endpoint map:", RESUME);

        status =
        RpcBindingVectorFree(                       /* free server binding handles  */
            &binding_vector
        );
        CHECK_STATUS(status, "Can't free server binding handles:", RESUME);

        puts("\nServer quit!");
    }
    RpcEndExcept;
} /* END SERVER INITIALIZATION */
/*************************************************************************/
/***              MIDL_user_allocate / MIDL_user_free             ***/
/*************************************************************************/

void * __RPC_API
MIDL_user_allocate
            (
             size
             )
size_t size;
{
    unsigned char * ptr;
    ptr = malloc( size );
    return ( (void *)ptr );

}

void __RPC_API
MIDL_user_free
```

Example D–5: Server Initialization of the Inventory Application (continued)

```
            (
             object
            )
void * object;
{
    free (object);
}
```

Example D–6: The Automatic Client File of the Inventory Application

```
/* FILE NAME: client.c */
/******************** Client of the inventory application ********************/
#include <stdio.h>
#include <stdlib.h>
#include "inv.h"                  /* header file created by the IDL compiler */

char instructions[] = "Type character followed by appropriate argument(s).\n\
    Is part available?              a  [part_number]\n\
    What is part name?              n  [part_number]\n\
    Get part description.           d  [part_number]\n\
    What is part price?             p  [part_number]\n\
    What is part quantity?          q  [part_number]\n\
    What are subparts of this part? s  [part_number]\n\
    Order part.                     o  part_number  quantity\n\
    REDISPLAY                       r\n\
    EXIT                            e\n";

main()
{
    part_record part;            /* structure for all data about a part  */
    part_list   *subparts;       /* pointer to parts list data structure */
    account_num account = 1234;  /* a user account number                */

    int i, num_args, done = 0;
    long result;
    char input[100], selection[20], quantity[20];

    puts(instructions);
    part.number = 0;
    strcpy(quantity, "");
    while(!done) {               /* user makes selections and each is processed */
       printf("Selection: "); fflush(stdout); gets(input);
       num_args = sscanf(input, "%s%ld%s", selection, &(part.number), quantity);

       switch (tolower(selection[0])) {
       case 'a': if (is_part_available(part.number))
                    puts("available: Yes");
                 else
                    puts("available: No");
                 break;
       case 'n': whatis_part_name(part.number, part.name);
                 printf("name:%s\n", part.name);
                 break;
       case 'd': part.description = get_part_description(part.number);
                 printf("description:\n%s\n", part.description);
```

Example D-6: The Automatic Client File of the Inventory Application (continued)

```
                    if(part.description != NULL)
                        free(part.description);      /* free memory allocated */
                    break;
        case 'p': whatis_part_price(part.number, &(part.price));
                    printf("price:%10.2f\n", part.price.per_unit);
                    break;
        case 'q': whatis_part_quantity(part.number, &(part.quantity));
                    if(part.quantity.units == ITEM)
                        printf("total items:%ld\n", part.quantity.total.number);
                    else if(part.quantity.units == GRAM)
                        printf("total grams:%10.2f\n", part.quantity.total.weight);
                    else if(part.quantity.units == KILOGRAM)
                        printf("total kilos:%10.2f\n", part.quantity.total.weight);
                    break;
        case 's': whatare_subparts(part.number, &subparts);
                    for(i = 0; i < subparts->size; i++)
                        printf("%ld  ", subparts->numbers[i]);
                    printf("\ntotal number of subparts:%ld\n", subparts->size);
                    free(subparts);         /* free memory for conformant struct */
                    break;
        case 'o': if(num_args < 3) {
                        puts("Not enough arguments");
                        break;
                    }
                    /* Assume KILOGRAM units and assign quantity input */
                    part.quantity.units = KILOGRAM;
                    part.quantity.total.weight = atof(quantity);
                    result = order_part(part.number, &(part.quantity), account);
                    if(result > 0) {
                      if(part.quantity.units == ITEM)
                        printf("order:%ld items\n", part.quantity.total.number);
                      else if(part.quantity.units == GRAM)
                        printf("order:%10.2f grams\n", part.quantity.total.weight);
                      else if(part.quantity.units == KILOGRAM)
                        printf("order:%10.2f kilos\n", part.quantity.total.weight);
                    }
                    else { /* error cases */
                        if(result == -1) puts("Invalid part number");
                        else if(result == -2) puts("Invalid quantity");
                        else if(result == -3) puts("Invalid account number");
                    }
                    break;
        case 'r':   /* redisplay selection or bad input displays instructions */
        default: puts(instructions);  break;
        case 'e': done = 1;  break;
        } /*end case */
    } /* end while */
} /* end main() */

/*************************************************************************/
/***                MIDL_user_allocate / MIDL_user_free             ***/
/*************************************************************************/
```

Example D-6: The Automatic Client File of the Inventory Application (continued)

```
void * __RPC_API
MIDL_user_allocate
            (
             size
            )
size_t size;
{

    unsigned char * ptr;
    ptr = malloc( size );
    return ( (void *)ptr );

}

void __RPC_API
MIDL_user_free
            (
             object
            )
void * object;
{
    free (object);
}
```

Example D-7: The Makefile for the Implicit Client

```
# FILE NAME: Makefile
# Makefile for the inventory application implicit client
#
# definitions for this make file
#
APPL=inv
IDLCMD=midl
NTRPCLIBS=rpcrt4.lib rpcns4.lib libcmt.lib kernel32.lib

!include <ntwin32.mak>


## NT c flags
cflags = -c -W0 -Gz -D_X86_=1 -DWIN32 -DMT /I. /I.. /nologo

## NT nmake inference rules
   $(cc) $(cdebug) $(cflags) $(cvarsmt) $<
   $(cvtomf)

#
# COMPLETE BUILD of the application
#
all:    lclient.exe interface client.exe

#
# INTERFACE BUILD
#
interface: $(APPL).h $(APPL)_c.obj

#
# LOCAL BUILD of the client application to test locally
```

Example D-7: The Makefile for the Implicit Client (continued)

```
#
local:      lclient.exe
lclient.exe: lclient.obj lmanager.obj invntry.obj
    $(link) $(linkdebug) $(conflags) -out:lclient.exe -map:lclient.map \
      lclient.obj lmanager.obj invntry.obj \
      $(NTRPCLIBS)

#
# CLIENT BUILD
#
client:     client.exe
client.exe: client.obj getbind.obj intbind.obj $(APPL)_c.obj
    $(link) $(linkdebug) $(conflags) -out:client.exe -map:client.map \
      client.obj getbind.obj intbind.obj $(APPL)_c.obj  \
      $(NTRPCLIBS)


# client and server sources
client.obj:  client.c     $(APPL).h
getbind.obj: getbind.c
intbind.obj: intbind.c

# Local client sources
invntry.obj: ..\invntry.c
              $(cc) $(cdebug) $(cflags) $(cvarsmt) /DLOCAL /I. /I.. \
                  /Foinvntry.obj ..\invntry.c
lclient.obj: client.c $(APPL).h
              $(cc) $(cdebug) $(cflags) $(cvarsmt) /DLOCAL /I. /I.. \
                  /Folclient.obj client.c
lmanager.obj: ..\manager.c $(APPL).h
              $(cc) $(cdebug) $(cflags) $(cvarsmt) /DLOCAL /I. /I.. \
                  /Folmanager.obj ..\manager.c

# client stubs
$(APPL)_c.obj: $(APPL)_c.c
$(APPL)_x.obj: $(APPL)_x.c

# generate stubs, auxiliary and header file from the IDL file
$(APPL).h $(APPL)_i.acf $(APPL)_c.c $(APPL)_x.c : ..\$(APPL).idl
    $(IDLCMD) ..\$(APPL).idl /acf $(APPL)_i.acf

# clean up for fresh build
clean:
    del $(APPL)_?.c
    del *.obj
    del $(APPL).h
    del *.map
    del *.pdb


clobber: clean
    if exist client.exe  del client.exe
    if exist lclient.exe del lclient.exe
    if exist server.exe  del server.exe
```

Example D–8: An ACF File for Implicit Binding

```
/* FILE NAME: inventory.acf (implicit version)*/
/* This Attribute Configuration File is used in conjunction with the      */
/* associated .idl file (inventory.idl) when the IDL compiler is invoked. */
[
implicit_handle(handle_t global_binding_h)  /* implicit binding method */
]
interface  inv          /* The interface name must match the .idl file. */
{
}
```

Example D–9: The Implicit Client of the Inventory Application

```
/* FILE NAME: client.c */
/******* Client of the inventory application with implicit method ***********/
#include <stdio.h>
#include <stdlib.h>
#include "inv.h"                /* header file created by the IDL compiler */
#include "..\status.h"

char instructions[] = "Type character followed by appropriate argument(s).\n\
    Is part available?              a  [part_number]\n\
    What is part name?              n  [part_number]\n\
    Get part description.           d  [part_number]\n\
    What is part price?             p  [part_number]\n\
    What is part quantity?          q  [part_number]\n\
    What are subparts of this part? s  [part_number]\n\
    Order part.                     o  part_number  quantity\n\
    REDISPLAY                       r\n\
    EXIT                            e\n";

main()
{
    part_record part;           /* structure for all data about a part   */
    part_list   *subparts;      /* pointer to parts list data structure  */
    account_num account = 1234; /* a user account number                 */
    unsigned long   status;        /* error status                       */

    int i, num_args, done = 0;
    long result;
    char input[100], selection[20], quantity[20];

    puts(instructions);
    part.number = 0;
    strcpy(quantity, "");

#ifndef LOCAL                       /* find server in name service database */
    do_import_binding("", &global_binding_h);
#endif

    status = RpcBindingReset(global_binding_h);
    CHECK_STATUS(status, "Can't reset binding handle", ABORT);

    while(!done) {              /* user makes selections and each is processed */
        printf("Selection: "); fflush(stdout);  gets(input);
        num_args = sscanf(input, "%s%ld%s", selection, &(part.number), quantity);

        switch (tolower(selection[0])) {
```

Example D-9: The Implicit Client of the Inventory Application (continued)

```
case 'a': if (is_part_available(part.number))
              puts("available: Yes");
          else
              puts("available: No");
          break;
case 'n': whatis_part_name(part.number, part.name);
          printf("name:%s\n", part.name);
          break;
case 'd': part.description = get_part_description(part.number);
          printf("description:\n%s\n", part.description);
          if(part.description != NULL)
              free(part.description);       /* free memory allocated */
          break;
case 'p': whatis_part_price(part.number, &(part.price));
          printf("price:%10.2f\n", part.price.per_unit);
          break;
case 'q': whatis_part_quantity(part.number, &(part.quantity));
          if(part.quantity.units == ITEM)
              printf("total items:%ld\n", part.quantity.total.number);
          else if(part.quantity.units == GRAM)
              printf("total grams:%10.2f\n", part.quantity.total.weight);
          else if(part.quantity.units == KILOGRAM)
              printf("total kilos:%10.2f\n", part.quantity.total.weight);
          break;
case 's': whatare_subparts(part.number, &subparts);
          for(i = 0; i < subparts->size; i++)
              printf("%ld  ", subparts->numbers[i]);
          printf("\ntotal number of subparts:%ld\n", subparts->size);
          free(subparts);          /* free memory for conformant struct */
          break;
case 'o': if(num_args < 3) {
              puts("Not enough arguments");
              break;
          }
          /* Assume KILOGRAM units and assign quantity input */
          part.quantity.units = KILOGRAM;
          part.quantity.total.weight = atof(quantity);
          result = order_part(part.number, &(part.quantity), account);
          if(result > 0) {
            if(part.quantity.units == ITEM)
              printf("order:%ld items\n", part.quantity.total.number);
            else if(part.quantity.units == GRAM)
              printf("order:%10.2f grams\n", part.quantity.total.weight);
            else if(part.quantity.units == KILOGRAM)
              printf("order:%10.2f kilos\n", part.quantity.total.weight);
          }
          else { /* error cases */
            if(result == -1) puts("Invalid part number");
            else if(result == -2) puts("Invalid quantity");
            else if(result == -3) puts("Invalid account number");
          }
          break;
case 'r':  /* redisplay selection or bad input displays instructions */
```

Example D-9: The Implicit Client of the Inventory Application (continued)

```
        default:  puts(instructions);  break;
        case 'e': done = 1;  break;
        } /*end case */
    } /* end while */
} /* end main() */
/***********************************************************************/
/***             MIDL_user_allocate / MIDL_user_free             ***/
/***********************************************************************/

void * __RPC_API
MIDL_user_allocate
        (
          size
          )
size_t size;
{

    unsigned char * ptr;
    ptr = malloc( size );
    return ( (void *)ptr );

}

void __RPC_API
MIDL_user_free
          (
            object
            )
void * object;
{
    free (object);
}
```

Example D-10: The do_import_binding Procedure

```
/* FILE NAME: getbind.c */
/* Get binding from name service database. */
#include <stdio.h>
#include "inv.h"
#include "..\status.h"

void do_import_binding(entry_name, binding_h)
char                entry_name[];        /* entry name to begin search   */
rpc_binding_handle_t *binding_h;          /* a binding handle             */
{
    unsigned long   status;              /* error status                 */
    RPC_NS_HANDLE   import_context;      /* required to import           */
    char            protseq[20];         /* protocol sequence            */

    status =
    RpcNsBindingImportBegin(        /* set context to import binding handles */
      RPC_C_NS_SYNTAX_DEFAULT,          /* use default syntax           */
      (unsigned char *)entry_name,      /* begin search with this name  */
      inv_v1_0_c_ifspec,               /* interface specification (inv.h) */
      NULL,                            /* no optional object UUID required */
```

Example D-10: The do_import_binding Procedure (continued)

```
        &import_context                 /* import context obtained          */
    );
    CHECK_STATUS(status, "Can't begin import:", RESUME);

    while(1) {
        status =
        RpcNsBindingImportNext(                 /* import a binding handle   */
            import_context,       /* context from rpc_ns_binding_import_begin */
            binding_h                 /* a binding handle is obtained        */
        );
        if(status != RPC_S_OK) {
            CHECK_STATUS(status, "Can't import a binding handle:", RESUME);
            break;
        }

        /** application specific selection criteria (by protocol sequence) *  */
        do_interpret_binding(*binding_h ,protseq);
        if(strcmp(protseq, "ncacn_ip_tcp") == 0)  /*select connection protocol*/
            break;
        else {
            status =
            RpcBindingFree(         /* free binding information not selected   */
                binding_h
            );
            CHECK_STATUS(status, "Can't free binding information:", RESUME);
        }
    } /*end while */

    status =
    RpcNsBindingImportDone(                     /* done with import context   */
        &import_context             /* obtained from rpc_ns_binding_import_begin */
    );
    return;
}
```

Example D-11: The do_interpret_binding Procedure

```
/* FILE NAME: intbind.c */
/* Interpret binding information and return the protocol sequence. */
#include <stdio.h>
#include <rpc.h>
#include "..\status.h"

void do_interpret_binding(binding, protocol_seq)
rpc_binding_handle_t binding;    /* binding handle to interpret          */
char                *protocol_seq;    /* protocol sequence to obtain     */
{
    unsigned long   status;             /* error status                   */
    unsigned char   *string_binding;    /* string of binding information   */
    unsigned char   *protseq;           /* binding component of interest   */

    status =
    RpcBindingToStringBinding(      /* convert binding information to string  */
        binding,                            /* the binding handle to convert */
        &string_binding                     /* the string of binding data    */
```

Example D-11: The do_interpret_binding Procedure (continued)

```
    );
    CHECK_STATUS(status, "Can't get string binding:", RESUME);

    status =
    RpcStringBindingParse(           /* get components of string binding  */
        string_binding,        /* the string of binding data            */
        NULL,                  /* an object UUID string is not obtained  */
        &protseq,              /* a protocol sequence string IS obtained */
        NULL,                  /* a network address string is not obtained */
        NULL,                  /* an endpoint string is not obtained     */
        NULL                   /* a network options string is not obtained */
    );
    CHECK_STATUS(status, "Can't parse string binding:", RESUME);

    strcpy(protocol_seq, (char *)protseq);

    /* free all strings allocated by other runtime routines       */
    status = RpcStringFree(&string_binding);
    status = RpcStringFree(&protseq        );
    return;
}
```

Example D-12: The Makefile for the Explicit Client

```
# FILE NAME: Makefile
# Makefile for the inventory application explicit client
#
# definitions for this make file
#
APPL=inv
IDLCMD=midl
NTRPCLIBS=rpcrt4.lib rpcns4.lib libcmt.lib kernel32.lib

!include <ntwin32.mak>


## NT c flags
cflags = -c -W0 -Gz -D_X86_=1 -DWIN32 -DMT /nologo

## NT nmake inference rules
    $(cc) $(cdebug) $(cflags) $(cvarsmt) /I. /I.. $<
    $(cvtomf)


#
# COMPLETE BUILD of the application
#
all:    local interface client server

#
# INTERFACE BUILD
#
interface: $(APPL).h $(APPL)_c.obj $(APPL)_s.obj $(APPL)_x.obj

#
# LOCAL BUILD of the client application to test locally
#
local:      lclient.exe
```

Example D-12: The Makefile for the Explicit Client (continued)

```
lclient.exe: lclient.obj manager.obj invntry.obj
    $(link) $(linkdebug) $(conflags) -out:lclient.exe -map:lclient.map \
        lclient.obj manager.obj invntry.obj \
        $(NTRPCLIBS)

#
# CLIENT BUILD
#
client:     client.exe
client.exe: client.obj getbind.obj intbind.obj $(APPL)_c.obj $(APPL)_x.obj
    $(link) $(linkdebug) $(conflags) -out:client.exe -map:client.map \
        client.obj getbind.obj intbind.obj $(APPL)_c.obj $(APPL)_x.obj \
        $(NTRPCLIBS)

#
# SERVER BUILD
#
server:     server.exe
server.exe: server.obj manager.obj invntry.obj $(APPL)_s.obj $(APPL)_x.obj
    $(link) $(linkdebug) $(conflags) -out:server.exe -map:server.map \
        server.obj manager.obj invntry.obj $(APPL)_s.obj $(APPL)_x.obj\
        $(NTRPCLIBS)


# client and server sources
client.obj:  client.c $(APPL).h
manager.obj: manager.c $(APPL).h
server.obj: ..\server.c $(APPL).h
            $(cc) $(cdebug) $(cflags) $(cvarsmt) /I. /I.. \
                /Foserver.obj ..\server.c
getbind.obj: ..\implicit\getbind.c
            $(cc) $(cdebug) $(cflags) $(cvarsmt) /I. /I.. \
                /Fogetbind.obj ..\implicit\getbind.c
intbind.obj: ..\implicit\intbind.c
            $(cc) $(cdebug) $(cflags) $(cvarsmt) /I. /I.. \
                /Fointbind.obj ..\implicit\intbind.c
invntry.obj: ..\invntry.c
            $(cc) $(cdebug) $(cflags) $(cvarsmt) /I. /I.. \
                /Foinvntry.obj ..\invntry.c

# Local client sources
lclient.obj: client.c $(APPL).h
            $(cc) $(cdebug) $(cflags) $(cvarsmt) /DLOCAL /I. /I.. \
                /Folclient.obj client.c

# client stubs
$(APPL)_c.obj: $(APPL)_c.c
$(APPL)_x.obj: $(APPL)_x.c

# compile the server stub
$(APPL)_s.obj : $(APPL)_s.c

# generate stubs, auxiliary and header file from the IDL file
$(APPL).h $(APPL)_c.c $(APPL)_x.c $(APPL)_s.c: $(APPL).idl
    $(IDLCMD) $(APPL).idl
```

Example D–12: The Makefile for the Explicit Client (continued)

```
# clean up for fresh build
clean:
    del $(APPL)_?.c
    del *.obj
    del $(APPL).h
    del *.map
    del *.pdb

clobber: clean
    if exist client.exe  del client.exe
    if exist lclient.exe del lclient.exe
    if exist server.exe  del server.exe
```

Example D–13: The MIDL File, Explicit Binding

```
/* FILE NAME: inv.idl */
[                                          /* brackets enclose attributes */
uuid(cbb7c850-0568-11ce-b719-08002b185ad7), /* universal unique identifier */
version(1.0),                              /* version of this interface   */
pointer_default(unique)                    /* pointer default             */
] interface  inv                           /* interface name              */
{
    const long MAX_STRING = 30;                 /* constant for string size  */

    typedef long     part_num;                    /* inventory part number   */

    typedef [string] char part_name[MAX_STRING+1];      /* name of part  */

    typedef [string, unique] char *paragraph;      /* description of part  */

    typedef enum {
        ITEM, GRAM, KILOGRAM
    } part_units;                            /* units of measurement    */

    typedef struct part_price {                         /* price of part  */
        part_units units;
        double     per_unit;
    } part_price;

    typedef union switch(part_units units) total {    /* quantity of part  */
        case ITEM:     long int number;
        case GRAM:
        case KILOGRAM: double   weight;
    } part_quantity;

    typedef struct part_list{                   /* list of part numbers   */
        long                     size;        /* number of parts in array  */
        [size_is(size)] part_num numbers[*];   /* conformant array of parts */
    } part_list;

    typedef struct part_record {                      /* data for each part */
        part_num       number;
        part_name      name;
        paragraph      description;
        part_price     price;
        part_quantity quantity;
```

Example D-13: The MIDL File, Explicit Binding (continued)

```
      part_list      subparts;
   } part_record;

   typedef long account_num;                          /* user account number */

   /*********************** Procedure Declarations ***********************/
   boolean is_part_available(        /* return true if in inventory    */
      [in] handle_t binding_h,     /* binding handle for explicit client */
      [in] part_num number              /* input part number */
   );

   void whatis_part_name(            /* get part name from inventory    */
      [in]  handle_t  binding_h,   /* binding handle for explicit client */
      [in]  part_num  number,          /* input part number */
      [in, out] part_name name          /* output part name   */
   );

   paragraph get_part_description(    /* return a pointer to a string    */
      [in]  handle_t  binding_h,   /* binding handle for explicit client */
      [in]  part_num  number
   );

   void whatis_part_price(           /* get part price from inventory   */
      [in]  handle_t   binding_h,  /* binding handle for explicit client */
      [in]  part_num   number,
      [out] part_price *price
   );

   void whatis_part_quantity(        /* get part quantity from inventory */
      [in]  handle_t      binding_h, /* binding handle for explicit client */
      [in]  part_num      number,
      [out] part_quantity *quantity
   );

   void whatare_subparts(            /* get list of subpart numbers     */
      [in]  handle_t  binding_h,   /* binding handle for explicit client */
      [in]  part_num  number,
      [out] part_list **subparts       /* structure containing the array  */
   );

   /* Order part from inventory with part number, quantity desired, and   */
   /* account number.  If inventory does not have enough, output lesser    */
   /* quantity ordered.  Return values:  1=ordered OK,                     */
   /* -1=invalid part, -2=invalid quantity, -3=invalid account.            */

   long order_part(   /* order part from inventory, return OK or error code */
      [in]      handle_t   binding_h, /* binding handle for explicit client */
      [in]      part_num       number,
      [in,out] part_quantity *quantity,              /* quantity ordered    */
      [in]      account_num   account
   );
} /* end of interface definition */
```

Example D-14: Remote Procedures, Explicit Binding

```
/* FILE NAME: manager.c */
/** Implementation of the remote procedures for the inventory application. **/
#include <stdio.h>
#include <stdlib.h>
#include "inv.h"

boolean is_part_available(binding_h, number)
handle_t binding_h;                        /* declare a binding handle */
part_num number;
{
   part_record *part;                      /* a pointer to a part record */
   int found;

   found = read_part_record(number, &part);
   if(found)
      return(TRUE);
   else
      return(FALSE);
}


void whatis_part_name(binding_h, number, name)
handle_t  binding_h;                       /* declare a binding handle */
part_num  number;
part_name name;
{
   part_record *part;                      /* a pointer to a part record */

   read_part_record(number, &part);
   strncpy((char *)name, (char *)part->name, MAX_STRING);
   return;
}


paragraph get_part_description(binding_h, number)
handle_t  binding_h;                       /* declare a binding handle */
part_num  number;
{
   part_record *part;                      /* a pointer to a part record */
   paragraph description;
   int size;

   if( read_part_record(number, &part) ) {
      /* Allocated data that is returned to the client must be allocated */
      /* with the MIDL_user_allocate stub support routine.              */
      size = strlen((char *)part->description) + 1;
      description = (paragraph)MIDL_user_allocate((unsigned)size);
      strcpy((char *)description, (char *)part->description);
   }
   else
      description = NULL;
   return(description);
}


void whatis_part_price(binding_h, number, price)
handle_t   binding_h;                       /* declare a binding handle */
```

Example D-14: Remote Procedures, Explicit Binding (continued)

```
part_num    number;
part_price  *price;
{
    part_record *part;                      /* a pointer to a part record */

    read_part_record(number, &part);
    price->units = part->price.units;
    price->per_unit = part->price.per_unit;
    return;
}


void whatis_part_quantity(binding_h, number, quantity)
handle_t        binding_h;                  /* declare a binding handle */
part_num        number;
part_quantity *quantity;
{
    part_record *part;                      /* a pointer to a part record */

    read_part_record(number, &part);
    quantity->units = part->quantity.units;
    switch(quantity->units) {
        case ITEM: quantity->total.number = part->quantity.total.number;
                break;
        case KILOGRAM:
        case GRAM: quantity->total.weight = part->quantity.total.weight;
                break;
    }
    return;
}


void whatare_subparts(binding_h, number, subpart_ptr)
handle_t  binding_h;                        /* declare a binding handle */
part_num  number;
part_list **subpart_ptr;
{
    part_record *part;                      /* pointer to a part record */
    int i;
    int size;

    read_part_record(number, &part);

    /* Allocated data that is output to the client must be allocated with   */
    /* the MIDL_user_allocate stub support routine.  Allocate for a         */
    /* part_list struct plus the array of subpart numbers. Remember the     */
    /* part_list struct already has an array with one element, hence the -1. */
    size = sizeof(part_list) + (sizeof(part_num) * (part->subparts.size-1));
    *subpart_ptr = (part_list *)MIDL_user_allocate((unsigned)size);

    /* fill in the values */
    (*subpart_ptr)->size = part->subparts.size;
    for(i = 0; i < (*subpart_ptr)->size; i++)
        (*subpart_ptr)->numbers[i] = part->subparts.numbers[i];
    return;
}
```

Example D-14: Remote Procedures, Explicit Binding (continued)

```
long int order_part(binding_h, number, quantity, account)
handle_t        binding_h;        /* declare a binding handle */
part_num        number;
part_quantity   *quantity;
account_num     account;
{
   part_record *part;             /* pointer to a part record */

   long error = 1;  /* assume no error to start */
   /* Test for valid input */
   if( !read_part_record(number, &part) ) /* invalid part number input */
      error = -1;
   else if(quantity->units == ITEM)        /* invalid quantity input    */
      error = (quantity->total.number <= 0) ? -2 : error;
   else if(quantity->units == GRAM || quantity->units == KILOGRAM)
      error = (quantity->total.weight <= 0.0) ? -2 : error;
   /* else if()    invalid account, not implemented */
   /*      error = -3;                             */
   if(error < 0)
      return(error);

   /* convert input quantity & units if units are not correct for part */
   if(quantity->units != part->quantity.units) {
      if(part->quantity.units == ITEM)      /* convert weight to items   */
         quantity->total.number = (long int)quantity->total.weight;
      else if(quantity->units == ITEM)       /* convert items to weight   */
         quantity->total.weight = (long float)quantity->total.number;
      else if(quantity->units == GRAM && part->quantity.units == KILOGRAM)
         quantity->total.weight /= 1000.0; /* convert grams to kilograms */
      else if(quantity->units == KILOGRAM && part->quantity.units == GRAM)
         quantity->total.weight *= 1000.0; /* convert kilograms to grams */
      quantity->units = part->quantity.units;
   }

   /* check if enough in inventory for this order */
   switch(part->quantity.units) {
   case ITEM:
      if(part->quantity.total.number > quantity->total.number)
         /* reduce quantity in inventory by amount ordered */
         part->quantity.total.number -= quantity->total.number;
      else {
         /* order all available and reduce quantity in inventory to 0 */
         quantity->total.number = part->quantity.total.number;
         part->quantity.total.number = 0;
      }
      break;
   case KILOGRAM:
   case GRAM:
      if(part->quantity.total.weight > quantity->total.weight)
         /* reduce quantity in inventory by amount ordered */
         part->quantity.total.weight -= quantity->total.weight;
      else {
         /* order all available and reduce quantity in inventory to 0.0 */
         quantity->total.weight = part->quantity.total.weight;
```

Example D–14: Remote Procedures, Explicit Binding (continued)

```
            part->quantity.total.weight = 0.0;
        }
        break;
    }

    write_part_record(part);      /* update inventory */

    return(1); /* order ok */
}
```

Example D–15: The Explicit Client of the Inventory Application

```
/* FILE NAME: client.c */
/******* Client of the inventory application with explicit method ***********/
#include <stdio.h>
#include <stdlib.h>
#include "inv.h"                    /* header file created by the IDL compiler */
#include "status.h"

char instructions[] = "Type character followed by appropriate argument(s).\n\
    Is part available?            a  [part_number]\n\
    What is part name?            n  [part_number]\n\
    Get part description.         d  [part_number]\n\
    What is part price?           p  [part_number]\n\
    What is part quantity?        q  [part_number]\n\
    What are subparts of this part? s  [part_number]\n\
    Order part.                   o  part_number  quantity\n\
    REDISPLAY                     r\n\
    EXIT                          e\n";

main()
{
    part_record part;              /* structure for all data about a part   */
    part_list   *subparts;         /* pointer to parts list data structure */
    account_num account = 1234;    /* a user account number                */
    unsigned long   status;            /* error status                     */

    handle_t    binding_h;         /* declare a binding handle */

    int i, num_args, done = 0;
    long result;
    char input[100], selection[20], quantity[20];

    puts(instructions);
    part.number = 0;
    strcpy(quantity, "");

#ifndef LOCAL                           /* find server in name service database */
    do_import_binding("", &binding_h);
#endif

    status = RpcBindingReset(binding_h);
    CHECK_STATUS(status, "Can't reset binding handle", ABORT);

    while(!done) {               /* user makes selections and each is processed */
      printf("Selection: ");  fflush(stdout);  gets(input);
```

```
num_args = sscanf(input, "%s%ld%s", selection, &(part.number), quantity);

switch (tolower(selection[0])) {
case 'a': if (is_part_available(binding_h, part.number))
              puts("available: Yes");
          else
              puts("available: No");
          break;
case 'n': whatis_part_name(binding_h, part.number, part.name);
          printf("name:%s\n", part.name);
          break;
case 'd': part.description =
              get_part_description(binding_h, part.number);
          printf("description:\n%s\n", part.description);
          if(part.description != NULL)
              free(part.description);       /* free memory allocated */
          break;
case 'p': whatis_part_price(binding_h, part.number, &(part.price));
          printf("price:%10.2f\n", part.price.per_unit);
          break;
case 'q': whatis_part_quantity(binding_h, part.number, &(part.quantity));
          if(part.quantity.units == ITEM)
              printf("total items:%ld\n", part.quantity.total.number);
          else if(part.quantity.units == GRAM)
              printf("total grams:%10.2f\n", part.quantity.total.weight);
          else if(part.quantity.units == KILOGRAM)
              printf("total kilos:%10.2f\n", part.quantity.total.weight);
          break;
case 's': whatare_subparts(binding_h, part.number, &subparts);
          for(i = 0; i < subparts->size; i++)
              printf("%ld  ", subparts->numbers[i]);
          printf("\ntotal number of subparts:%ld\n", subparts->size);
          free(subparts);          /* free memory for conformant struct */
          break;
case 'o': if(num_args < 3) {
              puts("Not enough arguments");
              break;
          }
          /* Assume KILOGRAM units and assign quantity input */
          part.quantity.units = KILOGRAM;
          part.quantity.total.weight = atof(quantity);
          result =
            order_part(binding_h, part.number, &(part.quantity), account);
          if(result > 0) {
            if(part.quantity.units == ITEM)
              printf("order:%ld items\n", part.quantity.total.number);
            else if(part.quantity.units == GRAM)
              printf("order:%10.2f grams\n", part.quantity.total.weight);
            else if(part.quantity.units == KILOGRAM)
              printf("order:%10.2f kilos\n", part.quantity.total.weight);
          }
          else { /* error cases */
            if(result == -1) puts("Invalid part number");
```

Example D-15: The Explicit Client of the Inventory Application (continued)

```
                    else if(result == -2) puts("Invalid quantity");
                    else if(result == -3) puts("Invalid account number");
                }
                break;
        case 'r':   /* redisplay selection or bad input displays instructions */
        default:  puts(instructions);  break;
        case 'e': done = 1;  break;
        } /*end case */
    } /* end while */
} /* end main() */

/**********************************************************************/
/***              MIDL_user_allocate / MIDL_user_free           ***/
/**********************************************************************/

void * __RPC_API
MIDL_user_allocate
            (
            size
            )
size_t size;
{

    unsigned char * ptr;
    ptr = malloc( size );
    return ( (void *)ptr );

}

void __RPC_API
MIDL_user_free
            (
            object
            )
void * object;
{
    free (object);
}
```

The Rfile Application

The remote file client (*rfile.c*) copies ASCII data from the client to the server. The source can be a data file or the standard input of the client. The target on the server system is either a file or the server standard output. The `rfile` application demonstrates some advanced features of RPC application development including:

- Using a context handle with a context rundown procedure.

- Using the explicit binding method with a primitive binding handle.

- Finding a server using strings of binding information.

How to Run the Application

To run the server of the distributed application, type the following:

```
C:\SERVER> nmake server
C:\SERVER> server
```

To run the client of the distributed application to transfer ASCII data, use an ASCII text file as input and a new data file on the server host as output. Type the following:

```
C:\CLIENT> nmake client
C:\CLIENT> client input_file  host  output_file
```

You can also send ASCII data from the client keyboard (*stdin*) by using the following client command:

```
C:\CLIENT> client ""  host  output_file
Using stdin.  Type input:
data
data
```

Application Files

Makefile contains descriptions of how the application is compiled. Some files depend on the header file *status.h* from the arithmetic application for the CHECK_STATUS macro. See Example E-1.

rfile.idl contains descriptions of the data types and procedures for the interface. See Example E-2.

client.c interprets the user input by calling the application-specific procedure *get_args*. A binding handle representing the information about a client-server relationship is obtained from strings of binding information. The remote procedure *remote_open* is called to open the server target file. A buffer is allocated for a conformant array. The application loops, reading source data and sending the data to the target with a remote procedure call to *remote_send*. Finally, the remote procedure *remote_close* is called to close the target file. See Example E-3.

getargs.c interprets the user input to obtain the name of a local client ASCII file of source data, the server host to use, and the server target file. See Example E-4.

strbind.c contains the *do_string_binding* procedure that shows how to find a server from strings of binding information. A host name or network address is input, and then combined with a generated protocol sequence to create a valid binding handle, which is returned as a parameter. See Example E-5.

crndwn.c is the implementation of a context rundown procedure. The server stub calls this procedure automatically if communication breaks between a client and the server which is maintaining context for the client. For this application, the context is a file handle of a server data file. This context rundown procedure closes the file. See Example E-6.

manager.c is the implementation of the remote procedures defined in the `rfile` interface. See Example E-7.

server.c initializes the server with a series of runtime calls prior to servicing remote procedure calls. In this application, all available protocol sequences are registered. The server is not advertised in a name service database. The server's dynamic endpoints are added to the server's local endpoint map. A client finds this server by constructing a string binding containing a protocol sequence and the host name or network address. See Example E-8.

Example E-1: The Makefile for the Remote File Application

```
# FILE NAME: Makefile
# Makefile for the remote file  application
#
# definitions for this make file
#
APPL=rfile
IDLCMD=midl
NTRPCLIBS=rpcrt4.lib rpcns4.lib libcmt.lib kernel32.lib
```

Example E-1: The Makefile for the Remote File Application (continued)

```
# Include Windows NT macros
!include <ntwin32.mak>

# NT c flags
cflags = -c -W0 -Gz -D_X86_=1 -DWIN32 -DMT /nologo

# NT nmake inference rules
    $(cc) $(cdebug) $(cflags) $(cvarsmt) $<
    $(cvtomf)

#
# COMPLETE BUILD of the application
#
all:    interface client.exe server.exe

#
# INTERFACE BUILD
#
interface: $(APPL).h $(APPL)_c.obj $(APPL)_s.obj $(APPL)_x.obj

#
# CLIENT BUILD
#
client:     client.exe
client.exe: client.obj getargs.obj strbind.obj $(APPL)_c.obj $(APPL)_x.obj
    $(link) $(linkdebug) $(conflags) -out:client.exe -map:client.map \
        client.obj getargs.obj strbind.obj $(APPL)_c.obj $(APPL)_x.obj \
        $(NTRPCLIBS)

#
# SERVER BUILD
#
server:     server.exe
server.exe: server.obj manager.obj crndwn.obj $(APPL)_s.obj $(APPL)_x.obj
    $(link) $(linkdebug) $(conflags) -out:server.exe -map:server.map \
        server.obj manager.obj crndwn.obj $(APPL)_s.obj $(APPL)_x.obj\
        $(NTRPCLIBS)

# client and server sources
client.obj:  client.c  $(APPL).h
manager.obj: manager.c $(APPL).h
server.obj:  server.c  $(APPL).h
crndwn.obj:  crndwn.c  $(APPL).h
getargs.obj: getargs.c
strbind.obj: strbind.c

# Local client sources
lclient.obj: client.c $(APPL).h
            $(cc) $(cdebug) $(cflags) $(cvarsmt) /DLOCAL \
                /Folclient.obj client.c
lmanager.obj: manager.c $(APPL).h
            $(cc) $(cdebug) $(cflags) $(cvarsmt) /DLOCAL \
                /Folmanager.obj manager.c
```

Example E-1: The Makefile for the Remote File Application (continued)

```
# client stubs
$(APPL)_c.obj: $(APPL)_c.c
$(APPL)_x.obj: $(APPL)_x.c

# compile the server stub
$(APPL)_s.obj : $(APPL)_s.c

# generate stubs, auxiliary and header file from the IDL file
$(APPL).h $(APPL)_c.c $(APPL)_x.c : $(APPL).idl
    $(IDLCMD) $(APPL).idl

# clean up for fresh build
clean:
    del $(APPL)_?.c
    del *.obj
    del $(APPL).h
    del *.map
    del *.pdb


clobber: clean
    if exist client.exe  del client.exe
    if exist lclient.exe del lclient.exe
    if exist server.exe  del server.exe
```

Example E-2: The MIDL File of the Remote File Application

```
/* FILE NAME: rfile.idl */
[
uuid(A61E4024-A53F-101A-B1AF-08002B2E5B76),
version(1.0),
pointer_default(unique)
]
interface rfile              /* file manipulation on a remote system */
{
    typedef [context_handle] void *filehandle;
    typedef                  byte buffer[];

filehandle remote_open(       /* open for write                      */
    [in] handle_t binding_h,  /* explicit primitive binding handle   */
    [in, string] char name[], /* if name is null, use stdout in server */
    [in, string] char mode[]  /* values can be "r", "w", or "a"      */
);

long remote_send(
    [in] filehandle fh,
    [in, max_is(max)] buffer buf,
    [in] long max
);

void remote_close(
    [in,out] filehandle *fh
);
}
```

Example E-3: A Client File of the Remote File Application

```
/* FILE NAME: client.c */
#include <stdio.h>
#include <stdlib.h>
#include <string.h>
#include "rfile.h"
#define MAX 200          /* maximum line length for a file */

main(argc, argv)
int argc;
char *argv[];
{
    FILE        *local_fh;           /* file handle for client file input */
    char        host[100];         /* name or network address of remote host */
    char        remote_name[100];               /* name of remote file */
    rpc_binding_handle_t binding_h;              /* binding handle */
    filehandle  remote_fh;                        /* context handle */
    buffer      *buf_ptr;            /* buffer pointer for data sent */
    int         size;                       /* size of data buffer */

    get_args(argc, argv, &local_fh, host, (char *)remote_name);
#ifndef LOCAL
    if(do_string_binding(host, &binding_h) < 0) {
        fprintf(stderr, "Cannot get binding\n");
        exit(1);
    }
#endif
    remote_fh = remote_open(binding_h, remote_name, (char *)"w");
    if(remote_fh == NULL) {
        fprintf(stderr, "Cannot open remote file\n");
        exit(1);
    }

    /* The buffer data type is a conformant array of bytes; */
    /* memory must be allocated for a conformant array.     */
    buf_ptr = (buffer *)malloc((MAX+1) * sizeof(buffer));

    while( fgets((char *)buf_ptr, MAX, local_fh) != NULL) {
        size = (int)strlen((char *)buf_ptr); /* data sent will not include \0 */
        if( remote_send(remote_fh, (*buf_ptr), size) < 1) {
            fprintf(stderr, "Cannot write to remote file\n");
            exit(1);
        }
    }
    remote_close(&remote_fh);
}
```

Example E-4: The get_args Procedure

```
/* FILE NAME: getargs.c */
#include <stdio.h>
#include <stdlib.h>
#include <string.h>

get_args(argc, argv, local_fh, host, remote_name)
int  argc;
```

Example E-4: The get_args Procedure (continued)

```c
char *argv[];
FILE **local_fh;
char host[];
char remote_name[];
{
   char local_name[100];

   switch(argc) {
   case 1:
   case 2: printf("Usage: %s [local_file] host [remote_file]\n", argv[0]);
           puts("Use \"\" for local stdin.");
           exit(0);
           break;
   case 3: strcpy(local_name, argv[1]);  /* use the same file name */
           strcpy(remote_name, local_name);
           strcpy(host, argv[2]);
           break;
   default: strcpy(local_name, argv[1]);
            strcpy(host, argv[2]);
            strcpy(remote_name, argv[3]);
            break;
   }
   if(strlen(local_name) == 0) {
      (*local_fh) = stdin;
      puts("Using stdin.  Type input:");
   }
   else
      if( ( (*local_fh) = fopen(local_name, "r")) == NULL ) {
         puts("Cannot open local file");
         exit(1);
      }
   return;
}
```

Example E-5: The do_string_binding Procedure

```c
/* FILE NAME: strbind.c */
/* Find a server binding handle from strings of binding information        */
/* including protocol sequence, host address, and server process endpoint. */
#include <stdio.h>
#include "rfile.h"
#include "status.h"                         /* contains the CHECK_STATUS macro */

int do_string_binding(host, binding_h) /*return=0 if binding valid, else -1 */
char            host[];        /* server host name or network address input   */
rpc_binding_handle_t *binding_h;    /* binding handle is output               */
{
   RPC_PROTSEQ_VECTOR    *protseq_vector;   /* protocol sequence list          */
   unsigned char         *string_binding;  /* string of binding information */
   unsigned long         status;           /* error status                    */
   int                   i, result;

   status =
   RpcNetworkInqProtseqs(    /* obtain a list of valid protocol sequences    */
      &protseq_vector                  /* list of protocol sequences obtained */
```

Example E-5: The do_string_binding Procedure (continued)

```
    );
    CHECK_STATUS(status, "Can't get protocol sequences:", ABORT);

    /* loop through protocol sequences until a binding handle is obtained */
    for(i=0; i < protseq_vector->Count; i++) {

        status =
        RpcStringBindingCompose(     /* make string binding from components  */
            NULL,                       /* no object UUIDs are required      */
            protseq_vector->Protseq[i], /* protocol sequence                 */
            (unsigned char *)host,      /* host name or network address      */
            NULL,                       /* no endpoint is required           */
            NULL,                       /* no network options are required   */
            &string_binding             /* the constructed string binding    */
        );
        CHECK_STATUS(status, "Can't compose a string binding:", RESUME);

        status =
        RpcBindingFromStringBinding(   /* convert string to binding handle  */
            string_binding,             /* input string binding              */
            binding_h                   /* binding handle is obtained here */
        );
        CHECK_STATUS(status, "Can't get binding handle from string:", RESUME);
        if(status != RPC_S_OK) {
            result = -1;
            CHECK_STATUS(status, "Can't get binding handle from string:", RESUME);
        }
        else
            result = 0;

        status =
        RpcStringFree(                      /* free string binding created   */
            &string_binding
        );
        CHECK_STATUS(status, "Can't free string binding:", RESUME);
        if(result == 0)  break;                     /* got a valid binding */
    }

    status =
    RpcProtseqVectorFree(            /* free the list of protocol sequences   */
        &protseq_vector
    );
    CHECK_STATUS(status, "Can't free protocol sequence vector:", RESUME);
    return(result);
}
```

Example E-6: The Context Rundown of the Remote File Application

```
/* FILE NAME: crndwn.c */
#include <stdio.h>
#include "rfile.h"

void filehandle_rundown(remote_fh)
filehandle remote_fh;               /* the context handle is passed in  */
{
    fprintf(stderr, "Server executing context rundown\n");
```

Example E-6: The Context Rundown of the Remote File Application (continued)

```
   if( (FILE *)remote_fh != stdout )
      fclose( (FILE *)remote_fh );  /* file is closed if client is gone */
   remote_fh = NULL;               /* must set context handle to NULL  */
   return;
}
```

Example E-7: Remote Procedures of the Remote File Application

```
/* FILE NAME: manager.c */
#include <stdio.h>
#include <string.h>
#include <io.h>
#include <errno.h>
#include "rfile.h"

filehandle remote_open(binding_h, name, mode)
rpc_binding_handle_t binding_h;
char                 name[];
char                 mode[];
{
   FILE *FILEh;

   if(strlen((char *)name) == 0)                      /* no file name given */
      if(strcmp((char *)mode, "r") == 0)
         FILEh = NULL;                        /* cannot read nonexistent file */
      else FILEh = stdout;                            /* use server stdout */

   else if(_access((char *)name, 0) == 0)              /* file exists */
      if(strcmp((char *)mode, "w") == 0)
         FILEh = NULL;                        /* do not overwrite existing file */
      else FILEh = fopen((char *)name, (char *)mode);  /* open read/append */

   else                                       /* file does not exist */
      if(strcmp((char *)mode, "r") == 0)
         FILEh = NULL;                        /* cannot read nonexistent file */
      else FILEh = fopen((char *)name, (char *)mode);  /* open write/append */

   return( (filehandle)FILEh );       /* cast FILE handle to context handle */
}


long int remote_send(fh, buf, max)
filehandle fh;
buffer buf;
long int max;
{
   /* write data to the file (context), which is cast as a FILE pointer */
   return( fwrite(buf, max, 1, fh) );
}


void remote_close(fh)
filehandle *fh;  /* the client stub needs the changed value upon return */
{
   if( (FILE *)(*fh) != stdout )
      fclose( (FILE *)(*fh) );
   (*fh) = NULL;           /* assign NULL to the context handle to free it */
```

Example E-7: Remote Procedures of the Remote File Application (continued)

```
    return;
}
```

Example E-8: Server Initialization of the Remote File Application

```
/* FILE NAME: server.c */
#include <stdio.h>
#include "rfile.h"                        /* header created by the idl compiler */
#include "status.h"                       /* contains the CHECK_STATUS macro    */
main ()
{
    unsigned long       status;           /* error status                       */
    rpc_binding_vector_t  *binding_vector; /* binding handle list               */

    status =                              /* error status */
    RpcServerRegisterIf(                  /* register interface with the RPC runtime */
        rfile_v1_0_s_ifspec,             /* handle for interface specification    */
        NULL,
        NULL
    );
    CHECK_STATUS(status, "Can't register interface", ABORT);

    status =
    RpcServerUseAllProtseqs(              /* establish protocol sequences  */
        RPC_C_PROTSEQ_MAX_REQS_DEFAULT,   /* queue length for remote calls */
        NULL                              /* no security descriptor        */
    );
    CHECK_STATUS(status, "Can't establish protocol sequences", ABORT);

    status =
    RpcServerInqBindings(                 /* get set of this server's binding handles */
        &binding_vector
    );
    CHECK_STATUS(status, "Can't get binding handles", ABORT);

    status =
    RpcEpRegister(                        /* add endpoint to local endpoint map   */
        rfile_v1_0_s_ifspec,             /* handle for interface specification    */
        binding_vector,                   /* vector of server binding handles      */
        NULL,                             /* no object UUIDs to register           */
        (unsigned char *)"remote_file server"   /* annotation (not required) */
    );
    CHECK_STATUS(status, "Can't add endpoints to local endpoint map:", ABORT);

    puts("Listening for remote procedure calls...");
    RpcTryFinally
    {
        status =
        RpcServerListen(                             /* listen for remote calls   */
            1,                                       /* Minimum number of threads */
            RPC_C_LISTEN_MAX_CALLS_DEFAULT,          /* Maximum number of threads */
            NULL
        );
        CHECK_STATUS(status, "rpc listen failed:", RESUME);
    }
```

Example E-8: Server Initialization of the Remote File Application (continued)

```
    RpcFinally
    {
        puts("Removing endpoints from local endpoint map.");
        status =
        RpcEpUnregister(              /* remove endpoints from local endpoint map */
            rfile_v1_0_s_ifspec,          /* handle for interface specification */
            binding_vector,               /* vector of server binding handles   */
            NULL                          /* no object UUIDs to unregister       */
        );
        CHECK_STATUS(status,"Can't remove endpoints from endpoint map:", RESUME);

        status =
        RpcBindingVectorFree(                     /* free set of binding handles */
            &binding_vector
        );
        CHECK_STATUS(status, "Can't free binding handles and vector", ABORT);
    }
    RpcEndFinally
}

/***************************************************************************/
/***                MIDL_user_allocate / MIDL_user_free              ***/
/***************************************************************************/
void * __RPC_API
MIDL_user_allocate
            (
            size
            )
size_t size;
{
    unsigned char * ptr;
    ptr = malloc( size );
    return ( (void *)ptr );

}

void __RPC_API
MIDL_user_free
            (
            object
            )
void * object;
{
    free (object);
}
```

The Windows
Phonebook Application

The phonebook application demonstrates a simple Windows client interface to a Microsoft RPC application. The Windows client looks up names in a phonebook database file maintained by the phonebook server (*phnbkd.exe*). The client does not use the Microsoft Locator name service, so you need to supply the server host name or address to a dialog box in the client interface.

How to Build and Run the Application

To build and run the server of the distributed application, type the following:

```
C:\SERVER> nmake phnbkd.exe
C:\SERVER> phnbkd
```

To build and run the Windows client of the distributed application, type the following:

```
C:\CLIENT> nmake phnbk.exe
C:\CLIENT> phnbk
```

Enter a hostname or address into the **Server Host Name** dialog box. Try the browse feature first to see some names. Then enter names into the **Search String** dialog box.

Application Files

Makefile contains descriptions of how the application is compiled. See Example F-1.

phnbk.idl contains descriptions of the data types and procedures for the interface. See Example F-2.

phnbk.acf is an attribute configuration file that specifies implicit binding as the client binding method. See Example F-3.

wclient.c provides a Windows user interface to the server (*phnbkd.exe*). The client invokes remote procedure calls based on user actions. See Example F-4.

wphnbk.def is a Windows module definition file. It defines the name of the application, the type of image to be produced, and other attributes of the application. See Example F-5.

wphnbk.h is a header file that defines constants used in *wphnbk.c* and in the resource file *wphnbk.rc*. See Example F-6.

wphnbk.rc is a Windows resource file. It describes the size and appearance of the Windows dialog box and of the controls (such as buttons and edit boxes) used by the application. See Example F-7.

manager.c is the implementation of the remote procedures defined in the phnbk interface. The remote procedures look up names contained in the *phnbk.txt* database file. See Example F-8.

server.c initializes the server with a series of runtime calls prior to servicing remote procedure calls. This application specifies to use the TCP/IP protocol sequence. The server is not advertised in a name service database. The server's dynamic endpoints are added to the server's local endpoint map. A client finds this server by constructing a string binding containing a protocol sequence and the host name or network address. See Example F-9.

phnbk.txt is an ASCII file containing the database of names used by the phonebook server. We created it using a text editor. You can add your own lines to this file. Make sure lines are under 100 characters in length. See Example F-10.

Example F-1: The Makefile for the Windows Phonebook Application

```
#
#
# Build phnbk client and server for Windows NT
#
#
!INCLUDE <ntwin32.mak>

includes =  -I.

all : phnbk.exe phnbkd.exe

#
# Link simple client
#
phnbk.exe: wclient.obj wphnbk.obj phnbk_c.obj
    $(link) $(linkdebug) $(guiflags) -out:phnbk.exe \
      wclient.obj phnbk_c.obj wphnbk.obj \
      rpcrt4.lib rpcns4.lib rpcndr.lib $(guilibs)


#
```

Example F-1: The Makefile for the Windows Phonebook Application (continued)

```
# Link server
#
phnbkd.exe: server.obj manager.obj phnbk_s.obj
    $(link) $(linkdebug) $(conflags) -out:phnbkd.exe \
     `server.obj manager.obj phnbk_s.obj \
      rpcrt4.lib rpcns4.lib rpcndr.lib $(conlibs)
#
# .RES
#
wphnbk.obj: wphnbk.rc
  rc -r wphnbk.rc
  cvtres -$(CPU) wphnbk.res
#
# Compile simple client source code
#
wclient.obj: wclient.c phnbk.h
    $(cc) $(cflags) $(cvars) $(scall) $(includes) wclient.c

#
# Compile server source code
#
server.obj: server.c phnbk.h
    $(cc) $(cflags) $(cvars) $(scall) $(includes) server.c

manager.obj: manager.c phnbk.h
    $(cc) $(cflags) $(cvars) $(scall) $(includes) manager.c


#
# Compile client stubs
#
phnbk_c.obj : phnbk_c.c phnbk.h
    $(cc) $(cflags) $(cvars) $(scall) $(includes) phnbk_c.c

##
#    $(cc) $(cflags) $(cvars) $(scall) $(includes) phnbk_x.c

#
# Compile server stubs
#
phnbk_s.obj : phnbk_s.c
    $(cc) $(cflags) $(cvars) $(scall) $(includes) phnbk_s.c

#phnbk_y.obj : phnbk_y.c
#    $(cc) $(cflags) $(cvars) $(scall) $(includes) phnbk_y.c

#
# Generate stubs and header file from interface definition
#
phnbk.h : phnbk.idl phnbk.acf
    midl phnbk.idl


#
# Clean up for fresh build
#
clean :
```

Example F–1: The Makefile for the Windows Phonebook Application (continued)

```
    del phnbk_*.*
    del *.obj
    del phnbk.h

#
# Clean up all byproducts of build
#
clobber : clean
    del phnbk.exe
    del phnbkd.exe
    del *.res
```

Example F–2: The MIDL File of the Windows Phonebook Application

```
/*
**   Interface definition file for implicit phnbk client
*/

[
 uuid(F2FE85A0-0C28-1068-A726-AA0004007EFF),
 version(1.0),
 pointer_default(ref)]
interface phnbk
{
/*
** Constant for maximum line size
*/
const long LINESIZE = 100;

/*
** Flag for hitting end of phonebook file
*/
const short END = -1;

/*
** Flag for normal completion of operation
*/
const short NORMAL = 0;

/*
** Define all possible operations on phonebook file
*/
typedef enum
            {
            FIRSTMATCH,
            NEXTMATCH,
            BROWSE,
            RESET,
            BROWSE_RESET
            } operations;

/*
** Perform some operation on the phonebook
*/
short
lookup
```

Example F-2: The MIDL File of the Windows Phonebook Application (continued)

```
    (
    [in]            short  operation,
    [in,string]   char   search_string[LINESIZE],
    [out,string]  char   return_string[LINESIZE]
    );
}
```

Example F-3: The ACF File of the Windows Phonebook Application

```
[implicit_handle (handle_t xhandle)] interface phnbk {}
```

Example F-4: Client File of the Windows Phonebook Application

```
/*
**
**
** MODULE: wclient.c
**
**
** PROGRAM: Windows wphnbk application
**
**
**
**
*/

#include <windows.h>
#include <stdlib.h>
#include <string.h>
#include <ctype.h>

#include "phnbk.h"
#include "wphnbk.h"


int             lookup_status;     /* lookup return status       */
error_status_t status;             /* rpc status                 */
unsigned char  input[LINESIZE];    /* 'find' search string       */
char            output[LINESIZE];   /* string returned from database */
char            oldmatch[LINESIZE];/* previous 'find' string     */
unsigned char  server[80];         /* string binding for server  */
short           operation;          /* operation requested        */
short           no_handle;          /* handle not initialized flag */
unsigned char  hostname[32];       /* phnbk server host name      */

long FAR PASCAL WndProc (HWND, WORD, WORD, LONG) ;

int
PASCAL WinMain
            (
            HANDLE hInstance,
            HANDLE hPrevInstance,
            LPSTR lpszCmdLine,
            int nCmdShow
            )
{
```

Example F-4: Client File of the Windows Phonebook Application (continued)

```
    char szAppName [] = "WPHNBK" ;
    HWND        hwnd ;
    MSG         msg;
    WNDCLASS    wndclass ;

    /*
    ** Initialize strings
    */
    input[0]    = '\0';
    output[0]   = '\0';
    oldmatch[0] = '\0';
    server[0]   = '\0';
    hostname[0] = '\0';

    no_handle = TRUE;

    /*
    ** Standard Windows stuff...
    */
    if (!hPrevInstance)
        {
        wndclass.style          = CS_HREDRAW | CS_VREDRAW;
        wndclass.lpfnWndProc    = (WNDPROC) WndProc ;
        wndclass.cbClsExtra     = 0 ;
        wndclass.cbWndExtra     = DLGWINDOWEXTRA ;
        wndclass.hInstance      = hInstance ;
        wndclass.hIcon          = LoadIcon(hInstance,szAppName);
        wndclass.hCursor        = LoadCursor ((HINSTANCE)NULL, IDC_ARROW) ;
        wndclass.hbrBackground  = (HBRUSH) (COLOR_WINDOW + 1) ;
        wndclass.lpszMenuName   = NULL ;
        wndclass.lpszClassName  = szAppName ;

        RegisterClass (&wndclass) ;
        }

    hwnd = CreateDialog (hInstance, szAppName, 0, NULL) ;

    ShowWindow (hwnd, nCmdShow) ;

    SetFocus ( GetDlgItem (hwnd, HOSTNAMEBOX ) );

    /*
    ** Start accepting messages
    */
    while ( GetMessage (&msg, NULL, 0, 0) )
        {
        TranslateMessage (&msg) ;
        DispatchMessage (&msg) ;
        }

    return msg.wParam ;
}

short
InitHandle
        (
        HWND hwnd
```

Example F-4: Client File of the Windows Phonebook Application (continued)

```
        )
{

    /*
    ** Read server host name
    */
    GetDlgItemText (hwnd, HOSTNAMEBOX, hostname, 16 );

    /*
    ** Warn user if they haven't specified a host name
    */
    if (hostname[0] == '\0')
        {
        MessageBox
                (
                hwnd,
                "Please enter server host name",
                "ERROR",
                MB_OK
                );
        SetFocus ( GetDlgItem (hwnd, HOSTNAMEBOX) );
        return (-1);
        }

    /*
    ** Build server string binding
    */
    strcat (server, "ncacn_ip_tcp:");
    strcat (server, hostname);
    /*
    ** Convert the character string binding into an RPC handle
    */
    status = RpcBindingFromStringBinding
                (
                server,
                &xhandle
                );

    if (status)
        {
        MessageBox
                (
                hwnd,
                "Invalid string binding",
                "ERROR",
                MB_OK
                );
        exit (EXIT_FAILURE);
        }

    no_handle = FALSE;

    return (0);
```

Example F–4: Client File of the Windows Phonebook Application (continued)

```
}

void
ShowResult
        (
        HWND hwnd
        )
{
    /*
    ** Display lookup results, based on the context of
    **    the requested operation
    */
    if (operation == BROWSE)
        {
        /*
        ** BROWSE -- return next entry
        */
        if (lookup_status == NORMAL)
            /*
            ** Everything ok, display next entry
            */
            SetDlgItemText (hwnd,RESULTSBOX,output);
        else
            {
            /*
            ** Otherwise, we hit end of file...
            */
            SetDlgItemText (hwnd,RESULTSBOX,"");
            SetDlgItemText (hwnd,INFOBOX,"No more entries");
            }
        }
    else
        {
        /*
        ** Operation was a Find or Find Next...tailor message
        **    syntax to reflect the operation.
        */
        if (lookup_status == NORMAL)
            {
            /*
            ** Print results
            */
            SetDlgItemText (hwnd,RESULTSBOX,output);

            /*
            ** Determine if this was first match, or subsequent match
            */
            if (operation == FIRSTMATCH)
                SetDlgItemText (hwnd,INFOBOX,"Match found");
            else
                SetDlgItemText (hwnd,INFOBOX,"Another match found");
            }
```

Example F-4: Client File of the Windows Phonebook Application (continued)

```
        else
            /*
            ** Hit end of file during search
            */
            if (operation == FIRSTMATCH)
                SetDlgItemText (hwnd,INFOBOX,"Match not found");
            else
                SetDlgItemText (hwnd,INFOBOX,"No other matches found");
        }

    return;
    }


long
FAR PASCAL WndProc
                (
                 HWND hwnd,
                 WORD message,
                 WORD wParam,
                 LONG lParam
                )
    {
    /*
    ** We switch cursors to the hourglass during
    **     a lookup RPC.  This is for saving the
    **     regular pointer.
    */
    HCURSOR OldCursor;

    /*
    ** First thing, save the match string from last time around
    */
    strcpy (oldmatch, input);

    /*
    ** Switch on the incoming message type (standard Windows
    **     programming)
    */
    switch (message)
        {
        /*
        ** Got a button pushed
        */
        case WM_COMMAND:

            switch (wParam)
                {
                /*
                ** Either a Find or a Find Next
                */
                case FINDBUTTON:
                    if (no_handle)
                        if (InitHandle(hwnd)) break;
```

Example F-4: Client File of the Windows Phonebook Application (continued)

```
/*
** Clear current text
*/
SetDlgItemText(hwnd,RESULTSBOX,"");
SetDlgItemText(hwnd,INFOBOX,"");

/*
** Read the search string
*/
GetDlgItemText(hwnd,SEARCHBOX,input,32);

/*
** Make sure user entered a search string
*/
if (input[0] == (unsigned char) '\0')
    {
    MessageBox
            (
            hwnd,
            "Missing Search String!",
            "ERROR",
            MB_OK
            );
    /*
    ** Set focus back to SEARCHBOX so user can
    **     enter search string
    */
    SetFocus ( GetDlgItem (hwnd, SEARCHBOX) );
    }
else
    {
    /*
    ** Search string is present. Save existing
    **     pointer and display hourglass
    */
    OldCursor = SetCursor (LoadCursor(NULL,IDC_WAIT));
    ShowCursor (TRUE);

    /*
    ** Determine desired operation
    */
    if (strcmp(oldmatch,input))
        operation = FIRSTMATCH;
    else
        operation = NEXTMATCH;

    /*
    ** Perform the requested operation
    */
    lookup_status = lookup
                            (
                            operation,
                            input,
                            output
```

Example F-4: Client File of the Windows Phonebook Application (continued)

```
                                    );

            /*
            ** Restore pointer cursor
            */
            ShowCursor (FALSE);
            SetCursor ( OldCursor );

            /*
            ** Display lookup results
            */
            ShowResult(hwnd);
            }

        break;
    /*
    ** BROWSE -- return next entry
    */
    case BROWSEBUTTON:
        if (no_handle)
            if(InitHandle(hwnd)) break;
        /*
        ** Clear existing text and display status
        */
        SetDlgItemText(hwnd,RESULTSBOX,"");
        SetDlgItemText(hwnd,SEARCHBOX,"");
        SetDlgItemText(hwnd,INFOBOX,"Browsing...");

        /*
        ** Switch to hourglass cursor
        */
        OldCursor = SetCursor (LoadCursor(NULL,IDC_WAIT));
        ShowCursor (TRUE);


        operation = BROWSE;

        /*
        ** Perform the requested operation
        */
        lookup_status = lookup
                            (
                             operation,
                             input,
                             output
                            );

        /*
        ** Restore pointer cursor
        */
        ShowCursor (FALSE);
        SetCursor ( OldCursor );

        /*
```

Example F-4: Client File of the Windows Phonebook Application (continued)

```
                        ** Display operation results
                        */
                        ShowResult(hwnd);

                        break;

                /*
                ** User has requested a RESET.  This clears all
                **    text and rewinds the phonebook file
                */
                case RESETBUTTON:
                    if (no_handle)
                        if (InitHandle(hwnd)) break;
                    /*
                    ** Clear all text
                    */
                    SetDlgItemText(hwnd,RESULTSBOX,"");
                    SetDlgItemText(hwnd,INFOBOX,"");
                    SetDlgItemText(hwnd,SEARCHBOX,"");

                    input[0] = '\0';

                    operation = RESET;

                    /*
                    ** Perform the requested operation
                    */
                    lookup_status = lookup
                                        (
                                        operation,
                                        input,
                                        output
                                        );

                    break;

            }

        return 0 ;

    /*
    ** User has closed the application
    */
    case WM_DESTROY:
        if (!no_handle)
            {
            /*
            ** Free binding handle, post quit message and leave
            */
            status = RpcBindingFree
                        (
                        &xhandle
                        );
            }

        PostQuitMessage (0) ;
```

Example F-4: Client File of the Windows Phonebook Application (continued)

```
            return 0 ;

        /*
        ** Ignore other messages
        */
        default:
            return DefWindowProc (hwnd, message, wParam, lParam) ;
        }
}
```

Example F-5: Window Module Definition File

```
;-----------------------------------
; WPHNBK.DEF module definition file
;-----------------------------------

NAME            WPHNBK

DESCRIPTION     'Windows RPC Phonebook'
EXETYPE         WINDOWS
STUB            'WINSTUB.EXE'
CODE            PRELOAD FIXED DISCARDABLE
DATA            PRELOAD FIXED MULTIPLE
HEAPSIZE        8192
STACKSIZE       8192
EXPORTS         WndProc
```

Example F-6: Header File

```
#define SEARCHBOX 102
#define RESULTSBOX 104
#define INFOBOX 106
#define FINDBUTTON 113
#define BROWSEBUTTON 112
#define RESETBUTTON 110
#define HOSTNAMEBOX 109
```

Example F-7: Resource File

```
#include <windows.h>
#include "wphnbk.h"

WPHNBK DIALOG  15, 33, 315, 102
CAPTION "Windows RPC Phonebook"
STYLE WS_OVERLAPPED | WS_BORDER | WS_CAPTION | WS_SYSMENU | WS_MINIMIZEBOX
CLASS "WPHNBK"
BEGIN
    CONTROL "Search String:", 100, "static", SS_LEFT | WS_CHILD,
        13, 18, 47, 10
    CONTROL "Input", 101, "button", BS_GROUPBOX | WS_TABSTOP | WS_CHILD,
        5, 3, 173, 32
    CONTROL "", 102, "edit", ES_LEFT | WS_BORDER | WS_TABSTOP | WS_CHILD,
        63, 17, 108, 12
    CONTROL "Search Results:", 103, "static", SS_LEFT | WS_CHILD,
        6, 50, 58, 7
    CONTROL "", 104, "edit", ES_LEFT | WS_BORDER | WS_TABSTOP | WS_CHILD,
        64, 48, 239, 12
```

Example F–7: Resource File (continued)

```
    CONTROL "Status:", 105, "static", SS_LEFT | WS_CHILD, 6, 80, 26, 8
    CONTROL "", 106, "edit", ES_LEFT | WS_BORDER | WS_TABSTOP | WS_CHILD,
        30, 78, 133, 12
    CONTROL "Output", 108, "button", BS_GROUPBOX | WS_TABSTOP | WS_CHILD,
        4, 36, 305, 31
    CONTROL "Information", 111, "button", BS_GROUPBOX | WS_TABSTOP | WS_CHILD,
        4, 68, 305, 31
    CONTROL "Find / Find Next", 113, "button",
        BS_PUSHBUTTON | WS_TABSTOP | WS_CHILD, 192, 6, 112, 14
    CONTROL "Reset", 110, "button", BS_PUSHBUTTON | WS_TABSTOP | WS_CHILD,
        192, 22, 50, 14
    CONTROL "Browse", 112, "button", BS_PUSHBUTTON | WS_TABSTOP | WS_CHILD,
        258, 22, 46, 14
    CONTROL "", HOSTNAMEBOX, "edit", ES_LEFT | WS_BORDER | WS_TABSTOP | WS_CHILD,
        228, 78, 76, 12
    CONTROL "Server Host Name:",107, "static", SS_LEFT | WS_CHILD,
        166, 80, 62, 8
END
```

Example F–8: Remote Procedures

```
/*
**
**
** MODULE: manager.c
**
**
** PROGRAM: phnbk application
**
**
**
**
**
*/

#include <stdio.h>
#include <string.h>
#include <malloc.h>
#include <stdlib.h>

#include "phnbk.h"

#ifdef WIN32
#endif

extern FILE *filehandle;        /* Phonebook file filehandle */
extern short previous_operation; /* Keeps track of previous operation */
/*
**
** FUNCTION:  getfileline
**
** PURPOSE:
**      Retrieve Lines from input file
**
```

Example F-8: Remote Procedures (continued)

```c
*/
int
getfileline
            (
            line,
            phone
            )
unsigned char * line;
FILE * phone;
{
    /*
    ** Each call of this routine returns a line of the
    **    phonebook file.  On EOF, it returns -1.
    */
    char ch;

    while ((ch = fgetc(phone)) != '\n' && ch != EOF)
        {
        /*
        ** Tabs are unpredictable, so substitute
        **    three spaces if you run across a tab...
        */
        if (ch == '\t')
            {
            *line++ = ' ';
            *line++ = ' ';
            *line++ = ' ';
            }
        else
            *line++ = ch;

        }

    *line++ = '\0';

    if (ch == EOF)
        return (END);
    else
        return (NORMAL);
}

/*
**
** FUNCTION:  lookup
**
** PURPOSE:
**    Look up entries in database
**
*/
short
lookup
        (
        op,
        stringin,
```

Example F-8: Remote Procedures (continued)

```
        stringout
        )
short op;
unsigned char stringin[LINESIZE];
unsigned char stringout[LINESIZE];
{
    unsigned char buf[LINESIZE];

    /*
    ** Switch on requested operation
    */
    switch (op)
        {
        case  RESET:
            /*
            **   Reset context
            */
            printf("Phonebook:\tRESET\n");

            rewind(filehandle);

            previous_operation = FIRSTMATCH;

            return(NORMAL);

            break;

        case  FIRSTMATCH:
            /*
            **   Look for first match of a string, starting at the
            **     beginning of the file...
            */
            printf("Phonebook:\tFIRSTMATCH\n");

            rewind(filehandle);

            break;


        case  NEXTMATCH:
            /*
            **   Nothing special here, fall out and continue search
            */
            printf("Phonebook:\tNEXTMATCH\n");
            break;


        case  BROWSE:
            /*
            **   A BROWSE operation just returns the next entry...
            **
            **   If the last operation was a BROWSE that got an EOF,
            **     then rewind and start cycling through again.
            */
            printf("Phonebook:\tBROWSE\n");

            if (previous_operation == BROWSE_RESET)
                rewind (filehandle);
```

Example F-8: Remote Procedures (continued)

```
            if ((getfileline(buf,filehandle)) != -1)
                {
                /*
                **  If not EOF, then just return next entry.
                */
                strcpy ((char *)stringout,(char *)buf);

                printf("Phonebook: \tFound %s\n", buf);

                previous_operation = BROWSE;

                return(NORMAL);
                }
            else
                {
                /*
                **  This allows the client to flag "no more entries"
                **  before cycling through the file again on
                **  another BROWSE request.
                */
                previous_operation = BROWSE_RESET;

                return(END);
                }
        }

    /*
    ** Keep track of previous operation in p_context
    */
    previous_operation = op;

    /*
    **  Either return the line of the file that contains a string
    **  match, or return -1...
    */
    while ((getfileline(buf,filehandle)) != -1)
        {
        if ((strstr((char *)buf, (char *)stringin)) != (char *) NULL)
            {
            printf("Phonebook: \tFound %s\n", buf);
            strcpy ((char *)stringout,(char *)buf);
            return(NORMAL);
            }
        }

    return(END);
}
```

Example F-9: Server Initialization

```
/*
**
**
** MODULE: server.c
**
```

Example F-9: Server Initialization (continued)

```
**
** PROGRAM: phnbk application
**
**
**
**
**
*/

#include <stdio.h>
#include <string.h>
#include <stdlib.h>
#include <malloc.h>

#include "phnbk.h"

#ifdef WIN32
#define MAIN_DECL _CRTAPI1

#else
#define MAIN_DECL
#include <dce/rpcexc.h>
#endif

#define IFSPEC phnbk_v1_0_s_ifspec

FILE * filehandle;          /* File handle used for phonebook file */
short previous_operation; /* Keeps track of previous phonebook operation */

int
MAIN_DECL main
            (
              ac,
              av
            )
int     ac;
char *av[];
{
    unsigned int            i;
    error_status_t          status;
    unsigned char           *string_binding;
    RPC_BINDING_VECTOR      *bvec;

    /*
    **
    ** Specify TCP/IP as a protocol sequences
    */
    status = RpcServerUseProtseq
              (
                "ncacn_ip_tcp",
                5,
                NULL
              );

    if (status != RPC_S_OK)
        {
```

Example F-9: Server Initialization (continued)

```
      printf("No available protocol sequences\n");
      exit(EXIT_FAILURE);
      }

/*
** register the server interface
*/
status = RpcServerRegisterIf
          (
          IFSPEC,
          NULL,
          NULL
          );

if (status != RPC_S_OK)
    {
    printf("Can't register interface \n");
    exit(EXIT_FAILURE);
    }

/*
** find out what binding information is actually available
*/
status = RpcServerInqBindings
          (
          &bvec
          );

if (status != RPC_S_OK)
    {
    printf("Can't inquire bindings \n");
    exit(EXIT_FAILURE);
    }

/*
** register with endpoint mapper
*/
status = RpcEpRegister
          (
          IFSPEC,
          bvec,
          NULL,
          (unsigned char *)"phnbk endpoint"
          );

if (status != RPC_S_OK)
    {
    printf("Can't register endpoint\n");
    exit(EXIT_FAILURE);
    }

/*
** Get the string bindings and print them
*/
for (i = 0; i < bvec->Count; i++)
```

Example F-9: Server Initialization (continued)

```
        {
        /*
        ** For each binding, convert it to a
        **     string representation
        */
        status = RpcBindingToStringBinding
                    (
                     bvec->BindingH[i],
                     &string_binding
                    );

        if (status != RPC_S_OK)
            {
            printf("Can't get string binding \n");
            exit(EXIT_FAILURE);
            }

        printf("%s\n", string_binding);
        }

    /*
    ** Open the phonebook file
    */
    filehandle = fopen("phnbk.txt","r");

    /*
    ** Server is all ready to start listening for client
    **     requests...
    */
    status = RpcServerListen
                (
                 1,
                 2,
                 0
                );

    if (status != RPC_S_OK)
        printf("Error: rpc_server_listen() returned \n");

    return (EXIT_FAILURE);
}
#ifdef WIN32

/****************************************************************************/
/***               MIDL_user_allocate / MIDL_user_free            ***/
/****************************************************************************/

void * __RPC_API
MIDL_user_allocate
            (
             size
            )
size_t size;
{

    unsigned char * ptr;
```

Example F-9: Server Initialization (continued)

```
    ptr = malloc( size );
    return ( (void *)ptr );


}

void __RPC_API
MIDL_user_free
            (
             object
            )
void * object;
{
    free (object);
}

#endif
```

Example F-10: Sample Input Data

```
Mickey Mouse            555-2345
Donald Duck             555-2342
Pluto                   555-4564
James T. Kirk           555-2342
Fred Flintstone         555-2342
Spider Man              555-2345
Bat Man                 555-2342
George Jetson           555-2342
Peter Pan               555-4312
John Doe                555-8888
Charlie Brown           555-2374
```

Index

About the Author

John Shirley is a consultant in the development of software and documentation, particularly in the field of distributed computing. He earned a B.A. from Alfred University with a dual major in mathematics and geology, an M.S. in geology from Miami University with a specialty in structural geology, and an M.S. in computer science from Pace University. John lives in Newtown, Connecticut.

Prior to consulting, John's career included six years in the oil industry as a geophysicist and international explorationist. His work included the analysis of seismic data from New Zealand, Australia, Turkey, Norway, the Dominican Republic, Jamaica, and the United States. He also worked as a software engineer developing programs for scientific instrument manufacturers.

Ward Rosenberry is a technical writing consultant and author concentrating on distributed computing and computer networking technologies. Ward has distinguished himself writing about the Open Software Foundation's Distributed Computing Environment since 1989, when he helped write Digital Equipment Corporation's original DCE design documents. He has since co-authored two other O'Reilly books about distributed computing: *Understanding DCE* and *Distributing Applications Across DCE and Windows NT*. He continues his close DCE involvement designing and developing DCE information both at Digital and at OSF and now operates a consulting firm, Rosenberry Associates, in Chelmsford, Massachusetts.

Ward graduated from the University of Lowell in 1979 with a B.A. in English. Ward, his wife Patricia Pestana, and their two children, William and John, live in North Chelmsford, Massachusetts.

Colophon

The animal on the cover of *Microsoft RPC Programming Guide* is a starfish, a marine invertebrate animal of the phylum *Echinodermata*, class *Asteroidea*. The approximately 1500 known living species of starfish are found throughout the world, at all ocean depths, and range in size from 1 cm to 68 cm wide. Most starfish have five arms, but can have as few as four or as many as 50.

Starfish are equipped with five double rows of outgrowths called tube feet. These tube feet, which are usually tipped with "suction cups," function in the respiratory process, enable the starfish to move, and are used to catch prey. The tube feet are connected via a water-vascular system unique to echinoderms. A ring canal in the disc-shaped body trunk connects to a radial canal in each arm, through which gaseous exchange takes place.

When a starfish needs to move, pressure in the water-vascular system causes the tube feet to become erect, lifting up the body. The tube feet then take small steps, moving the starfish slowly forward. One arm takes the lead in movement; when the direction changes, the lead shifts to another arm. Most of the time, however, starfish are sedentary creatures who prefer to stay anchored in one place. They will move to search for food, or if there is a change in external conditions.

The majority of starfish are predators, feeding on bivalves, crustaceans, and other echinoderms. By anchoring its arms on the sea floor, the starfish is able to use the suction pull of the tube feet to pry open the shells of bivalves. The starfish can then extrude its stomach through its mouth and into the tiny crevice of the bivalve shell, and begin the digestive process outside of its body.

Many species of starfish can reject an arm if it is injured in an attack. The body will generate a new arm, but this is a slow process that can take more than a year to complete. In a few speciess, the arm that has broken off will generate a body trunk and four new arms. At least one species of starfish eschews sexual reproduction in favor of this asexual mode, and has developed the ability to break off an arm at will.

Starfish usually reproduce by releasing eggs and sperm into the waves. The fertilized eggs form free-swimming larvae, although the female adult will provide some form of brood care in colder regions.

Edie Freedman designed the cover of this book, using a 19th-century engraving from the Dover Pictorial Archive. The cover layout was produced with Quark XPress 3.3 using the ITC Garamond font.

The inside layout was designed by Edie Freedman and Jennifer Niederst and implemented in gtroff by Lenny Muellner. The text and heading fonts are ITC Garamond Light and Garamond Book. The illustrations that appear in the book were created in Aldus Freehand 4.0 by Chris Reilley. This colophon was written by Clairemarie Fisher O'Leary, with assistance from Kiersten Nauman.

Programming

UNIX, C and MULTI-PLATFORM

Books from O'Reilly & Associates, Inc.

Fall/Winter 1994-95

Fortran/Scientific Computing

Migrating to Fortran 90

By James F. Kerrigan
1st Edition November 1993
389 pages, ISBN 1-56592-049-X

Many Fortran programmers do not know where to start with Fortran 90. What is new about the language? How can it help them? How does a programmer with old habits learn new strategies?

This book is a practical guide to Fortran 90 for the current Fortran programmer. It provides a complete overview of the new features that Fortran 90 has brought to the Fortran standard, with examples and suggestions for use. The book discusses older ways of solving problems—both in FORTRAN 77 and in common tricks or extensions—and contrasts them with the new ways provided by Fortran 90.

The book has a practical focus, with the goal of getting the current Fortran programmer up to speed quickly. Two dozen examples of full programs are interspersed within the text, which includes over 4,000 lines of working code.

Topics include array sections, modules, file handling, allocatable arrays and pointers, and numeric precision. Two dozen examples of full programs are interspersed within the text, which includes over 4,000 lines of working code.

"This is a book that all Fortran programmers eager to take advantage of the excellent feature of Fortran 90 will want to have on their desk." —*FORTRAN Journal*

High Performance Computing

By Kevin Dowd
1st Edition June 1993
398 pages, ISBN 1-56592-032-5

High Performance Computing makes sense of the newest generation of workstations for application programmers and purchasing managers. It covers everything, from the basics of modern workstation architecture, to structuring benchmarks, to squeezing more performance out of critical applications. It also explains what a good compiler can do— and what you have to do yourself. The book closes with a look at the high-performance future: parallel computers and the more "garden variety" shared memory processors that are appearing on people's desktops.

UNIX for FORTRAN Programmers

By Mike Loukides
1st Edition August 1990
264 pages, ISBN 0-937175-51-X

This handbook lowers the UNIX entry barrier by providing the serious scientific programmer with an introduction to the UNIX operating system and its tools. It familiarizes readers with the most important tools so they can be productive as quickly as possible. Assumes some knowledge of FORTRAN, none of UNIX or C.

C Programming Libraries

POSIX.4

By Bill Gallmeister
1st Edition Winter 1994-95 (est.)
400 pages (est.), ISBN 1-56592-074-0

A general introduction to real-time programming and real-time issues, this book covers the POSIX.4 standard and how to use it to solve "real-world" problems. If you're at all interested in real-time applications—which include just about everything from telemetry to transation processing—this book is for you. An essential reference.

POSIX Programmer's Guide

By Donald Lewine
1st Edition April 1991
640 pages, ISBN 0-937175-73-0

Most UNIX systems today are POSIX compliant because the Federal government requires it for its purchases. Given the manufacturer's documentation, however, it can be difficult to distinguish system-specific features from those features defined by POSIX. The *POSIX Programmer's Guide*, intended as an explanation of the POSIX standard and as a reference for the POSIX.1 programming library, helps you write more portable programs.

"If you are an intermediate to advanced C programmer and are interested in having your programs compile first time on anything from a Sun to a VMS system to an MSDOS system, then this book must be thoroughly recommended."
—Sun UK User

Understanding and Using COFF

By Gintaras R. Gircys
1st Edition November 1988
196 pages, ISBN 0-937175-31-5

COFF—Common Object File Format—is the formal definition for the structure of machine code files in the UNIX System V environment. All machine code files are COFF files. This handbook explains COFF data structure and its manipulation.

Using C on the UNIX System

By Dave Curry
1st Edition January 1989
250 pages, ISBN 0-937175-23-4

This is the book for intermediate to experienced C programmers who want to become UNIX system programmers. It explains system calls and special library routines available on the UNIX system. It is impossible to write UNIX utilities of any sophistication without understanding the material in this book.

"A gem of a book.... The author's aim is to provide a guide to system programming, and he succeeds admirably. His balance is steady between System V and BSD-based systems, so readers come away knowing both." —*SUN Expert*

Practical C Programming

By Steve Oualline
2nd Edition January 1993
396 pages, ISBN 1-56592-035-X

C programming is more than just getting the syntax right. Style and debugging also play a tremendous part in creating programs that run well. *Practical C Programming* teaches you not only the mechanics of programming, but also how to create programs that are easy to read, maintain, and debug. There are lots of introductory C books, but this is the Nutshell Handbook®! In this edition, programs conform to ANSI C.

"This book is exactly what it states—a practical book in C programming. It is also an excellent addition to any C programmer's library." —Betty Zinkarun, *Books & Bytes*

Programming with curses

By John Strang
1st Edition 1986
76 pages, ISBN 0-937175-02-1

Curses is a UNIX library of functions for controlling a terminal's display screen from a C program. This handbook helps you make use of the curses library. Describes the original Berkeley version of curses.

C Programming Tools

Software Portability with imake

By Paul DuBois
1st Edition July 1993
390 pages, ISBN 1-56592-055-4

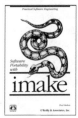

imake is a utility that works with *make* to enable code to be compiled and installed on different UNIX machines. *imake* makes possible the wide portability of the X Window System code and is widely considered an X tool, but it's also useful for any software project that needs to be ported to many UNIX systems.

This Nutshell Handbook®—the only book available on *imake*—is ideal for X and UNIX programmers who want their software to be portable. The book is divided into two sections. The first section is a general explanation of *imake*, X configuration files, and how to write and debug an *Imakefile*. The second section describes how to write configuration files and presents a configuration file architecture that allows development of coexisting sets of configuration files. Several sample sets of configuration files are described and are available free over the Net.

Managing Projects with make

By Andrew Oram & Steve Talbott
2nd Edition October 1991
152 pages, ISBN 0-937175-90-0

make is one of UNIX's greatest contributions to software development, and this book is the clearest description of *make* ever written. It describes all the basic features of *make* and provides guidelines on meeting the needs of large, modern projects. Also contains a description of free products that contain major enhancements to *make*.

"I use *make* very frequently in my day to day work and thought I knew everything that I needed to know about it. After reading this book I realized that I was wrong!
—Rob Henley, Siemens-Nixdorf

"If you can't pick up your system's *yp Makefile*, read every line, and make sense of it, you need this book."
—*Root Journal*

Checking C Programs with lint

By Ian F. Darwin
1st Edition October 1988
84 pages, ISBN 0-937175-30-7

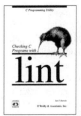

The *lint* program checker has proven time and again to be one of the best tools for finding portability problems and certain types of coding errors in C programs. *lint* verifies a program or program segments against standard libraries, checks the code for common portability errors, and tests the programming against some tried and true guidelines. *Linting* your code is a necessary (though not sufficient) step in writing clean, portable, effective programs. This book introduces you to *lint*, guides you through running it on your programs, and helps you interpret *lint's* output.

"I can say without reservation that this book is a must for the system programmer or anyone else programming in C."
—*Root Journal*

lex & yacc

By John Levine, Tony Mason & Doug Brown
2nd Edition October 1992
366 pages, ISBN 1-56592-000-7

Shows programmers how to use two UNIX utilities, *lex* and *yacc*, in program development. The second edition contains completely revised tutorial sections for novice users and reference sections for advanced users. This edition is twice the size of the first, has an expanded index, and now covers Bison and Flex.

Power Programming with RPC

By John Bloomer
1st Edition February 1992
522 pages, ISBN 0-937175-77-3

RPC, or remote procedure calling, is the ability to distribute the execution of functions on remote computers. Written from a programmer's perspective, this book shows what you can do with RPCs, like Sun RPC, the de facto standard on UNIX systems. It covers related programming topics for Sun and other UNIX systems and teaches through examples.

Multi-Platform Programming

Guide to Writing DCE Applications

By John Shirley, Wei Hu & David Magid
2nd Edition May 1994
462 pages, ISBN 1-56592-045-7

A hands-on programming guide to OSF's Distributed Computing Environment (DCE) for first-time DCE application programmers. This book is designed to help new DCE users make the transition from conventional, nondistributed applications programming to distributed DCE programming. In addition to basic RPC (remote procedure calls), this edition covers object UUIDs and basic security (authentication and authorization). Also includes practical programming examples.

"This book will be useful as a ready reference by the side of the novice DCE programmer." —*;login*

Distributing Applications Across DCE and Windows NT

By Ward Rosenberry & Jim Teague
1st Edition November 1993
302 pages, ISBN 1-56592-047-3

This book links together two exciting technologies in distributed computing by showing how to develop an application that simultaneously runs on DCE and Microsoft systems through remote procedure calls (RPC). Covers the writing of portable applications and the complete differences between RPC support in the two environments.

Understanding DCE

By Ward Rosenberry, David Kenney & Gerry Fisher
1st Edition October 1992
266 pages, ISBN 1-56592-005-8

A technical and conceptual overview of OSF's Distributed Computing Environment (DCE) for programmers, technical managers, and marketing and sales people. Unlike many O'Reilly & Associates books, *Understanding DCE* has no hands-on programming elements. Instead, the book focuses on how DCE can be used to accomplish typical programming tasks and provides explanations to help the reader understand all the parts of DCE.

Encyclopedia of Graphics File Formats

By James D. Murray & William vanRyper
1st Edition July 1994
928 pages (CD-ROM included), ISBN 1-56592-058-9

The computer graphics world is a veritable alphabet soup of acronyms; BMP, DXF, EPS, GIF, MPEG, PCX, PIC, RTF, TGA, RIFF, and TIFF are only a few of the many different formats in which graphics images can be stored.

The *Encyclopedia of Graphics File Formats* is the definitive work on file formats— the book that will become a classic for graphics programmers and everyone else who deals with the low-level technical details of graphics files. It includes technical information on nearly 100 file formats, as well as chapters on graphics and file format basics, bitmap and vector files, metafiles, scene description, animation and multimedia formats, and file compression methods.

Best of all, this book comes with a CD-ROM that collects many hard-to-find resources. We've assembled original vendor file format specification documents, along with test images and code examples, and a variety of software packages for MS-DOS, Windows, OS/2, UNIX, and the Macintosh that will let you convert, view, and manipulate graphics files and images.

Multi-Platform Code Management

By Kevin Jameson
1st Edition August 1994
354 pages (two diskettes included), ISBN 1-56592-059-7

For any programmer or team struggling with builds and maintenance, this book—and its accompanying software (available for fifteen platforms, including MS-DOS and various UNIX systems)—can save dozens of errors and hours of effort. A "one-stop-shopping" solution for code management problems, it shows you how to structure a large project and keep your files and builds under control over many releases and platforms. The building blocks are simple: common-sense strategies, public-domain tools that you can obtain on a variety of systems, and special utilities developed by the author. The book also includes two diskettes that provide a complete system for managing source files and builds.

Understanding Japanese Information Processing

By Ken Lunde
1st Edition September 1993
470 pages, ISBN 1-56592-043-0

Understanding Japanese Information Processing provides detailed information on all aspects of handling Japanese text on computer systems. It brings all of the relevant information together in a single book and covers everything from the origins of modern-day Japanese to the latest information on specific emerging computer encoding standards. Appendices provide additional reference material, such as a code conversion table, character set tables, mapping tables, an extensive list of software sources, a glossary, and more.

"A programmer interested in writing a computer program which will handle the Japanese language will find the book indispensable." —*Multilingual Computing*

"Ken Lunde's book is an essential reference for everyone developing or adapting software for handling Japanese text. It is a goldmine of useful and relevant information on fonts, encoding systems and standards."
—Professor Jim Breen, Monash University, Australia

Business

Building a Successful Software Business

By Dave Radin
1st Edition April 1994
394 pages, ISBN 1-56592-064-3

This handbook is for the new software entrepreneur and the old hand alike. If you're thinking of starting a company around a program you've written—and there's no better time than the present—this book will guide you toward success. If you're an old hand in the software industry, it will help you sharpen your skills or will provide a refresher course. It covers the basics of product planning, marketing, customer support, finance, and operations.

"A marvelous guide through the complexities of marketing high-tech products. Its range of topics, and Radin's insights, make the book valuable to the novice marketeer as well as the seasoned veteran. It is the Swiss Army Knife of high-tech marketing." —Jerry Keane, Universal Analytics Inc.

ORACLE Performance Tuning

By Peter Corrigan & Mark Gurry
1st Edition September 1993
642 pages, ISBN 1-56592-048-1

The ORACLE relational database management system is the most popular database system in use today. Organizations, ranging from government agencies to small businesses, from large financial institutions to universities, use ORACLE on computers as diverse as mainframes, minicomputers, workstations, PCs, and Macintoshes.

ORACLE offers tremendous power and flexibility, but at some cost. Demands for fast response, particularly in online transaction processing systems, make performance a major issue. With more organizations downsizing and adopting client-server and distributed database approaches, performance tuning has become all the more vital.

Whether you're a manager, a designer, a programmer, or an administrator, there's a lot you can do on your own to dramatically increase the performance of your existing ORACLE system. Whether you are running RDBMS Version 6 or Version 7, you may find that this book can save you the cost of a new machine; at the very least, it will save you a lot of headaches.

"This book is one of the best books on ORACLE that I have ever read.... [It] discloses many Oracle Tips that DBA's and Developers have locked in their brains and in their planners.... I recommend this book for any person who works with ORACLE, from managers to developers. In fact, I have to keep [it] under lock and key, because of the popularity of it."
—Mike Gangler

O'Reilly & Associates—
GLOBAL NETWORK NAVIGATOR™

The Global Network Navigator (GNN)™ is a unique kind of information service that makes the Internet easy and enjoyable to use. We organize access to the vast information resources of the Internet so that you can find what you want. We also help you understand the Internet and the many ways you can explore it.

In GNN you'll find:

Navigating the Net with GNN

 The *Whole Internet Catalog* contains a descriptive listing of the most useful Net resources and services with live links to those resources.

 The *GNN Business Pages* are where you'll learn about companies who have established a presence on the Internet and use its worldwide reach to help educate consumers.

 The *Internet Help Desk* helps folks who are new to the Net orient themselves and gets them started on the road to Internet exploration.

News

 NetNews is a weekly publication that reports on the news of the Internet, with weekly feature articles that focus on Internet trends and special events. The Sports, Weather, and Comix Pages round out the news.

Special Interest Publications

 Whether you're planning a trip or are just interested in reading about the journeys of others, you'll find that the *Travelers' Center* contains a rich collection of feature articles and ongoing columns about travel. In the *Travelers' Center*, you can link to many helpful and informative travel-related Internet resources.

The *Personal Finance Center* is the place to go for information about money management and investment on the Internet. Whether you're an old pro at playing the market or are thinking about investing for the first time, you'll read articles and discover Internet resources that will help you to think of the Internet as a personal finance information tool.

All in all, GNN helps you get more value for the time you spend on the Internet.

 The Best of the Web

GNN received "Honorable Mention" for **"Best Overall Site," "Best Entertainment Service,"** and **"Most Important Service Concept."**

The *GNN NetNews* received "Honorable Mention" for **"Best Document Design."**

Subscribe Today

GNN is available over the Internet as a subscription service. To get complete information about subscribing to GNN, send email to **info@gnn.com**. If you have access to a World Wide Web browser such as Mosaic or Lynx, you can use the following URL to register online: `http://gnn.com/`

If you use a browser that does not support online forms, you can retrieve an email version of the registration form automatically by sending email to **form@gnn.com**. Fill this form out and send it back to us by email, and we will confirm your registration.

O'Reilly on the Net—
ONLINE PROGRAM GUIDE

O'Reilly & Associates offers extensive information through our online resources. If you've got Internet access, we invite you to come and explore our little neck-of-the-woods.

Online Resource Center

Most comprehensive among our online offerings is the O'Reilly Resource Center. Here, you'll find detailed information and descriptions on all O'Reilly products: titles, prices, tables of contents, indexes, author bios, software contents, reviews... you can even view images of the products themselves. We also supply helpful ordering information: how to contact us, how to order online, distributors and bookstores world wide, discounts, upgrades, etc. In addition, we provide informative literature in the field: articles, interviews, and bibliographies that help you stay informed and abreast.

 The Best of the Web

The *O'Reilly Resource Center* was voted "**Best Commercial Site**" by users participating in "Best of the Web '94."

To access ORA's Online Resource Center:

Point your Web browser (e.g., `mosaic` or `lynx`) to:

`http://gnn.com/ora/`

For the plaintext version, `telnet` or `gopher` to:

`gopher.ora.com`

(telnet login: `gopher`)

FTP

The example files and programs in many of our books are available electronically via FTP.

To obtain example files and programs from O'Reilly texts:

`ftp` to:

`ftp.ora.com`

or

`ftp.uu.net`

`cd published/oreilly`

Ora-news

An easy way to stay informed of the latest projects and products from O'Reilly & Associates is to subscribe to "ora-news," our electronic news service. Subscribers receive email as soon as the information breaks.

To subscribe to "ora-news":

Send email to:
listproc@online.ora.com

and put the following information on the first line of your message (not in "Subject"):
subscribe ora-news "your name" **of** "your company"

For example:
subscribe ora-news Jim Dandy of Mighty Fine Enterprises

Email

Many customer services are provided via email. Here's a few of the most popular and useful.

nuts@ora.com
> For general questions and information.

bookquestions@ora.com
> For technical questions, or corrections, concerning book contents.

order@ora.com
> To order books online and for ordering questions.

catalog@ora.com
> To receive a free copy of our magazine/catalog, "ora.com" (please include a postal address).

Snailmail and phones

O'Reilly & Associates, Inc.
103A Morris Street, Sebastopol, CA 95472
Inquiries: **707-829-0515, 800-998-9938**
Credit card orders: **800-889-8969** (Weekdays 6a.m.- 6p.m. PST)
FAX: **707-829-0104**

O'Reilly & Associates—
LISTING OF TITLES

INTERNET

!%@:: A Directory of Electronic Mail
    Addressing & Networks
Connecting to the Internet: An O'Reilly Buyer's Guide
Internet In A Box
The Mosaic Handbook for Microsoft Windows
The Mosaic Handbook for the Macintosh
The Mosaic Handbook for the X Window System
Smileys
The Whole Internet User's Guide & Catalog

SYSTEM ADMINISTRATION

Computer Security Basics
DNS and BIND
Essential System Administration
Linux Network Administrator's Guide (Winter '94/95 est.)
Managing Internet Information Services
Managing NFS and NIS
Managing UUCP and Usenet
sendmail
Practical UNIX Security
PGP: Pretty Good Privacy (Winter '94/95 est.)
System Performance Tuning
TCP/IP Network Administration
termcap & terminfo
X Window System Administrator's Guide: Volume 8
The X Companion CD for R6 (Winter '94/95 est.)

USING UNIX AND X

BASICS

Learning GNU Emacs
Learning the Korn Shell
Learning the UNIX Operating System
Learning the vi Editor
MH & xmh: Email for Users & Programmers
SCO UNIX in a Nutshell
The USENET Handbook (Winter '94/95 est.)
Using UUCP and Usenet
UNIX in a Nutshell: System V Edition
The X Window System in a Nutshell
X Window System User's Guide: Volume 3
X Window System User's Guide, Motif Ed.: Vol. 3M
X User Tools (with CD-ROM)

ADVANCED

Exploring Expect (Winter 94/95 est.)
The Frame Handbook
Learning Perl
Making TeX Work
Programming perl
sed & awk
UNIX Power Tools (with CD-ROM)

PROGRAMMING UNIX, C, AND MULTI-PLATFORM

FORTRAN/SCIENTIFIC COMPUTING

High Performance Computing
Migrating to Fortran 90
UNIX for FORTRAN Programmers

C PROGRAMMING LIBRARIES

Practical C Programming
POSIX Programmer's Guide
POSIX.4: Programming for the Real World
    (Winter '94/95 est.)
Programming with curses
Understanding and Using COFF
Using C on the UNIX System

C PROGRAMMING TOOLS

Checking C Programs with lint
lex & yacc
Managing Projects with make
Power Programming with RPC
Software Portability with imake

MULTI-PLATFORM PROGRAMMING

Encyclopedia of Graphics File Formats
Distributing Applications Across DCE and
    Windows NT
Guide to Writing DCE Applications
Multi-Platform Code Management
ORACLE Performance Tuning
Understanding DCE
Understanding Japanese Information Processing

BERKELEY 4.4 SOFTWARE DISTRIBUTION

4.4BSD System Manager's Manual
4.4BSD User's Reference Manual
4.4BSD User's Supplementary Documents
4.4BSD Programmer's Reference Manual
4.4BSD Programmer's Supplementary Documents
4.4BSD-Lite CD Companion
4.4BSD-Lite CD Companion: International Version

X PROGRAMMING

Motif Programming Manual: Volume 6A
Motif Reference Manual: Volume 6B
Motif Tools
PEXlib Programming Manual
PEXlib Reference Manual
PHIGS Programming Manual (soft or hard cover)
PHIGS Reference Manual
Programmer's Supplement for Release 6 (Winter '94/95 est.)
Xlib Programming Manual: Volume 1
Xlib Reference Manual: Volume 2
X Protocol Reference Manual, R5: Volume 0
X Protocol Reference Manual, R6: Volume 0
    (Winter '94/95 est.)
X Toolkit Intrinsics Programming Manual: Vol. 4
X Toolkit Intrinsics Programming Manual,
    Motif Edition: Volume 4M
X Toolkit Intrinsics Reference Manual: Volume 5
XView Programming Manual: Volume 7A
XView Reference Manual: Volume 7B

THE X RESOURCE

A QUARTERLY WORKING JOURNAL FOR X PROGRAMMERS

The X Resource: Issues 0 through 13
    (Issue 13 available 1/95)

BUSINESS/CAREER

Building a Successful Software Business
Love Your Job!

TRAVEL

Travelers' Tales Thailand
Travelers' Tales Mexico
Travelers' Tales India (Winter '94/95 est.)

AUDIOTAPES

INTERNET TALK RADIO'S "GEEK OF THE WEEK" INTERVIEWS

The Future of the Internet Protocol, 4 hours
Global Network Operations, 2 hours
Mobile IP Networking, 1 hour
Networked Information and
    Online Libraries, 1 hour
Security and Networks, 1 hour
European Networking, 1 hour

NOTABLE SPEECHES OF THE INFORMATION AGE

John Perry Barlow, 1.5 hours

O'Reilly & Associates—
INTERNATIONAL DISTRIBUTORS

Customers outside North America can now order O'Reilly & Associates books through the following distributors. They offer our international customers faster order processing, more bookstores, increased representation at tradeshows worldwide, and the high-quality, responsive service our customers have come to expect.

EUROPE, MIDDLE EAST, AND AFRICA

(except Germany, Switzerland, and Austria)

INQUIRIES

International Thomson Publishing Europe
Berkshire House
168-173 High Holborn
London WC1V 7AA
United Kingdom
Telephone: 44-71-497-1422
Fax: 44-71-497-1426
Email: ora.orders@itpuk.co.uk

ORDERS

International Thomson Publishing Services, Ltd.
Cheriton House, North Way
Andover, Hampshire SP10 5BE
United Kingdom
Telephone: 44-264-342-832 (UK orders)
Telephone: 44-264-342-806 (outside UK)
Fax: 44-264-364418 (UK orders)
Fax: 44-264-342761 (outside UK)

GERMANY, SWITZERLAND, AND AUSTRIA

International Thomson Publishing GmbH
O'Reilly-International Thomson Verlag
Attn: Mr. G. Miske
Königswinterer Strasse 418
53227 Bonn
Germany
Telephone: 49-228-970240
Fax: 49-228-441342
Email: anfragen@orade.ora.com

THE AMERICAS, JAPAN, AND OCEANIA

O'Reilly & Associates, Inc.
103A Morris Street
Sebastopol, CA 95472 U.S.A.
Telephone: 707-829-0515
Telephone: 800-998-9938 (U.S. & Canada)
Fax: 707-829-0104
Email: order@ora.com

ASIA

(except Japan)

INQUIRIES

International Thomson Publishing Asia
221 Henderson Road
#05 10 Henderson Building
Singapore 0315
Telephone: 65-272-6496
Fax: 65-272-6498

ORDERS

Telephone: 65-268-7867
Fax: 65-268-6727

AUSTRALIA

WoodsLane Pty. Ltd.
Unit 8, 101 Darley Street (P.O. Box 935)
Mona Vale NSW 2103
Australia
Telephone: 61-2-979-5944
Fax: 61-2-997-3348
Email: woods@tmx.mhs.oz.au

NEW ZEALAND

WoodsLane New Zealand Ltd.
21 Cooks Street (P.O. Box 575)
Wanganui, New Zealand
Telephone: 64-6-347-6543
Fax: 64-6-345-4840
Email: woods@tmx.mhs.oz.au

Here's a page we encourage readers to tear out...

O'REILLY WOULD LIKE TO HEAR FROM YOU

Please send me the following:

❏ *ora.com*

O'Reilly's magazine/catalog, containing behind-the-scenes articles and interviews on the technology we write about, and a complete listing of O'Reilly books and products.

❏ *Global Network Navigator*™

Information and subscription.

Please print legibly

Which book did this card come from?

_____

Where did you buy this book?
  ❏ Bookstore   ❏ Direct from O'Reilly
  ❏ Bundled with hardware/software   ❏ Class/seminar

Your job description: ❏ SysAdmin   ❏ Programmer
  ❏ Other_____

What computer system do you use?   ❏ UNIX
  ❏ MAC   ❏ DOS(PC)   ❏ Other _____

Name _____ Company/Organization Name _____

Address _____

City _____ State _____ Zip/Postal Code _____ Country _____

Telephone _____ Internet or other email address (specify network) _____

Nineteenth century wood engraving
of the horned owl from the O'Reilly
& Associates Nutshell Handbook®
Learning the UNIX Operating System

POST CARD

O'Reilly & Associates, Inc., 103A Morris Street, Sebastopol, CA 95472-9902

BUSINESS REPLY MAIL

FIRST CLASS MAIL   PERMIT NO. 80   SEBASTOPOL, CA

Postage will be paid by addressee

O'Reilly & Associates, Inc.
103A Morris Street
Sebastopol, CA 95472-9902